"An authoritative, engaging guide to being happy together! Filled with personal stories, practical recommendations, and scientific research from positive psychology!"
—Angela Duckworth, *New York Times* bestselling author of *Grit*, founder and CEO of Character Lab, and Christopher H. Browne Distinguished Professor of Psychology, University of Pennsylvania

"Suzie Pileggi Pawelski and James Pawelski provide practical, evidence-based advice about how each of us can make the most out of our romantic relationships. Intimate relationships can be the source of lasting joy or excruciating heartache depending on how they're managed. *Happy Together* is the definitive guidebook on how to navigate this most important aspect of our lives. I wish I would've had this book twenty years ago. Read it . . . you can thank me later."
—Larry King, Peabody Award–winning television and radio host

"*Happy Together* is one of the most powerful books on relationships I have ever read. Loaded with ideas and research, this book unlocks the keys to building a healthy relationship that will strengthen both partners and create more well-being for many others in the process!"
—Tom Rath, #1 *New York Times* bestselling author of *StrengthsFinder 2.0* and *Are You Fully Charged?*

"Suzie and James masterfully show that happily ever after doesn't come from a perfect, problem-free life. Rather, it comes from knowing how to adapt with your partner to the range of joys and adversities we all experience. Weaving together empirical research, philosophical wisdom, and real-life examples, *Happy Together* demonstrates the central importance of emotional agility for romantic relationships—and shows you how to cultivate it with your partner."
—Susan David, #1 *Wall Street Journal* bestselling author of *Emotional Agility*, cofounder of the Institute of Coaching at McLean Hospital, and psychologist, Harvard Medical School

"Suzie and James beautifully weave ancient wisdom with modern research, personal stories with universal truths, the art of love with the science of love. Relationships are potentially the number one predictor of happiness. This book can help you to realize—to make real—this potential. Read it, together or alone, read it now."
—Tal Ben-Shahar, *New York Times* bestselling author of *Happier* and *Being Happy* and Harvard University lecturer

"I loved it! *Happy Together* is a pioneering book filled with helpful advice and engaging exercises that will make your relationship stronger and more fulfilling. Every couple needs to read it!"
—Jon Gordon, *Wall Street Journal* bestselling author of *The Energy Bus* and *The Power of Positive Leadership*

"I believe the main purpose in life is to grow in our capacity to give and receive love. *Happy Together* is a must-read for anyone seeking this purpose in their romantic relationship."   —Marci Shimoff, #1 *New York Times* bestselling author of *Happy for No Reason*

"Falling in love is easy. Falling in love with the right person is harder. And staying in love is harder still. But it's possible. In their clear, engaging, and thoughtful book, Suzie and James Pawelski combine the wisdom of Aristotle with the empirical research of modern psychology to show us how. Combining poignant anecdotes (including many tales from their own relationship), research findings, and lots of very practical advice, in *Happy Together*, the Pawelskis provide both a 'how to' and a 'why to' guide that will help people nurture and sustain lasting loving relationships. It takes work to stay in love, but it's worth the effort, and *Happy Together* is a luminous roadmap for that effort."
        —Barry Schwartz, bestselling author of *The Paradox of Choice*, *Why We Work*, and *Practical Wisdom* with Kenneth Sharpe

"With the high-level perspective of decades in the field of happiness, and the intimate understanding of the challenges of long-term intimacy from their own relationship, Suzie and James Pawelski have created an accessible playbook for anyone seeking what we all seek: deep and meaningful love that lasts. Together, they teach us that there is no quick fix to happiness together—nor should there be. Rather, with a little bit of work and a lot of will, there is indeed a way to bring out the best in ourselves and those we love most. You'll be happy you read this book."   —Larry Smith, creator of the Six-Word Memoir project and *New York Times* bestselling book series

"A philosopher, a psychologist, and a journalist walk into a bar. Grab your partner and walk in after them! Because as this book shows, what they know can help you live happily ever after."   —Yakov Smirnoff, comedian, actor, and writer

"As a movie producer, I'm well aware that movies can contribute to the illusory simplicity of 'happily ever after,' but movies can also show us that nothing worthwhile can be accomplished without effort. The movie hero who wants to achieve something has to do something, to take action over and over again in order to reach his or her goal. Suzie and James have written a book that gives us science-based steps to take to accomplish that 'happily ever after' and to show couples how to become the heroes of their own love story—from first kiss till death do they part."
        —Lindsay Doran, producer of *Sense and Sensibility* and *Nanny McPhee*

"Reading *Happy Together* is like a visit to a romantic relationship gym. The book is a beautifully written guide on how to use the principles of positive psychology to develop and to enhance intimate relationships. The authors, both positive psychology experts, also frankly share their own marital experiences to show, rather than tell, couples how to grow together. This book will make an imaginative gift to any couple planning on making a life together or wishing to enhance an already established relationship." —George E. Vaillant MD, professor of psychiatry, Harvard Medical School and author of *Triumphs of Experience*

"If your marriage occasionally disappoints you or is not quite up to your expectations, the Pawelskis bring advice from the field of positive psychology to help you enrich your relationship. Recognizing the strengths of both partners, savoring and gratitude, and knowing that love is an action verb are highly related to the most rewarding partnerships. The authors offer both an excellent description of how to improve one's relationships, and also exercises to practice these activities." —Ed Diener, leading positive psychology researcher and Gallup senior scientist

"Wishing for your 'happily ever after' is never enough. Thankfully, science can step in to offer real hope. *Happy Together* is an accessible guide that can help any couple cultivate positive emotions rather than just wish and wait for them. Take it to heart and use the science of well-being to create a lifetime of happiness together." —Barbara Fredrickson, PhD, author of *Love 2.0* and *Positivity*

"In this groundbreaking book, Suzie and James Pawelski explore the how of being happy together. Based on scientific research, framed by ancient wisdom, informed by their own insights and experience, and presented in a clear and engaging style, their book is a practical and powerful guide to building love that lasts." —Sonja Lyubomirsky, professor of psychology, University of California, Riverside, and author of *The How of Happiness* and *The Myths of Happiness*

"There's no more fitting, knowledgeable, or loving couple than Suzie and James to share with the world how to achieve and experience the 'happily ever after' we've all dreamed about. They detail with wit, warmth, and personal examples how a romantic team is at its best when each player helps the other reach his or her highest potential. The Pawelskis' insightful application of positive psychology and accessible style make *Happy Together* a must-have on my list of key resources in the space." —Deborah K. Heisz, cofounder, CEO, and editorial director of Live Happy

"The Pawelskis have done the seemingly impossible: They have shown us how to realistically build long-lasting love, despite the inevitable hardships of relationships. Equipped with the tools of positive psychology and the philosophy of Aristotle, you will be able to have relationships that are deeper, wiser, more mutually inspiring, and, of course, happier." —Scott Barry Kaufman, director of the University of Pennsylvania's Imagination Institute and author of *Wired to Create*

"Suzie and James have knocked it out of the park with a practical guide to lasting love. I highly recommend this book to anyone who wants to know the real keys to a happy, fulfilling relationship, backed by years of research."
—Valorie Burton, bestselling author of
Successful Women Think Differently and *Happy Women Live Better*

"Actually DO what this book presents and you will no doubt elevate the most important aspect of your life—your loving relationships."
—Neal Mayerson, PhD, chairman of the VIA Institute and president of the Manuel D. and Rhoda Mayerson Foundation and the Mayerson Company

"*Happy Together* presents a powerful case for 'finding and feeding the good in ourselves and our partners' to build satisfying, sustainable relationships. I especially enjoyed the exercises included throughout the book. This message aligns perfectly with the Institute for Integrative Nutrition, where we consider positive relationships a crucial and primary food for health and happiness."
—Joshua Rosenthal, founder and director
of the Institute for Integrative Nutrition

"It has arrived—your relationship gym! *Happy Together* is an artful, intelligent, and user-friendly integration of the best science to improve your romantic relationships. If every new couple read and followed the insights and exercises in Suzann Pileggi and James Pawelski's new book, relationship therapists would be out of business and flourishing relationships would become the norm. Our romantic relationship can be our source of greatest tension or our wellspring of greatest strength. Pileggi and Pawelski show us we can choose the latter by creating synergies of relational character strength through savoring, passion, strengths conversations, and much more."
—Ryan M. Niemiec, author of *Character Strengths Interventions* and
Mindfulness and Character Strengths, and education director of
the global VIA Institute on Character

"Couples the world over fall in love and then fall into normality and taking each other for granted. Many relationships wither and some die. But it doesn't have to be that way. As this book so powerfully shows, we can all learn how to retain the vitality in our relationships and make them thrive. Suzie and James beautifully demonstrate through scientific research and engaging anecdotes that the true joy of a good relationship is to value each other, grow as individuals, and become stronger together. This book will change lives for the better."
—Sir Anthony Seldon, author, cofounder of Action for
Happiness, and vice chancellor, University of Buckingham

"What do you get when a master teacher of positive psychology and a successful journalist fall in love, marry, and start a family? The answer to this riddle is *Happy Together*, an inspiring, engaging, and practical book on how to develop, deepen, and enrich intimate relationships. Melding empirical research, personal experience, and narratives of couples, Suzann Pileggi Pawelski and

James Pawelski have written the first major work on the application of positive psychology to love, intimacy, and how to build an enduring and deeply satisfying relationship. This book speaks to couples looking to enhance their relationship, clinicians working with individuals and couples, and anyone who wants to know how successful relationships really work."

—Richard F. Summers, MD, clinical professor of psychiatry and senior residency adviser, Perelman School of Medicine of the University of Pennsylvania, and author of *Psychodynamic Therapy: A Guide to Evidence Based Practice* and *Positive Psychiatry: A Casebook*

"Happy Together is about real magic, not the kind that you read about in fairy tales, but the magic that comes from one of the most powerful experiences in the world, the unconditional acceptance of another human being. Romantic love is easy, common, and all too fleeting. *Happy Together* is about something much more important, the kind of bond that sustains us through joy and sorrow both, the alchemy that turns passionate lovers into partners for life. If you've ever suspected that there must be a secret to a happy relationship, you were right. The secret is here. It's essential reading if you want to stay connected for good."

—Michael Baime, MD, director of the Penn Program for Mindfulness, University of Pennsylvania

"This superb book, by one of the most popular couples in positive psychology, meshes strong science with clear applications and sound exercises. It is a must-read for all of us who want to better understand our romantic relationship and how best to improve it."

—Robert J. Vallerand, PhD, author of the award-winning book *The Psychology of Passion*, Canada Research Chair on Motivational Processes and Optimal Functioning, and professor of social psychology, Université du Québec à Montréal

"The science of positive psychology can guide and inform powerful interventions and applications. *Happy Together* is a must-read exemplar of how to use evidence-based positive psychology principles to improve one of the most powerful predictors of happiness and well-being—our most significant relationships."

—Stewart I. Donaldson, professor of psychology and community and global health, Claremont Graduate University, editor of *Scientific Advances in Positive Psychology* and *Applied Positive Psychology: Improving Everyday Life, Schools, Work, and Society*

"This pioneering, important book is must reading for any couple who wants proven ways to enhance passion, love, and long-term stability. It takes grit to weather the challenges that occur in any marriage, but these positive psychology leaders have given us new tools and fresh evidence to help us survive and thrive in 'green cape' relationships."

—Caroline Adams Miller, MAPP, author of *Creating Your Best Life* and *Getting Grit*

"*Happy Together* is my kind of book: it convinces me with research, inspires me with stories, enlightens me with quizzes, and motivates me with exercises to be a better man and a better husband. I'm using it cover to cover in my own relationship—and recommending it to everyone I know!"

—David J. Pollay, bestselling author of *The Law of the Garbage Truck* and founder of PollayCoaching.com

"Reading *Happy Together* is like having husband-and-wife team Suzann and James Pawelski as your personal trainer for your marriage or future healthy relationship. Talk about packed with thought-provoking and action-focused relationship exercises! You can do these on your own or with your partner to learn how to cultivate the REAL 'happily ever after.'"

—Margaret H. Greenberg, MAPP, and Senia Maymin, PhD and MAPP, bestselling authors of *Profit from the Positive*

"For anyone in a relationship or looking for a relationship, *Happy Together* is a must-read. Using research and real-life examples, Suzie and James Pawelski explore what it *really* means to live happily ever after. This is not your typical 'couple's therapy' book—it is packed with illuminating and often counterintuitive insights about how to find and build love that lasts. Read it with a highlighter in hand—there is actionable advice and timeless wisdom on every page. I am going to prescribe it to every couple I know."

—Samantha Boardman, MD, Weill Cornell Medical College

Happy Together

Using the Science of
Positive Psychology
to Build Love
That Lasts

Suzann Pileggi Pawelski, MAPP
and James O. Pawelski, PhD

A TarcherPerigee Book

tarcherperigee

An imprint of Penguin Random House LLC
375 Hudson Street
New York, New York 10014

Most TarcherPerigee books are available at special quantity discounts for
bulk purchase for sales promotions, premiums, fund-raising, and educational
needs. Special books or book excerpts also can be created to fit specific needs.
For details, write: SpecialMarkets@penguinrandomhouse.com.

ISBN 9780143130598 (paperback)
ISBN 9781524704421 (e-book)

Printed in the United States of America

Book design by Katy Riegel

Contents

Foreword

I WISH POSITIVE PSYCHOLOGY had existed when I became a psychologist more than fifty years ago. More to the point, I wish this book had been written back then. At that time, the best we had to offer individuals was a few guidelines for how to be less miserable, and the best we had to offer couples was instruction on how to fight less destructively. This book takes a very different approach: Instead of trying to minimize the bad, it focuses on how couples can optimize the good in their relationships.

I have dedicated my life to the scientific study and evidence-based practice of how we can lead better lives. When I entered the field of psychology, the focus was on the study and treatment of mental illness, and I began my career studying helplessness and depression, looking for ways to heal what is worst in human experience.

As my career progressed, I became dissatisfied with psychology's fixation on mental illness. Even if we could somehow find a way to cure all psychological problems, I realized, that would not automatically lead to the mental health we all want. Even if we were wholly successful in curing all psychological problems, which we are not, the best we could ever get to is zero. So as a complement to the psychology of suffering, I proposed positive psychology, which would focus on the things that make life worth living.

When my colleagues and I launched positive psychology twenty years ago, we envisioned a field that would articulate an evidence-based vision of how to live well. This scientific approach would enable individuals to make wise choices in the various domains of life and help societies build thriving schools, businesses, families, and communities.

Positive psychology is well on its way to realizing this vision. Researchers are illuminating successful approaches to learning, managing, relating to, and serving others. And dedicated practitioners are using this research to transform education, business, medicine—and our society at large.

This is the first book to apply positive psychology research to romantic relationships. It shows we are no longer stuck trying to help couples fight in less damaging ways. Going beyond that, we can help couples focus on flourishing. My PERMA model of flourishing, for example, consists of five elements of a fulfilling life: Positive emotions, Engagement, Relationships, Meaning, and Accomplishment. Relationships, of course, are right at the center of PERMA. Indeed, relationships may be the most important part of a happy and flourishing life. Chris Peterson, my colleague, friend, and a cofounder of positive psychology, summed up our entire field in three words: *Other people matter.*

Suzie Pileggi Pawelski and James Pawelski are just the right authors for this book. I first met Suzie ten years ago, when she was accepted into the third class of our Master of Applied Positive Psychology (MAPP) program at the University of Pennsylvania. Zestful and tenacious, she was an excellent student, and as a writer, she has an uncanny knack for making academic research findings accessible and fun.

I have known James even longer, having met him soon after the launch of positive psychology. He was a bright, energetic young philosopher with a deep interest in the conceptual underpinnings of positive psychology and its potential for improving human experience. He was after a living, applicable kind of philosophy of the sort William James, his hero, wished for. I was so impressed with James that I invited him to join me at Penn, where he has thrived as the director of the MAPP program, an award-winning teacher, the executive director of the International Positive Psychology Association (IPPA), and the leader of research on the arts, humanities, and human flourishing.

Impressive as Suzie and James are as individuals, they are even more effective as a couple. They are qualified to write this book, not just because of their expertise in the field of positive psychology but also because of their dedication to its application in their own marriage. They live their work.

Positive psychology has deep roots in philosophy, and by beginning with them, Suzie and James present the scientific research in an especially clear and powerful way. Their discussions of Aristotle and William James, for example, are engaging and organically connected to the remarkable range of positive psychology research they cover on passion, positive emotions, savoring, and character strengths. Their Interaction Model of Relationships marks a significant advance in our understanding of foundational elements of positive psychology.

This book emphasizes that though relationships aren't easy, they can be improved through the practice of key skills. As Suzie likes to say, "Love is an action verb." The book also emphasizes that relationships work better when you focus not on what you can get out

of them but on what you can put into them—and *become* through
them. Suzie and James make a strong case for the power of better
romantic relationships to help us become better people. This is certainly something my wife, Mandy, and I have experienced: We
have become better people because of our relationship.

I now invite you to see for yourself why the approach in this
book is so effective. Dive into the ancient wisdom and the contemporary science, complete the insightful exercises, and apply what
you learn in your relationship today!

Martin E. P. Seligman, PhD

Wynnewood, PA

Introduction:
Becoming Happy Together

BEING HAPPY TOGETHER with your partner or spouse is one of the greatest joys life has to offer. We all want to be happy, of course. And connecting with others is a multiplier of our happiness, making it more frequent, more sustained, and more satisfying. Being happy with others is the easiest and most natural thing in the world.

Until it isn't.

Then, being happy together becomes one of the greatest *challenges* life has to offer. In these times, the "together" part gets in the way, making happiness seem impossible. We are then tempted to think that if it weren't for people—or these *particular* people—being in our lives, we could be happy.

And to make things even more complicated, it's often the very same people who make us both happy *and* unhappy.

Although the information and exercises in this book can be applied to any kind of relationship, our focus here is on romantic relationships. The effects of romantic relationships on our happiness are enormous. When they are going well, it's hard to imagine anything making us happier; when they are not going well, it's difficult to see how anything could make us more miserable.

So how about you? How is your romantic relationship going? And why are you interested in a book about being happy together with your partner? Is it because you are currently in a romantic relationship that's going well and you want it to continue to grow? Or are you experiencing the opposite—feeling stuck in a romantic relationship that doesn't feel very romantic anymore and looking for ways of getting your partnership back on track? Perhaps you have turned to this book out of desperation, because you feel like whatever love you find simply doesn't last, with your relationships ending in messy breakups or even divorce. Or maybe it's because you are not in a romantic relationship right now and you want to prepare yourself to be a good partner when you do find a significant other.

These are all great reasons for picking up this book, and we want to assure you that you've come to the right place—not because reading this book will magically and effortlessly create your dream relationship for you. Nothing can do that. But because this book is chock-full of insights and exercises based on decades of scientific research by leading figures in the field of positive psychology.

Although this research has been applied in a wide variety of contexts—from education to coaching, from economics to business, and from medicine to law—this is the first book applying positive psychology to romantic relationships. The two of us have each been working in positive psychology for more than a decade, benefiting from the wide-ranging research on how to live a flourishing life. When we got married, we found that our life together opened up vast new opportunities—and challenges—for applying this research. Although there were many relevant studies in the field that could be of great help to couples like us, no one had brought them together into an easily accessible format. Suzie had begun to do just that in her writing, with a cover story titled "The Happy Couple" for *Scientific American Mind*.

As we continued to work on applying positive psychology research in our own relationship, Suzie suggested we put together a workshop to see if other couples would find this information valuable, as well. So in 2013 we offered a workshop on "Romance and Research" at the International Positive Psychology Association's Third World Congress on Positive Psychology. We were shocked at the number of people who packed the room and were deeply encouraged by their overwhelmingly positive response to this material. Since then, we have given Romance and Research™ workshops around the world. We are enormously grateful to those who have attended these workshops, as they have helped us learn new insights in the application of positive psychology research to romantic relationships. They have also encouraged us to continue this work and to write about it for a larger audience.

We are now excited to be able to present this work in book format. And we offer it to all those who are—or hope to be—in romantic relationships and want to make them the happiest, healthiest, and most fulfilling they can be. We want to be clear we are not claiming that we as a couple have it all figured out, that our relationship is one blissful moment after another, and that if you follow our instructions, you too will live happily ever after. (Trust us, it's not sunshine and rainbows all the time for us, either!) Instead of fairy-tale endings, we believe in brave beginnings and informed efforts, not so we can magically find the relationship of our dreams, but so we can wisely create beautiful relationships in the real world.

Note that this book is not titled *13 Steps to a Blissful Marriage*, *The Complete Guide to Happily Ever After*, or *Everything You Need to Know About Romantic Relationships*. Although such titles seem appealing in the easy promises they offer, we believe they are fundamentally misleading. Marriages are not meat loafs, in which mastering a few steps will yield perfect results every time. Nor are they so simple that anyone can provide a complete guide to them, since each and every marriage or partnership is affected by myriad complications, starting with the two people in it. The truth is, real human relationships can be delightful, uplifting, and satisfying, yet are often messy and frustrating—and sometimes heartbreaking. The important thing to keep in mind is that, as with any human endeavor, we can get better at relationships through well-directed effort.

We believe in the importance of working on our relationships just like we work on our bodies at the gym. Fitness doesn't come magically; it's the result of sustained effort. And this effort needs to be directed wisely. This is why we turn to trainers for advice. And any good trainer will tell you how important it is to develop good exercise habits that can make it easier to get to the gym and keep going on our routines. This is true of relationships, as well. Sustained effort and habits are essential. And once we begin to see the fruits of our labor, and enjoy greater understanding and better interactions with our partners, we naturally become motivated to work even harder. Eventually, the hard work doesn't seem to be so "hard" or "work" at all, but rather becomes natural and fun behavior we want to keep doing. To help us direct our efforts wisely in our "relationship gym," we will need to look to leading researchers in the field of positive psychology for their evidence-based advice. Since positive psychology is steeped in a rich philosophical tradition, we will also look to great thinkers such as Aristotle, who extolled the value of "the good life" and expounded on what good relationships look like, and William James, who emphasized the importance of cultivating healthy habits through continual effort and directed attention.

There is far more sound psychological and philosophical advice on how to be happy together than we could possibly include in a single volume, so we have tried to select some of the best advice and put it together in a way that is clear and immediately applicable. We encourage you to go through this book with your significant other, if possible, since working together through this material can help you learn about each other and bond as a couple. If that is not possible—if you're not in a relationship right now, or if your partner would rather not accompany you for any reason—never fear. You can still benefit tremendously from this material.

As you read this book, please do make time to do the exercises in each chapter. Going to the gym doesn't help you unless you actually work out while you're there. And while you can learn a lot of facts and gain some intellectual insights from just reading this book, it is in actually putting this material into practice in your life that you stand to benefit most from it. You can complete the exercises with your significant other, with a friend or family member, or on your own. But please do complete them!

Whether you are newlyweds or newly single, whether you have been married for fifty years or have not yet been in a romantic relationship, we invite you to think of this book as an invitation to the relationship gym, where we can all benefit from the advice of psychologists and philosophers to help us actively build love that lasts.

CHAPTER 1

Is Love Really
All You Need?

*J*ANUARY 16, 2010, *was an unusually sunny and balmy Saturday for the dead of winter in Philadelphia. I began that day like any other, with an outdoor run, this time in workout tights and a lightweight T-shirt rather than my heavy fleece and usual winter running attire. The mild weather was a welcome respite from the typical frigid temperatures this time of year, not only because it came after one of the biggest snowstorms in the city's recent history, but also because it was the perfect start to an extraordinary day I'll never forget—a day I had dreamt about all my life. My wedding day. As I ran through the familiar winding roads of my childhood hometown with the sun's golden rays warming my face, I thought to myself that the glorious sunshine boded well for a lifetime of happiness. I mounted the final hill, feeling triumphant.*

Six hours later, clad in an exquisite Vienna ball gown, I stood at the altar of the Cathedral Basilica of Saints Peter and Paul, the largest Catholic church in Pennsylvania. I was beaming from having just wed James, the handsome and brilliant man who had captured my heart, dazzling me with his witty charm, sensitive soul, and elegant mind. We have a promising and happy future ahead, *I thought to myself. As we stepped off the altar hand in hand, I smiled at our loved ones who had come out to witness and share in our celebration of love. The notes of Beethoven's symphonic "Ode to Joy," performed by the trumpeter and organist we'd hired for this special day, floated around us as we walked slowly down the aisle.*

James joined right in, intoning the lyrics in his powerful baritone voice—and in German! "Why am I not surprised?" I laughed to myself, watching him joyfully singing along to the music.

I was suddenly catapulted back to another time when James surprised me with his knowledge. A month or two before our first kiss, we happened to be lingering on the steps of this very cathedral. I showed him a book I was reading, The Confessions of Saint Augustine, *and we discussed our mutual admiration for this classic. After a while, James asked me what time it was, and wanting to impress him I responded cheekily, "What then is time?" Without missing a beat, he launched into Augustine's original question in Latin, "Quid est ergo tempus?" Then he continued to quote Augustine in English, "If no one asks me, I know. If I wish to explain it to him who asks, I do not know."[1] I was floored. My intention had been to impress* him, *but now it was* I *who was impressed! The butterflies that always fluttered in my stomach when I was in his presence now broke into full choreographic celebration.*

Like on that first day standing on the cathedral steps together discussing Augustine, I couldn't but feel happy! It was like my past and present had merged together, and time stood still. (What then is time, indeed!) Now once again we stood on the same church steps together, but instead of James reciting Augustine's famous passage on time, he—my modern-day philosopher-poet husband—was soulfully singing the lyrics to "Ode to Joy." Written by yet another genius philosopher, the German poet Friedrich Schiller, the lyrics address another universal topic: the value of an enduring relationship.

Whoever has created an abiding friendship,
Or has won a true and loving wife,

All who can call at least one soul theirs,
Join in our song of praise. . . . [2]

I felt full of vitality and positive emotions. It was the perfect day to
begin our lives together. A natural-born optimist, I was certain that this
loving feeling would last forever.

SITTING ON THE BALCONY of our high-rise condominium in Philadelphia, I gaze into the distance at the midnight blue Delaware River. The sun warming my shoulders on this unusually mild winter afternoon takes me back to another unseasonably warm day. My wedding day.

All you need is love, love. Love is all you need. The Beatles' legendary lyrics play in my head.

I can remember thinking that day that the warm, positive feeling of love coursing through James and me would be enough to carry us through our life together, be it the good times or the bad. I assumed a happy, long-lasting marriage was as simple as coasting along side by side on those loving feelings. *We have plenty of love to carry us through anything*, I remember thinking on that sunny January day.

Now, after years of marriage, I'm sitting here pondering whether love really *is* all you need. If so, what about those inevitable times when you are not feeling so loving toward your partner or spouse? When, to quote the Righteous Brothers' famous lyrics, "You've lost that lovin' feelin'?" because despite your repeated requests, your spouse continually forgets—or even worse, ignores!—your pleas to exercise, be on time, clean up the home office, or [insert your own favorite irritation here]. Then what?

Do we have to *feel* loving all the time to *be* loving?

If so, then James and I are in serious trouble. But then so is every other couple I know. So if it's not mere feelings that do it, what, then, does make a couple happy together over the long term? What is the key to building love that lasts?

SO HOW DO YOU GET
TO HAPPILY EVER AFTER?

After spending nearly half my life—almost twenty years—working in media and communications in New York City and then getting married a bit later in life (at forty), I am only now realizing the extent to which I have been influenced by how relationships are popularly portrayed. Unlike my husband, James, who spent more time listening to Beethoven's beautiful symphonies than the Beatles' peppy love songs growing up, I had a preconceived notion of what marriage should look like based upon what I'd seen and heard in popular media. I still believed in storybook romances, as so many young women (and men) do. If you listen to popular media, you know you fall in love, get married, and live happily ever after. End of story.

And I fell for this fairy tale—hook, line, and sinker.

The problem with fairy tales, though, is that they focus only on the first two parts of the story: falling in love and getting married. In the first part of the story, you dream of finding and falling in love with your perfect partner, that special someone you want to spend the rest of your life with. You invest an enormous amount of time and effort into finding a mate: going on countless dates, signing up for innumerable online dating apps, and madly scanning profiles or swiping left and right in a furious search for the perfect person. Once you find that special someone, of course, you dive into all the courting, dating, meeting of the friends and families— and if things go well, the eventual proposal.

This brings you to the second part of the story: getting married.

During the engagement period, you immerse yourself in meticulous preparation for the wedding: searching for the perfect dress, choosing the venue, selecting the band, finding the best photographer, and creating the menu, not to mention figuring out the seating chart. The list goes on. And on. And *on*. (Speaking for myself, it seems that I made many more deliberate decisions about details in the few intense months of preparation for my wedding than I did in the first few years of my marriage!)

And these activities are all for just one day! Sound familiar?

Falling in love is an amazing experience, and a wedding can be magical (ours certainly was!). It's definitely worth putting effort into these two parts of the story. The problem is that fairy tales don't say anything about the third (and longest) part of the story, except that the couple "lived happily ever after." We are given no hint about how we can actually go about doing so. But if we want the marriage—the happily ever after—to last a lifetime, shouldn't we actually spend more time in meticulous preparation for all those years to come than for the single day that kicks it off? We have all kinds of help (from family, friends, wedding planners, caterers, you name it) to get ready for our special day, but what about the years (and decades) that follow? Who will help us prepare for those? Imagine if a fraction of all the time and attention we put into our wedding day were put into our marriages! Not just in the planning of the wedding but in the long journey that comes afterward! If we invested equal energy into what happens after "I do," wouldn't we be more prepared for what happens down the road and increase our chances for the long-term success of our relationship?

In other areas of our lives, of course, we expect to have to put in careful work to achieve the results we are looking for. No one expects that landing our first job will automatically lead to a successful career, that planting a few seeds will inevitably yield a garden full of delicious, home-grown vegetables, or that the simple act of buying a gym membership will effortlessly tone our bodies and allow us to fit into smaller-sized jeans.

So back to my original question: What, then, makes a couple happy together? Clearly, it can't just be falling in love or planning a magical wedding day. What comes next? If we're prepared to work hard to turn a job into a career, seeds into healthy vegetables, and a gym membership into fitness, what steps can we take to turn a memorable wedding day into a lifelong, fulfilling, and happy marriage? Since we're never told in storybook romances the details of the happily ever after, it seems it's just supposed to happen automatically. Of course, that's not how things work in the real world. So where can we turn for advice on this crucial question?

In my own life, the key has been the wedding favors. Allow me to explain.

After my career in media and corporate communications, I started a new career as a freelance writer, studying research outcomes in the (then) new field of positive psychology and publishing articles on them. James was also working in this field, directing and teaching in the Master of Applied Positive Psychology (MAPP) program at the University of Pennsylvania, which is how we met. Given this background in positive psychology, we had a great interest in what makes a couple happy—especially when we started our own relationship!

It just so happens that at the same time I was also writing a cover story titled "The Happy Couple" for *Scientific American Mind* magazine.[3] My article addressed how couples can create happier marriages by applying the science of positive psychology to their relationships. Specifically, it focused on research supporting three key activities for flourishing: cultivating positive emotions in your daily life, developing a harmonious or healthy passion, and remembering to seek out and celebrate the good times rather than just focusing on fixing problems.

Coincidentally, as luck (or perhaps destiny) would have it, the article ended up hitting newsstands the month we walked down the aisle. If impending marriage alone doesn't create pressure enough for any couple embarking on the new adventure of a life journey together, having your cover article heralding "The Happy Couple" from newsstands everywhere while you exchange vows sure does!

There was, however, one lucky advantage to this timing. We realized copies of my article would make great wedding favors, reminding us (and our guests) that happily ever after doesn't simply *happen*. And in the spirit of celebration, we decided to take some liberties with the accompanying pictures, replacing the stock photos of smiling couples with fun pictures of the two of us. We then rolled the articles into scrolls and tied them with ribbons embossed with "Happily Ever After" that I had stumbled upon at our local craft store.

The wedding favors were a hit, and although we didn't realize it at the time, they were the seeds of what would eventually grow into this book. As we began our life together as a newly minted couple with a shared interest in positive psychology, human nature, and helping others, we were both naturally curious to dig deeper into what makes a couple happy together, particularly once the excitement of the wedding day and the initial newlywed bliss have faded. Ever since then, we have been on a personal and professional journey to discover what leads to marital longevity and satisfaction.

My article, we realized, just scratched the surface of the ways in which positive psychology research could be helpful for developing healthy romantic relationships. And now that we were married, talks about what makes a happy couple went from interesting discussions to necessary investigations. I suggested we write this book together as a way of digging deeper into the science and its application. James agreed, seeing it as a shared project we could undertake to help develop and strengthen our own marriage and at the same time provide a resource that could be helpful to others.

In the rest of this chapter, we'd like to introduce you to positive psychology and explain why it's such an important area of research for people in romantic relationships. Our favorite way of introducing the field is through an interactive thought experiment James devised.

WHAT IS POSITIVE PSYCHOLOGY?

While browsing at a local flea market, you stumble across what looks like a magic lamp in one of the stalls. Just for fun, you rub it—and to your amazement, out pops a genie! The genie calls you by name and says she's been waiting to meet you for a long time. She says she is so impressed with you that she wants to transform you into a superhero. Before she can do so, though, she needs to know what color you would like your cape to be. She gives you two options. Choosing a red cape will give you powers, or "cape-abilities" (sorry, we couldn't help ourselves!), to fight *against* unfair and unjust things in the world we want to discourage or end, things such as poverty, disease, prejudice, hatred, and war. Choosing a green cape will give you cape-abilities to fight *for* the things in the world we want to encourage and promote: things like abundance, health, justice, love, and peace. The genie tells you that you can choose only one of the capes. Take a moment right now to consider: Which cape would you choose? And why?

You may think the red cape is the responsible choice, since there is so much suffering in the world that should be stopped immediately. Or you may prefer it because you feel it's easier for people to agree on how to put the red cape to use. It's often easier to see eye-to-eye on what problems need to be addressed than on what opportunities should be realized. Alternatively, you may choose the green cape, because you feel that would be more uplifting. Or perhaps because you realize there are at least times when realizing an opportunity can also solve a problem. Increased love and understanding in a relationship, for example, can ease much of the tension that may otherwise lead to frustrations and fights. So which cape *should* you choose?

The point of this exercise is not to argue that one is right and the other wrong. Instead, the point we want to emphasize is that they are different. Whichever cape you choose—and for whatever reason you choose it—you can be a successful superhero. If you choose the red cape, you will look for problems to solve. Since there are many problems in this world, you will find plenty of them and have a meaningful life fixing things that are wrong. Alternatively, if you choose the green cape, you will look for opportunities. Since there are many opportunities in this world, you will find plenty of them and have a meaningful life helping to realize them.

Although choosing either the red or the green cape is fine if you want meaning in your life, it's not going to work if you're aiming for happiness. Without getting too technical (although James would certainly like to!), this is because happiness is not merely the opposite of unhappiness. Simple opposites are ones in which you can't have both at the same time. Think about a toilet seat. It's either up or it's down (depending, no doubt, on who used it last!). If you know it's not up, then it must be down; if you know it's not down, then it must be up. But happiness is not like a toilet seat. In the case of happiness and unhappiness, you can have one or the other—or neither, or both. In fact, most of us would probably say that our lives at any given moment (except for our wedding day, of course!) are a combination of happy and unhappy. We nearly always are feeling some levels of happiness and unhappiness at the same time. To be happy, we certainly need to be able to protect ourselves from things that threaten and harm us. By itself, though, the power to fight against unhappiness doesn't automatically produce happiness. As we will see in chapter 4, for example, getting rid of sadness does not automatically produce joy, and getting rid of anger does not automatically yield love. So having just a red cape or just a green cape is not sufficient if we want to be happy.

The good news is that we don't need to be limited by genies trying to force us to choose between red and green capes. In fact, we don't need genies at all! Our *genes* have already equipped us with the power to fight against the things we don't want in our lives and to cultivate those we do. In essence, nature has already given us a reversible cape with a red side and a green side. The challenge is that most of us find it much easier to use the red than the green side of the cape. This is because our evolutionary history has instilled in us the ability to look for, anticipate, and avoid danger in order to survive. Psychologists call this our "negativity bias."[4] We typically know when we have problems, because they scream at us to get our attention and we're programmed to listen up. But amid all the noisy problems and worries in our lives, we don't always recognize the opportunities for improvement or greater happiness that surround us, because they simply whisper their possibilities . . . and then pass by without a fuss.

Here is where positive psychology comes in. Taking into account that most of us tend to overuse the red side of our reversible cape, positive psychology uses scientific research to discover and teach us how we can use the green side of our cape more frequently and effectively.

Positive psychology is a science that focuses on human strengths and potential and celebrates what's best in life. It emphasizes goals, well-being, satisfaction, happiness, interpersonal skills, perseverance, talent, wisdom, and personal responsibility. Positive psychologists study the impact of concepts such as passion, gratitude, savoring, and spirituality on our well-being in order to understand what qualities and feelings make life really fulfilling and worth living. The ultimate goal of this research is to help people cultivate and benefit from these qualities in their own lives and relationships.

Positive psychology is based on the uplifting tenet that we can learn to improve our lot in life. Many people feel stuck with the cards they've been dealt and believe their happiness is a result of what happens to them. Positive psychology, by contrast, emphasizes that happiness is largely a result of how we choose to respond to what happens to us. By learning how to respond more positively to the events in our lives, we can strongly influence the quality of our experience.

Positive psychology was launched in 1998 by University of Pennsylvania psychology professor Martin Seligman when he was president of the American Psychological Association (APA). During his presidential address at the APA convention that year, he observed that in the second half of the twentieth century, psychology had become largely a science of healing, focused on diagnosing and treating a growing range of mental illnesses. Acknowledging that this work is important, he pointed out that psychology had, unfortunately, neglected the complementary study of what makes life most worth living, citing as examples "optimism, courage, work ethic, future-mindedness, interpersonal skill, the capacity for pleasure and insight, and social responsibility." He argued that psychology's original purpose had been to help "make the lives of all people more fulfilling and productive," and that to achieve this purpose, it had to balance its important emphasis on repairing the worst things in life with the equally important work of building the best things in life to understand and promote the actions that "lead to well-being, to positive individuals, to flourishing communities, and to a just society."[5] His address was a smashing hit, with his colleagues giving him a standing ovation—and positive psychology was launched.

Seligman was one of a handful of psychology researchers who had begun exploring positive topics—what we are calling the green side of our capes. Others included Mihaly Csikszentmihalyi, then of the University of Chicago, with his research on flow experiences (times when we get so caught up in what we are doing that we lose a sense of time—and even of ourselves as existing outside the activity), and Ed Diener, then of the University of Illinois, with his research on subjective well-being (what it feels like to be you on the inside and how satisfied you are with your life).

At the time positive psychology was founded, James was a newly minted PhD in philosophy. Having read Seligman's 1991 book, *Learned Optimism*,[6] he was intrigued by the empirical research into the causes of depression and the evidence-based suggestions for how we can cultivate flexible and adaptive optimism in our lives, making it more likely for us to be successful, happy, and healthy and to enjoy flourishing relationships. James was fascinated that psychologists were turning to questions of how to live life well, and that they were bringing new, empirical methods to bear on inquiries that had been occupying philosophers for thousands of years. Shortly afterward, he attended the first public conference on positive psychology and immediately hit it off with the man everyone called "Marty." They began collaborating on various projects, and a few years later Marty invited James to join him in the Positive Psychology Center at the University of Pennsylvania to help develop the world's first degree program in positive psychology: the MAPP program.

Around this time, Suzie left her job as a vice president at a large public relations firm in New York City and became a freelance writer. She was soon intrigued by this new field of positive psychology. After devouring *Learned Optimism* in one sitting, she returned to Penn, her alma mater, to study positive psychology. During her time there, she observed that relatively little work had been done applying positive psychology research to relationships, and after completing her studies, she pitched an article on this topic to *Scientific American Mind*. As she worked on "The Happy Couple," she realized even more clearly how crucial this area is and how important it is to develop it further.

APPLYING POSITIVE PSYCHOLOGY TO ROMANTIC RELATIONSHIPS

Positive psychologists value relationships greatly. In fact, Christopher Peterson, one of the leading figures in positive psychology, argued that you could summarize positive psychology in three words: *Other people matter.*[7] And Seligman identifies relationships as one of the five key elements of flourishing in his model of well-being. Called PERMA, this model includes Positive emotions, Engagement, Relationships, Meaning, and Accomplishment.[8] While each element is important to a well-balanced life, we believe positive relationships may be *the* most important. Scientific evidence, as well as our own personal experiences, supports our belief. We evolved as social animals, after all. And having someone to share things with can add even more meaning to a great life.

Before the advent of positive psychology, the discipline of psychology was largely focused on disease and dysfunction—in other words, on things that need to be fixed (the red-cape approach). And psychological research on relationships was largely relegated to explorations of what goes wrong in them. To this day, most relationship books focus on fixing problems couples face. By contrast, we will take a green-cape approach in this book, which is the first one to apply positive psychology research to romantic relationships.

Red-cape efforts are important, of course, but if they are not balanced by green-cape approaches and behaviors—which are the actual practices that create and sustain happiness, satisfaction, and enjoyment in a relationship—then those efforts are much less likely to succeed.

That's why we set out to study and understand how we can apply positive psychology principles to romantic relationships and balance the reactive red-cape mindset with the more proactive green-cape perspective. In reviewing the scientific literature, we found four areas that are especially important in making relationships last.

1. *Passion* fuels our relationships, and many other aspects of our lives, including our leisure activities and our work. As every romantic understands, it's important to know how to cultivate passion. But as positive psychology research shows, it's important to cultivate the *right kind* of passion. The wrong kind can actually be damaging and worse than not having any passion at all. We'll explore which kind to encourage and which to avoid in relationships, as well as effective (and fun!) ways to do just that.

2. *Positive emotions* are more than merely pleasant feelings to enjoy; they can also have ongoing positive consequences in our lives, like making us more creative. And although we often think of positive emotions as being the *result* of good things happening in our lives, they can *cause* good things to happen, as well. In the context of relationships, positive emotions are not simply indicators that things are going well; they can also help us take actions that will keep the relationship healthy. Most relationships begin in a burst of positive emotions, but we are likely to experience fewer of them as the relationship develops and we settle into it over time. Although it's

important to respect the full range of emotions that are a part of the human experience and allow yourself to feel and acknowledge them when they come up, it's especially important, as a relationship matures, to learn how to cultivate positive emotions in yourself and toward your partner.

3. *Savoring* helps us make the most of positive emotions and other good experiences. Often, we take these kinds of experiences for granted, enjoying them for a brief moment and then moving on with our busy lives. Research on savoring shows us the value of intentionally opening ourselves as fully as we can to the positive moments while they are happening, of remembering positive moments from our past, and of anticipating positive moments in the future.

4. *Character* is a key part of who we are and how we relate to others. Knowing what our particular character strengths are and how to cultivate them can help us guide our lives and direct our efforts in ways that are likely to yield the greatest results. It can also help us contribute in better ways to our relationships. Knowing the strengths of our significant others, and sharing our strengths with them, can help us avoid some of the frictions and frustrations that can arise from differences in our personalities, and it can help make the relationship itself greater than the sum of its parts.

These areas of research will form the core of our investigation throughout this book. In part 1, we will examine some of the characteristics of a healthy relationship. We will begin with ancient wisdom by exploring what Aristotle had to say about cultivating good relationships and then move to scientific research on passion, positive emotions, and savoring and the roles they play in creating lasting love. Each chapter begins with anecdotes that illustrate a key aspect of healthy relationships, then examines what the research says about it, and ends with an exercise we invite you to undertake with your significant other. Remember, this is a relationship gym, so do be sure to complete the exercises with your romantic partner to build your relationship muscles! If your significant other is unable or unwilling to participate, or if you don't have a romantic partner in your life right now, feel free to complete the exercises on your own, or with a friend or family member. In part 2, we will examine key ways to cultivate healthy relationships by focusing on character strengths, a foundational area of research in positive psychology. We will adapt them to relationships by means of an Interaction Model we have developed and will teach you how to use.

So let's get started! In the next chapter, we will take you on a journey back in time for a look into Aristotle's *Nicomachean Ethics*, one of the most important philosophical works exploring what constitutes the good life and good relationships. This will help provide a powerful framework we will use to apply positive psychology research to relationships. But first, be sure to take a few minutes to complete the following exercise to help you apply what we have discussed in this chapter and prepare you for the chapters to come.

"CAPE-ABILITY" PRACTICE EXERCISE

Spend a few minutes thinking about your relationship and the typical interactions you have with your partner. Write down your answers to the following questions:

- Which side of your reversible cape do you tend to use more? The red side or the green side? Explain.

- How might your relationship be improved if you used the green side of your cape more often and more effectively?
- What concrete steps can you take to make better use of the green side of your cape in your relationship?

PART 1

The Philosophy and Psychology Behind Long-Lasting Love

CHAPTER 2

What Aristotle Can Teach Us About Building Love That Lasts

*M*ELVIN, A SOCIALLY *awkward middle-aged man who hasn't had much experience dating, is at a fine restaurant with Carol, a warm-hearted and quick-witted woman he's been seeing, in what seems, perhaps, to be Melvin's earnest attempt to finally win her over. Up to this point, their relationship has been rocky, to say the least. Carol recounted to Melvin how she felt when they first met: "I thought you were handsome, but then you spoke." Throughout their relationship Melvin's actions and words, regardless of his intentions, have tended to offend rather than uplift Carol. On this particular evening, he finally musters up the courage to be vulnerable with her and says something touching and profound that leaves her speechless. He tells her, "You make me want to be a better man."*

If this sounds familiar to you, it's probably because it's a famous scene from the 1997 Academy Award–winning film *As Good as It Gets*, in which Jack Nicholson plays Melvin, a curmudgeonly writer, and Helen Hunt portrays Carol, a spunky waitress and single mom who's been down on her luck lately.[1] They both received Oscars for

their brilliant and nuanced portrayals of these believable and lov-
able characters with all their quirks.

Now contrast this popular movie scene with a famous scene
from another critically acclaimed and Oscar-nominated film, *Jerry
Maguire*, in which the leading man, Jerry, played by Tom Cruise,
suddenly returns to his estranged wife. He surprises a stunned and
teary-eyed Dorothy, portrayed by Renée Zellweger, in a room
packed full with her friends and family, with the declaration "You
complete me."[2]

These two scenes present very different reasons for being in a
relationship. Melvin wants to be with Carol because he sees how
good she is and this motivates him to want to become a better version of himself. Jerry, by contrast, feels like Dorothy is his other
half, that he is not whole without her. We invite you to consider
your own reasons for being in a relationship, either one you are in
now or one you would like to be in at some point in the future. Are
your motivations more like Melvin's or more like Jerry's?

Jerry's perspective is very much like the pop-culture or storybook-
romance view Suzie mentioned having fallen for hook, line, and
sinker growing up. This concept of soul mates, the romantic notion
that there is but one unique, idealized person who will forever
complete us and lead us to happily ever after, is a popular theme in
religion, literature, poetry, and philosophy. It goes back at least
to Plato, who presents a fascinating take on it in one of his most
important dialogues, *Symposium*.

In this dialogue, Plato tells the story of a dinner party in which
the guests each take a turn describing and praising love. One of the
guests is Aristophanes, an award-winning comic playwright from
Athens, who claims love is nothing other than our desire to find the
person who completes us. He backs up his claim by regaling the
guests with an ingenious myth about human nature. Long ago,
Aristophanes begins, humans had spherical bodies with four arms

and four legs growing out of them. They had two faces, each with a set of ears, placed on opposing sides of their round heads. And they had two sets of sex organs. If they were ever in a hurry, they could move rapidly by putting out all their limbs and rolling along like a gymnast doing cartwheels.

These humans were very powerful, Aristophanes continues, and they were quite ambitious. So much so that they tried to ascend to heaven so they could attack the gods. Naturally, this alarmed the gods, who had a meeting to decide what to do. They didn't want to destroy the humans with thunderbolts, because they would then lose the worship and the sacrifices the humans brought them. But they clearly had to do something. At last, Zeus had an idea. He decided to cut them in half, so each would have only two arms and two legs and only one face. This would serve to weaken them, and at the same time increase their sacrifices, since it would double their number. So he sliced each person in half, with the warning that if they didn't behave, he would slice them in half again and they would have to go around hopping on one leg. He then told Apollo to turn each person's head around (so they could see the cut and be reminded to behave themselves) and then heal the wounds. Apollo drew the skin over each person's wound and pulled it together like a pouch with a drawstring, creating what we now call our navels.

Unfortunately, Zeus's plan didn't quite work out as he had intended. The humans, used to being whole and now feeling lonely, spent all their time searching for their other half. And when they found the other person, they embraced each other and did not let go, hoping to grow back into a whole again. They couldn't do anything in this condition, so the gods weren't getting their sacrifices. Worse still, the human pairs began dying from starvation. Zeus quickly realized further action was needed, so he moved their genitals around to the front of each person. That way, when they came together and embraced, they would find satisfaction in intercourse and then be able to go about their other duties, remembering to eat and to offer sacrifices to the gods.

This explains, Aristophanes concludes, why love draws us to find our other half. Originally, he says, there were three genders, not just two. In addition to males and females, there used to be androgynous humans, who were made up of male and female elements. If we were originally part of an androgynous human, then we are drawn to members of the opposite sex. Women who were part of a female whole are lesbians, who look for another woman to complete them, and men who were part of a male whole are gay and thus attracted to other men. Because of our history, we long for wholeness and are driven to find our other half, who completes us. Once we find this person, we want nothing other than to be with him or her as much as we possibly can.[3]

Although this myth is comical in certain ways, it is also profoundly serious, as it tries to explain that deep feeling of connection and recognition we sometimes feel when meeting another person. Two thousand years after Aristophanes and in a very different culture, these feelings were explored by another playwright who has had an enormous influence on our views of romantic relationships. William Shakespeare wrote a number of plays in which characters fall in love at first sight. The most famous of these lovers are no doubt Romeo and Juliet. Although scholars have debated whether Shakespeare's depictions were meant to celebrate or undermine this experience, his dramatizations certainly popularized it.

Today, the term *soul mate* is often used to capture some of these perspectives of what an ideal romantic relationship should look like. Don't get us wrong: We're all for experiencing deep feelings of connection, and we understand they can sometimes occur very early in a relationship. With that said, though, there are several dangers that can arise if we expect another person to be the soul mate that completes us. First, it can make us start to think of relationships as a matter of fate. We may come to believe these moments of connection are completely beyond our control and even influence. If we believe there is nothing we can do to prepare ourselves for these romantic lightning strikes, we may not have much motivation to focus on our own self-development, to cultivate the kinds of intrapersonal and interpersonal skills that are foundational for any kind of romantic relationship and that contribute to the success of a long-term commitment.[4] We may also not notice important clues about our partner and our relationship. Although a sense of sacredness can be beneficial in a marriage,[5] an overly rigid sense of fate may be detrimental, especially if it motivates us to disregard important information, including alarming red flags, as we move forward in the relationship.

A second danger that can arise from expecting another person to complete us is that we may become overly reliant on that person. We may fall prey to a kind of codependency in which we have a hard time developing as a full human being because we are leaning on our partner to fulfill us in a way that encourages or enables our immaturity, insecurity, or imbalance. Healthy relationships are characterized by a kind of interdependence,[6] in which the other person doesn't so much complete us as complement us. In this kind of relationship, each person can be secure, mature, and whole in him- or herself, while at the same time being vulnerable and open to the other, appreciating the unique strengths the other person brings to the relationship, and benefiting from a mutual giving and receiving of support.

A third danger in this perspective is that a sense of being completed by another person—great as it may feel in the moment—can be very difficult to sustain. This is because we are all continually in the process of becoming something we never were before.[7] So what "completes" us at one point in our lives is likely to be very different from what does so at some other point. And if our relationship is based on our completing someone else, we may feel pressured to try to continue to be what that person needs instead of who we most truly are and who we are becoming. Perhaps it should not be surprising that the romanticized tales of relationships we discussed in the previous chapter often simply end with the claim that the couple lived happily ever after. If instead of these formulaic endings, the tales went on to recount what actually happened in the rest of the couples' lives, we would no doubt see how unsustainable many of those relationships really were.

But what about the view that relationships succeed to the extent to which partners sacrifice themselves for each other? According to this popular perspective, only when individuals give up their autonomy can the relationship flourish. But this common approach actually flies in the face of strong scientific evidence. This point was made to us recently by Ed Deci, who along with Richard Ryan (both psychology researchers at the University of Rochester) developed *self-determination theory* (SDT), one of the best-supported theories of human motivation. SDT distinguishes between two types of motivation:

- *Autonomous motivation*, in which "you do something with a full sense of willingness, volition, and choice, either because it is interesting to you or personally valued and important to you."
- *Controlled motivation*, in which "you do something because you were seduced or coerced to do it—for example, with rewards or threats of punishment—and your experience is one of pressure, obligation, and tension."[8]

"Couples can accommodate without mutual autonomy," Ed told us. "You can persevere in the relationship, but you won't feel deeply satisfied and joyful about it." So instead of giving up autonomy in a relationship, Ed advises, couples should follow the research indicating that the healthiest relationships are ones in which each person supports the autonomous motivation of the other. In other words, instead of requiring the other person to be what we need, we work to help him become who *he* is. And instead of obligating us to become what he needs, he frees us to be who *we* are. This does not mean, of course, that we don't provide our partner with as much support as we can. What it does mean, though, is that we are not defined by what the other person lacks.

Although the scene in which Jerry tells Dorothy she completes him is a very impassioned and powerful one, we suspect his motivations for continuing the relationship will cause problems in the long run. Jerry values Dorothy instrumentally, because she completes him. The perspective here is very self-oriented, and the underlying danger is that if Dorothy stops completing him, Jerry will stop loving her.

If Jerry's approach to relationships is problematic, what about Melvin's?

WHAT MELVIN GOT RIGHT

We all know what a platonic friendship is, right? A nonsexual relationship. What about an Aristotelian friendship? What is that? Although you've likely never heard this term before, we believe it's a concept everyone interested in romantic relationships should know about. So let's dig into it now.

Aristotle holds that love is the greatest external good.[9] And he says we tend to love three different kinds of things: those that are useful, those that are pleasurable, and those that are good. He claims, furthermore, that there is a kind of friendship that corresponds to each of these categories. Let's take a look at each, in turn.

The first type of friendship is between people who find each other useful. They may see in their relationship an opportunity for profit, often focusing on financial gain. They may, for example, decide to create a mutually beneficial business partnership. This kind of relationship, indeed, may be very profitable, Aristotle says, but he also points out problems that tend to arise with it. Since the whole basis of the friendship is what each person can get out of it, it is self-oriented and can quickly lead to quarrels if one or the other partner feels he or she is being shortchanged. And such quarrels often spell the end of friendships like these. If either partner feels the relationship is no longer useful to them, they will likely simply cut off the relationship and move on.

The second type of friendship Aristotle describes is between people who find it pleasurable to be with each other. This type of friendship is higher than the first, Aristotle says, because friends who come together for profit may not actually enjoy spending time with each other. But friends who come together for pleasure are often witty and do actually enjoy each other's company. They may, for example, like to get together on the weekends and go out for a good time on the town. Aristotle notes that these friendships can, indeed, be very pleasant, but he also observes that problems can quickly arise in these kinds of relationships, as well. As with friendships of utility, friendships of pleasure are also self-oriented, with the goal for each person being the pleasure they can get from it. And if the friendship somehow stops leading to pleasure, the friends will likely quickly part, with the relationship coming to an end. Both of these types of friendships, Aristotle says, are instrumental. We enter into them because of something we can get out of them. And when we stop getting what we want from them—profit or pleasure—we see no value in the relationship, and it simply dies.

This brings us to the third type of friendship. This kind of friendship, Aristotle says, is based on the good. Two people are attracted to each other because of the good they see in the other person. They value the other person's character and want to help it continue to grow and develop in healthy directions. The good they see in the other person may also inspire them to want to become better themselves. This type of friendship, Aristotle argues, is not self-oriented or instrumental. Each person is focused not on him- or herself, but on the other person. The partners love each other for who they are, and not for what they can get out of the relationship. Aristotle holds that this type of friendship will probably be much more enduring than the first two, since it is likely to be brought to an end only if one of the persons involved becomes corrupt and stops being good. Aristotle contends that friendship based on goodness is the truest kind, superior to the other two. Additionally, he says, these kinds of friendships, although they are not motivated by the quest for profit or pleasure, often do turn out to be useful and pleasurable, as well as good.[10]

After getting married, Suzie asked James why Aristotle's observations need to be limited to just friendships. "What if we apply his philosophy to romantic relationships, as well? What if we see ourselves not just as lovers, but as Aristotelian lovers, focusing on appreciating the good in the other person and supporting each other's growth and development?" James embraced this idea wholeheartedly. And that's how Aristotle became part of the foundation of our marriage—and of the framework for applying positive psychology research to romantic relationships.

Think about your relationship from the standpoint of Aristotle's analysis of friendship. Like friendships, marriages and other romantic relationships can occur on any of the three levels. To what degree have you and your partner been drawn together by utility, pleasure, or goodness? Relationships of utility focus on how each partner can profit from the relationship. This could include immediate or long-term financial security, social standing, or some other type of gain. Relationships of pleasure focus on how each partner can find enjoyment in the relationship. This could come from strong physical attraction, sexual relations, a shared sense of humor, or enjoyment of similar interests, activities, and hobbies. Relationships of goodness are focused on the other person. They are not motivated by what each person can get from the relationship, but rather by the goodness each person sees in the other.

Like Aristotle, we find nothing wrong with profit or pleasure as a part of a healthy relationship. And you may well have been initially drawn to your partner because of one or both of these. But if that's *all* you are focused on at this point, then your relationship may be unnecessarily unstable and not yet fully developed. Aristotle observes that marriages tend to provide profit and pleasure, and if they are between people of good character, they can reach the third level of friendship, as well.[11] We, too, believe that profit and pleasure may well result from a marriage. But they are not good foundations for a mature relationship, since they are self-focused motivations that make the relationship conditional on our needs being met. Focusing on the good in the other person and supporting its development should be the emphasis of the relationship, with profit and pleasure being likely and welcome secondary effects.

This is what Melvin got right. He saw the good in Carol, and that's what attracted him to her. Not only did he value her for who she was, but he was also motivated to become a better person. Aristotle points out that this often happens in such relationships. When we are with others of good character, it motivates us to improve our own character, as well. New York University Stern School of Business social psychologist Jonathan Haidt, author of *The Happiness Hypothesis*, refers to these experiences as ones of being moved or "elevated" by "witnessing acts of virtue or moral beauty."[12] Elevation, an "other-praising" emotion, causes "warm, open feelings in the chest" and inspires people to behave more virtuously themselves. When we are uplifted or elevated, our hearts are opened and our thoughts are more focused on others than on ourselves. We seek ways to make positive changes to enhance our relationships, and we experience moral growth and heightened positive emotions, like that of hope, and ultimately love.[13]

Like Aristotle, we classify love as the greatest external good. Love of the good in the other person is a great foundation for a healthy relationship. We would say that Melvin and Carol became Aristotelian lovers. In contrast to Jerry, whose love depended on the overpowering but unsustainable feeling that Dorothy completed him, Melvin's love depended on the strong and stable valuing of who Carol was as a person. It's unclear what Jerry's love would motivate him to do besides making sure Dorothy continues to complete him, no matter the direction in which either grows in the future. Melvin, on the other hand, is motivated to become a better man, and no doubt to support Carol in her efforts to become a better woman. This is why our bets are on Melvin and Carol's relationship, and why our ideal in our own marriage is to be Aristotelian lovers. It's also why we are working to grow our relationship in this direction and to support others in the development of similar ideals.

Becoming Aristotelian lovers is a great way to be happy together. But happiness can mean a lot of different things. What kind of happiness should Aristotelian lovers aim for?

WHAT THEN IS HAPPINESS?

As you think about your life and your relationship, how would you define happiness? Is it the feeling that comes when you're having fun? Is it the sense of security you get when your needs are met? Is it the realization that you are understood and accepted for who you really are? Is it the conviction that you and your partner can take on anything together? Is it the assurance that you are living a meaningful life? All of the above? None of the above? Something different?

The more we think about what happiness is, the more complicated it can seem. We might be tempted to resort to Augustine's clever answer about time: "If no one asks me, I know. If I wish to explain it to him who asks, I do not know."[14] But before we settle on this answer from Augustine, let's have a little chat with Aristotle. Imagine Aristotle, with a rustle of robes, walks in on you as you are reading this book. He's got a few questions for you:

ARISTOTLE: Hi! I'm Aristotle. What are you up to?

You: I'm reading a great book on relationships.

ARISTOTLE: I recommend you not call a book great until you've finished it. But why are you reading this book?

You: To learn how to have better relationships.

ARISTOTLE: So why do you want to have better relationships?

You: Because I think this will increase my happiness.

ARISTOTLE: And why do you want to be happy?

You: I just do. Doesn't everybody?

ARISTOTLE: Ha! I knew you would wind up here eventually. I could have started with any of your actions, and if I were to continue to ask why long enough, you would eventually wind up with the same answer: because you think it will lead to happiness. This is what motivates all of your actions, whether you realize it or not—and whether or not they actually do result in happiness. That's the first thing to remember about happiness: *Any actions we take are intended to be instrumental for happiness.* The second thing to remember about happiness is that we want it for its own sake. *Happiness itself is not instrumental.* We don't want it for any other reason than that we want it. It's what all humans ultimately want.

You: [*You ponder Aristotle's words. He seems a bit self-assured, bordering on arrogant. But you have to admit that his observations do ring true. The more you think about what he just said, though, the more you realize he didn't actually define happiness.*] Well, you may be right, Aristotle. But you haven't actually told me what happiness is.

Aristotle: You're not going to let me get away with anything, are you? I like that! Well, what do people generally think happiness is?

You: A lot of people think it's pleasure.

Aristotle: Bah! That's ridiculous. Pleasure may be a proper life for cattle, but human beings are capable of so much more than that!

You: Well, other people think happiness lies in fame and honor.

Aristotle: How can it be that people in your time are still caught up in these superficial things? We depend on others for fame and honor. But happiness needs to be something under our own control.

You: Well, what about wealth? Money seems to control everything these days.

Aristotle: We had similar problems in our day, too. But wealth can't be happiness, since we want money for the security it brings or for the things it can buy, and not—like happiness—for its own sake.

You: What then is happiness?

Aristotle: I thought you'd never ask! Human happiness lies in doing well what we are uniquely suited for.

You: Say *what*?

Aristotle: OK, let's break that down. What is the goal of a flute player?

You: To play music?

ARISTOTLE: Yes, that's exactly right! And what is the goal of a
sculptor?

YOU: To create art.

ARISTOTLE: Excellent! And would you agree that the goal of a
flute player is not just to play music but to play it well, and that
the goal of a sculptor is to create excellent art?

YOU: Sure.

ARISTOTLE: OK, so what is the goal of a human being?

YOU: Just one? We have many goals!

ARISTOTLE: Yes, but what is the ultimate goal?

YOU: To live, I guess.

ARISTOTLE: That's not a bad answer. But remember, we are
looking for what we are *uniquely* suited for. Even plants are
well suited for living. So nutrition and growth are not unique
to humans.

YOU: True. Well, how about the senses? Plants don't have senses.
We're uniquely suited for seeing, hearing, touching, smelling,
and tasting.

ARISTOTLE: Yes, except animals can do this, as well. I'll give
you a hint: *Think* about your answer very carefully.

YOU: Oh, of course! We can think in ways plants and animals
cannot.

ARISTOTLE: Yes! You got it! Our rationality sets us uniquely
apart. So human happiness lies in using our rational capacities well. That's why I'm such a happy guy! And with that, I'll
have to take my leave. I'm due back in Athens to teach my
next class at my school, the Lyceum. You should stop by
sometime. You'd be an excellent student!

As you recover from your encounter with Aristotle—thinking
about his insight, his wit, and the way the cut of his robe accented
his wise demeanor— we should go over several important points on

the connection between happiness and relationships that he didn't have time to make before he had to rush off to class.

First, let's consider happiness. The word Aristotle uses for happiness is *eudaimonia*, a compound word constructed from the Greek *eu* (good) and *daimon* (god, spirit, demon). It carries with it connotations of good fortune and divinity, of what might be called blessedness.[15] Aristotle observed that there was near-universal agreement in his day that the good life is a life of *eudaimonia*. But problems arose when people gave their opinions on what the eudaimonic life consists of. Similar disagreements on what happiness is continue today, as well.

If you have young children or nieces or nephews, chances are they will give answers similar to those of our young son, Liam, if you ask them what happiness is. For him, it's eating ice cream and cookies, playing, and going to the zoo. If you ask us as his parents what we most want for our son, we will say that we want him to be happy. Does this mean our highest aspiration for him is that he will have plenty of ice cream and cookies, playdates, and visits to the zoo in his life? Although we hope his life is not devoid of these things, this is not what we mean when we say we want him to be happy. Instead, we mean that we want him to be fulfilled, to be able to find satisfying and meaningful ways to use his interests and talents in the service of something larger than himself. Although the term *eudaimonia* is usually translated as happiness, it means more than just a pleasant mood and refers to overall well-being or flourishing. We will continue to use the word *happiness* in this book, but please keep in mind that we are using it less in the childlike sense and more in the parental sense, with Aristotle's rich and comprehensive notion of *eudaimonia* in mind.

Second, we need to say a little more about what Aristotle means by "rationality." When we think of rationality, we may immediately think of something academic or intellectual. And Aristotle certainly has a lot to say about this type of rationality. But he emphasizes a different kind, as well. *Practical* rationality is what we need, he says, when we want to learn how to do things well. And if our goal is to live well and have healthy relationships, we need to use our practical rationality to develop moral virtues. This may sound moralistic, if we think of virtues in a Victorian sense of following rigidly prescribed rules for thinking and behaving. But Aristotle actually has something very different—and much more attractive and useful—in mind. In part 2, we will explore what that is.

Finally, we need to say something about the way practical rationality is connected to good relationships. Aristotle emphasizes that being a moral person requires more than just having practical rationality; we must put it to use. To become an Olympic champion, he points out, strength in itself is not enough to win the prize. We must do more than merely show up on the sidelines and look good. If we want to win, we have to get in the game and compete.[16] Similarly, in relationships, it is not enough just to *know* the good in ourselves and in our partners to achieve the rewards of goodness. We actually have to act and interact appropriately. So satisfying relationships require active virtue, and not merely a theoretical knowledge of how we should behave. Furthermore, it is not enough simply to be virtuous once. Just as one workout at the gym is not enough to become fit, so happiness in our lives and in our romantic relationships is not a function of a single virtuous deed (alas, if only it were!); rather, it emerges when active virtue is practiced over an entire lifetime.[17]

OUR APPROACH TO BEING HAPPY TOGETHER

Inspired by Aristotle's insights about friendship, our ideal for romantic relationships is the goal of becoming Aristotelian lovers. In this ideal, relationships are characterized by three interrelated elements. First, partners love the good they see in each other. This does not mean they ignore the benefits that can arise from their relationship, or the pleasure that may come from being in each other's company. But their relationship is not founded on these things. And loving the good they see in each other does not imply that they expect their partner to be perfect or that they are naively blind to their partner's flaws. In fact, being particularly adept at seeing the good in each other no doubt makes Aristotelian lovers especially good at the second element that characterizes them: They are committed to each other's well-being and supportive of their growth. Because they see the good in each other so clearly, they also have a unique perspective on their true potential, and they do what they can to help each other achieve it. This does not mean that they demand their partner change or try to force them into their own view of what they should be. Rather, they provide support and perspectives to help their partner do their own growing. Third, Aristotelian lovers are inspired to become better people themselves. They value the ways their partner's unique character and patient love help them see more clearly what it means to be a good person and how they themselves can realize more of their own potential. They realize this is something they will need to work at, and don't simply rely on their partner to do it for them. But they welcome the partnership and the support toward mutual growth.

There are various ways, of course, that couples can help each other grow and develop into better people. Going back to the thought experiment in the previous chapter, we want to underscore the value of the reversible cape. It is certainly important to know how to use the red side well. It can be helpful to have someone point out your vices so you can see what you need to change. But we think it's at least as important—and a whole lot more motivating—to have someone focus on your virtues and lovingly help you understand, identify, and expand the good that is already in you. For this reason, as well as the fact that the green side of the cape often gets short shrift, we will be focusing in this book on how to use that side more frequently and effectively in our quest to become Aristotelian lovers.

In the rest of part 1, we will turn to positive psychology research to learn how we can cultivate Aristotelian love in three specific areas: passion, emotions, and savoring. For each area, we will rely on leading researchers to help us define what the good is, then we will provide information and exercises to help you find and feed that good in yourself and in your partner.

Before we move on, though, remember that this is a relationship gym. And that means it's time for an exercise. To get the full benefit of what we've discussed in this chapter, think carefully about the questions in the following exercise and write down thoughtful answers about your relationship.

ARISTOTELIAN LOVERS PRACTICE EXERCISE

Take a few moments to think about the movie examples from *As Good as It Gets* and *Jerry Maguire* that we explored at the beginning of the chapter. Recall specifically the two different types of sentiments their main characters express to their partners: "You make me want to be a better man" vs. "You complete me." Consider what you think they mean in the context of a relationship. Think about some of the potential upsides and downsides of each.

Now think about your own romantic relationship or marriage. Or the relationship you'd like to be in if you're currently not part of a couple. Does your relationship or intended relationship have more characteristics of one than the other? If so, what might this mean for the future of your relationship?

Finally, consider how adopting the principles of Aristotelian love could positively influence you, your partner, and your relationship. To what degree is your relationship motivated by what you can each get out of it? By benefits, such as financial security or social standing? Or by pleasures, such as physical attraction, sexual relations, and similar interests or hobbies? To what degree is your relationship motivated by the good you see in the other person and the good you would like to develop in yourself? What might you do to move closer to becoming Aristotelian lovers? How might a greater use of the green side of your cape be of help?

CHAPTER 3

Promoting Passion in Your Partnership

AMIT, A HANDSOME, Ivy League-educated single man from a close-knit family, moved to New York City soon after finishing graduate school. Things were going quite well for him in most areas of his life: His career was progressing nicely, and he had a great group of friends and an active social life. The only thing missing was a meaningful romantic relationship. Then he met Padma. She was gorgeous, intelligent, fit, sexy, and stylish. The attraction was instant. And magnetic. Love at first sight, he thought. He had finally met his match. He was wildly drawn to her and couldn't stay away from her. An intensely passionate relationship ensued. He began spending a majority of his time with her. He couldn't believe how lucky he was to have met this beautiful woman. They soon married, and lived happily ever after.

Hollywood may like to stop there, but unfortunately real life doesn't. Let's take a closer look at how happily ever after actually turned out for Amit and Padma. They had two beautiful children together. And life was good . . . for a while. But eventually, the magnetic passion that initially attracted them to each other began to subside, as it naturally does in a long-term relationship. As he spent more time with his wife, Amit began to see her controlling and selfish nature, something that to this point had been masked by his initial intense feelings for her. Sadly, he realized that they both had more of an obsession rather than a love for each other and that he was in an emotionally unhealthy and unstable relationship. He tried to keep the marriage together for the sake of their children and because he came from a family and culture in which divorce was not tolerated. Eventually, though, he realized he needed to exit the marriage to protect his psychological health and that of his children. While happier after the split, he did not want to be single for the rest of his life. And in spite of his sad experience, he was still overpoweringly attracted to the same sort of woman as his ex-wife. "I found myself falling into the same kind of roller-coaster relationships with other women," he told us.[1]

IS IT LOVE OR LOVESICKNESS?

Like Amit, many people think of this type of intense yearning and instant magnetic attraction to their partner as an essential part of romantic passion. And why wouldn't we, when it's advertised everywhere? From *Billboard* music charts to blockbuster films, pop culture helps contribute to creating and perpetuating this notion of romantic passion as an uncontrollable feeling of being swept away. Popular songs with titles such as "I Can't Live Without You," "Every Breath You Take," and "You're My Everything" abound and suggest that a desperate longing and an all-consuming love are what characterize a great relationship. It's no wonder so many of us come to believe this is what love should always look and feel like.

According to Robert Vallerand, professor of social psychology at the University of Quebec at Montreal and past president of the Canadian Psychological Association and the International Positive Psychology Association, this romanticized view of love can actually be harmful to our well-being and our relationships.[2] A leading researcher on the psychological concept of passion and its role in our lives and our romantic relationships, Vallerand argues such unbridled emotional experiences do not actually exemplify ideal love, but rather a kind of *obsessive passion*, in which the passion controls the person, who then feels swept away.[3] In other words, the intense ardor and infatuation one person feels toward the object of her affection seems to take over the rational part of her brain that controls her emotions and actions. Many of us may experience a milder version of these feelings at the beginning of our relationships—it sometimes may be what helps cement our attraction to our partner. But as the relationship progresses, these intense feelings naturally subside, with thriving relationships continuing to be sustained by a calmer, healthier kind of passion.

To be clear, passion is a very important part of a successful relationship. The key, though, is to cultivate the *right kind* of passion to ensure you and your partner will not only survive but thrive over the long haul.[4] The problem is, many of us wind up confusing love with obsessive passion, which causes us to jump into relationships too quickly and then give up on them just as abruptly the minute the intensity fades. And our culture doesn't help, with its insistence that couples should be living happily and passionately ever after, or else they're doing it wrong. Amit is a perfect example of someone who is confusing love with obsessive passion. Take a look at the language he uses to describe his relationship experiences. He doesn't say he *chooses* the women he becomes romantically involved with, but rather he *falls for* them. It's like some other force has taken over. At first, as Amit can attest, it can be exhilarating. It's a thrilling joyride along the autobahn . . . but at full speed and with blinders on. Being this controlled by your passion makes it impossible to navigate safely the sharp turns in life's road. Unable to see and think clearly, we can't make wise or healthy choices in our relationships, which make them more likely to crash and burn. In these cases, we're not in love; we're love*sick*.

Of course, the temptation is to think these kinds of relationships are just part and parcel of the human experience. Pain and passion go hand in hand. To some extent, of course, this is true. When we open ourselves up to love, we also open ourselves up to pain. The psychologist Roy Baumeister has written about the pain of unrequited love,[5] and Elaine Hatfield has documented the feelings of emptiness, anxiety, and anger, along with the physical ailments we can experience when love goes wrong.[6] Neuroscientists have even mapped out the neurological and chemical changes that occur when love relationships end.[7] The danger here lies in conflating the results of the crashing and burning of obsessive passion with the normal, if difficult, outcome of problems in loving relationships. Normalizing the catastrophic results of obsessive passion makes it unlikely that those involved will learn from the experience and come to approach their relationships differently. They are unlikely ever to find a cure for their lovesick approach to relationships.

NOT EXACTLY THE STUFF OF PRINCE (OR PRINCESS) CHARMING

In his latest book, *The Psychology of Passion*, Vallerand explores obsessive passion in great detail. He argues that it is as damaging to a relationship as having no passion at all. His research has even found that those who are obsessively passionate tend to experience more negative emotions during sex and that women who are with these romantic partners report being less satisfied sexually—and less happy with the relationship in general.[8]

Vallerand argues that one of the reasons for these negative effects is that obsessive passion is often a function of an insecure sense of self. And this type of insecurity often results in a focus on one's own needs, at the expense of those of one's partner. As Phoebe, a television network executive who has had a string of obsessively passionate partners, put it when we interviewed her: "It's like a drug. Fast, fun, addictive, and lots of drama. However, it's not long-term and doesn't make for a lifelong partner. I may love this person, but it's never going to be about me. I'm never going to have someone to help me. It's going to be just me dealing with the bills, the kids. You are there to support them, to help *them* shine. Everything will help *their* goals. There are better packages. You need a better package deal. You can't just go for the impulsive."[9]

Amit agrees with Phoebe's assessment, stating that his ex-wife and the subsequent women he dated were incredibly attractive and alluring people—who were also almost exclusively focused on themselves. He was left holding the ball for all the responsibilities, like taking care of his children, the house, and the other aspects of life. He felt he couldn't rely on any of the women he met, and this naturally fostered a lack of trust that eventually led to each relationship ending in an ugly breakup.

ROMANTIC LOVE VS. OBSESSIVE PASSION

So what are we saying? That anytime you experience an overwhelming emotion in a relationship you should assume it's an obsessively passionate one and put an immediate stop to it? That healthy relationships are dispassionate and boring? Not at all! In the early stages of your relationship, you and your partner may well have thought about each other to the exclusion of almost everything else. You may have found yourself—or may currently be finding yourself, if you're still in those early stages—totally distracted at work, daydreaming at your desk about your date last night or your future together, rather than drafting that important document. Maybe you mentally replayed every word from your recent conversations together. There may have been a time when you felt butterflies in your stomach at the mere mention of your partner's name. And looking back on these times, you may well savor them deeply. While you may not have the same intensity of feelings now, and especially not with the frequency you experienced then, you may treasure the memory of these moments, and you may well consider them to be a foundational part of your current relationship.

Are we saying this means you are in an obsessive relationship? Of course not! These experiences are all natural, normal, and healthy. Life wouldn't be nearly as rich without these special moments, and you are right to enjoy and savor them. Problems can arise, however, if your relationship never moves past this stage. It can be difficult to differentiate between healthy relationships and obsessive ones in their early stages, since the throes of new romance can seem indistinguishable from obsessive passion. Temporarily losing yourself in the first weeks or months after meeting that special someone can be a normal part of a budding relationship. But if you find yourself losing interest in your relationships as soon as they begin to emerge from these early stages, that can be a warning sign that you're addicted to the rush of obsessive passion. A different indicator of obsessive passion is the permanent loss of your sense of self in your relationship. If the weeks and months turn into years, and you find that you or your partner still can't get your mind off the other or can't focus on work, enjoy hobbies, spend time with friends individually, or be apart from the other without constantly checking in, these are all red flags that you and your relationship may be in trouble. Possibly even *Fatal Attraction*[10] trouble. (In which case it might be advisable to run now—and quickly!)

So how do we know if the passion we're experiencing in our relationships is the good kind (harmonious) or the dangerous kind (obsessive)? It starts with some self-analysis. In 2013, Vallerand and his colleagues conducted a study of ninety-nine individuals who were in a committed romantic relationship for an average of three years.[11] Participants were asked to complete the Romantic Passion Scale,[12] a measure devised to determine the type of passion most prevalent in their relationship. Next, their close friends were asked to rate a series of statements on a scale from 1 (*do not agree at all*) to 7 (*completely agree*). For example, "Being in a relationship with his/her current romantic partner has made my friend stop doing activities that he/she used to really enjoy," and "Being in a relationship with his/her current romantic partner has made my friend neglect his/her relationships with his/her friends." Sure enough, the study results indicate that those in an obsessively passionate romantic relationship are more likely than those in a healthy, harmoniously passionate relationship to have friends who report that they have withdrawn from relationships and activities outside their romantic relationship.

This is what happened to Ed and Susan.

After meeting Ed, a handsome corporate attorney, Susan was so head-over-heels into him that she spent all her free time with him, to the exclusion of her friends and hobbies. Susan's friends initially brushed it off as the trappings of a new romance, but they eventually realized that the situation wasn't changing. Rarely did they see Susan. And when they did see her, she seemed to be a different person. She didn't spend much time engaging in the hobbies she had enjoyed before meeting Ed. An avid runner, sports enthusiast, and social butterfly, Susan seemed to have all but given up these activities for her partner. Her personality even seemed to change. And the few times she did arrange to meet up with a friend, she seemed to be at Ed's beck and call, literally. He was jealous when she spent time with her friends and was very controlling. Often he'd call her when she was out, and she'd immediately make a beeline back to his apartment out of fear of upsetting him or jeopardizing the relationship. In spite of her immediate responses, these episodes would often lead to heated arguments, in which he would yell that she didn't care about him. Eventually, he would calm down and apologize. He would resume his romantic overtures, and things would be good again. Until the next episode.

What Susan didn't realize was that the relationship was already in jeopardy, because its foundation was built on shaky ground: an unhealthy sort of passion that does not lead to long-lasting, healthy relationships. Why do so many of us find ourselves in relationships like these? And why, when we get out of one, do we so often get back into another just like it, as Amit and Phoebe experienced?

While it can be tough to break a habit like this, awareness is the first step in doing so. Identifying and acknowledging the pattern is paramount in order to make the necessary changes and choices when it comes to our lives and relationships. Relational habits are particularly difficult to break because our attractions are functions of deep-seated needs and expectations. According to one well-supported psychological theory, these needs and expectations are largely the result of relational norms that were modeled for us by our parents and other caregivers as we were growing up. This view, known as attachment theory, was developed in the 1960s and 1970s by John Bowlby and Mary Ainsworth, researchers who studied the attachment between children and their caregivers. In the 1980s the theory was extended to adult relationships, and it was discovered that interactions between adults had similarities to those between children and parents or caregivers. The core idea is that the way we predominantly learn to attach as children to our caregiver is how we attach as adults in our close relationships. The three main attachment styles are *secure*, *anxious*, and *avoidant*, and they describe the ways we perceive and respond to intimacy in our romantic relationships.[13]

According to attachment theory, secure individuals are comfortable with giving and receiving love, anxious individuals tend to be preoccupied with their relationships and worry about whether their partners love them back, and avoidant individuals tend to push others away in an attempt to preserve their independence. We believe obsessive passion is linked to anxious and avoidant attachment styles. Although this has not yet been confirmed experimentally, there are studies currently under way to test this hypothesis.

Amit's experience certainly seems to confirm our view. He observes that "the type of women I repeatedly dated were, in fact, quite a lot like my mom—who can be very difficult. She's beautiful, intensely passionate, and has self-centered, narcissistic tendencies." He definitely sees that his romantic relationships have often mimicked his parents' marriage, even though he realizes it was not ideal. "It's a pattern I have, and I'm trying to break it," he acknowledges.[14]

Social psychologist Phil Brickman made an insightful observation about the kinds of issues Amit is struggling with: While we are not responsible for our problems, we are responsible for the solutions.[15] Although we can't change the relationships our parents had or the role models we had in our childhood, we can see them through a different lens and educate—or more aptly, reeducate—ourselves on what constitutes a healthy relationship. As children we might not have had the right resources or tools, but as adults we can find what we need to change our perspectives and empower ourselves. We can throw out old scripts and create new ones, and we can cultivate the kinds of relationships that will benefit us, as well as our partners.

This holds true, for example, for passion. Few of us don't want passion in our lives and in our relationships. Yet, as we have already seen, the passion that is often modeled in relationships and in popular media is obsessive. As it turns out, passion can strengthen our relationships, but it has to be the right kind. How can we identify healthy passion, and what can we do to cultivate this type of passion in our relationships?

HERE'S TO A HEALTHIER, HARMONIOUS PASSION

Vallerand defines passion as a strong inclination toward a self-defining activity, object, person, or belief that we love, value, and invest time and energy in. When we are passionate about something, he argues, the activity or person becomes internalized in our identity.[16] Vallerand's view is in line with the influential self-expansion model of love, which says when we are in romantic relationships, we want to expand ourselves by including the other person within our self, and we associate that expansion of our self with the other.[17] Vallerand takes this a step further (and connects it to self-determination theory, which we discussed in chapter 2) by pointing out that there are two possible types of motivation for internalizing the other person in our identity. The motivation can be *controlled*, meaning the person feels obligated in some way to be a part of the relationship; or it can be *autonomous*, in which case the person willingly chooses to engage in the relationship. Controlled motivation tends to lead to relationships of obsessive passion, Vallerand argues, and autonomous motivation tends to lead to relationships with a healthy kind of passion, what he calls *harmonious passion*.[18]

Harmonious passion, in general, leads to cognitive and emotional advantages such as better concentration, a more positive outlook, and increased mental health.[19] So, for example, when it comes to our hobbies, if we have a harmonious passion for, say, soccer or music, we enjoy those activities when we are engaged in them. We don't feel like we should be doing something else instead. And when we are not engaged in those activities, we don't feel guilty for doing something else, nor are we so obsessed with the activity that we can't concentrate on our work, family life, or whatever else we are doing.

In the case of relationships in particular, harmonious passion helps partners maintain a healthy identity, increases intimacy, and enables couples to handle conflict better.[20] Rather than getting swept away by our partner, like Susan was in the preceding example, we retain our identity and maintain more of a balanced lifestyle, engaging in interests and activities outside of our relationship. Phoebe found out firsthand the difference between healthy and harmful passion when she stopped treading the same narrow and broken path to relationships and instead consciously carved out a new path that allowed room for many other aspects of her life: friends, career, hobbies, and personal interests. No longer did she devote the majority of her attention to one guy at the expense of everything else. Instead of neglecting herself, she learned the importance of nurturing all aspects of her life. She realized that what she had previously perceived as things that go with the territory in relationships—the turmoil, tribulations, and trust issues—soon disappeared. She no longer had room in her life for an obsessively passionate relationship and soon attracted—and became attracted to—Patrick, who became her husband.

Phoebe's relationship with Patrick brought an end to the tirades and torrents of tumultuous passion she had once craved and been swept up in. Instead, she developed an appreciation for a different and healthier type of passion, one that sated her and sustains her union today. In her relationship with Patrick, she still experiences those intense, intimate, and oh-so-enjoyable moments. Now, however, these moments lead to long-term happiness and contentment, rather than the negative feelings of fury and frustration that had been fueled by her previous string of lovesick liaisons and obsessively passionate relationships. She's reaping the rewards of a healthy love and feeling more creative and productive at work and at play. She and Patrick support one another and engage in fun, exhilarating activities they both enjoy, like dirt biking, which is how they initially met. She also continues to enjoy quality time with her girlfriends doing things she's always enjoyed, such as going to the beach, attending L.A. Lakers games, and planning weekend getaways. These diverse sources of fun in her life fuel the flame of her romantic relationship without triggering the obsessive passion that used to smother her and make her relationships go up in smoke. The harmonious passion she and Patrick share leads to more mature relationships and is a key factor in becoming Aristotelian lovers. What can we do to cultivate this type of passion?

HOW CAN WE CULTIVATE HARMONIOUS PASSION?

The good news is that passion is not an innate quality but rather something that can be learned and practiced, resulting in greater intimacy and stronger and more mature relationships. Before you can work on building a more harmonious passion in your relationship, however, it's important to find out what levels of obsessive and harmonious passion are already there. We invite you to do so by taking the following Romantic Passion Scale, which assesses both obsessive and harmonious romantic passion toward one's partner.

ROMANTIC PASSION SCALE[21]

This scale assesses the two types of passion we have been discussing: obsessive and harmonious. Begin by writing down the name of your spouse or partner, then answer the questions below in reference to your relationship with this person.

Name of my spouse or partner: _____

Using the scale below, please think of this person and indicate your level of agreement with each item.

Do Not Agree at All	Very Slightly Agree	Slightly Agree	Moderately Agree	Mostly Agree	Strongly Agree	Very Strongly Agree
1	2	3	4	5	6	7

1. My relationship with my partner is in harmony with the other activities in my life.   1 2 3 4 5 6 7

2. I have difficulty controlling my urge to be with my romantic partner.   1 2 3 4 5 6 7

3. The new things that I discover when I am with my partner allow me to appreciate my romantic relationship even more.   1 2 3 4 5 6 7

4. I have almost an obsessive feeling for my romantic partner.   1 2 3 4 5 6 7

5. My relationship with my partner reflects the qualities I like about myself.   1 2 3 4 5 6 7

6. My relationship with my partner is the only thing that really turns me on.   1 2 3 4 5 6 7

7. My relationship with my partner allows me to live a variety of experiences.   1 2 3 4 5 6 7

8. If I could, I would only be with my romantic partner.   1 2 3 4 5 6 7

9. My relationship with my partner is well integrated in my life.   1 2 3 4 5 6 7

10. My relationship with my partner is so exciting that I sometimes lose control over it.   1 2 3 4 5 6 7

11. My relationship with my partner is in harmony with other things that are part of me.   1 2 3 4 5 6 7

12. I have the impression that my relationship with my partner controls me.   1 2 3 4 5 6 7

13. I spend a lot of time with my romantic partner.

                                                 1 2 3 4 5 6 7

14. I love my romantic partner.   1 2 3 4 5 6 7

15. My romantic partner is important to me.

                                                 1 2 3 4 5 6 7

16. My romantic partner is part of who I am.

                                                 1 2 3 4 5 6 7

17. My romantic partner is part of my identity.

                                                 1 2 3 4 5 6 7

To score your results on the Romantic Passion Scale, do the following:

1. First, add together your answers to questions 1, 3, 5, 7, 9, and 11. The resulting sum represents the level of harmonious passion (HP) you have in your relationship.
2. Next, add together your answers to questions 2, 4, 6, 8, 10, and 12. The resulting sum represents the level of obsessive passion (OP) you have in your relationship.
3. Finally, add together your answers to questions 13 through 17. The resulting sum represents the level of general passion (GP) you have in your relationship.

INTERPRETING YOUR RESULTS

- If your OP score is higher than your HP score, this is a red flag indicating that you may well be obsessively passionate about your relationship.
- If your OP score is about the same as your HP score AND the scores are 30 or above, this is a red flag indicating that you may well be obsessively passionate about your relationship.

- If your OP score is about the same as your HP score AND the scores are below 30, this is a yellow flag indicating that you might be obsessively passionate about your relationship.
- If your OP score is below your HP score, this is a green flag indicating that you are probably harmoniously passionate about your relationship.
- If your OP score is below your HP score AND your HP score is above 30, this is a double green flag indicating that you are very likely harmoniously passionate about your relationship.
- If your GP score is below 20, you are reporting a low level of general passion in your relationship.
- If your GP score is between 20 and 24, you are reporting a moderate level of general passion in your relationship.
- If your GP score is 25 or higher, you are reporting a high level of general passion in your relationship.

Whatever your score on the Romantic Passion Scale, it's important not to focus so much on that initial intense attraction that you take harmonious passion for granted and risk losing yourself in obsessive passion. As Billy Joel reminds us in his song "A Matter of Trust":

Some love is just a lie of the heart
The cold remains of what began with a passionate start.

Cultivating harmonious passion, rather than obsessive passion, throughout our lives, can help ensure our relationships avoid that fate. And it's important for all of us, whether or not we tend toward obsessive passion, to foster harmonious passion in our relationships. Let's explore three specific ways for doing so.

STRATEGIES FOR CULTIVATING HARMONIOUS PASSION

#1: Work to develop greater trust with your partner and become more emotionally attuned to what he or she is feeling or may need. Trust is essential to all healthy romantic relationships; it's the foundation that can sustain you and your partner through inevitable rough times and help you emerge stronger and happier together on the other side. Vallerand emphasizes in his research that a lack of trust is associated with an all-consuming or obsessive passion.[22] This is because people who are obsessively passionate about their lovers, as we have already noted, tend to have an insecure sense of self and are thus preoccupied with protecting their ego rather than being attuned to their partner. John Gottman, professor emeritus of psychology at the University of Washington and leading marriage and relationship expert, echoes this point in his book *The Science of Trust*, in which he argues that "emotional attunement" to your partner is a fundamental skill for couples to cultivate if they want their relationship to last long-term. Being emotionally attuned to your partner is the essence of trust, and Gottman offers the acronym ATTUNE to outline the key elements of this type of connection: Attention, Turning toward, Tolerance, Understanding, Non-defensive responding, and Empathy.[23] This is a helpful way to remind us to turn toward our partner with our full attention, to be tolerant and understanding, and to communicate in a non-defensive, empathic way.

Of course, these are goals to work toward. None of us are perfect, so we realize it's not realistic to try to keep your relationship perpetually free of any twinges of unhealthy elements. Sometimes we catch ourselves not really actively listening to our partner, but rather feeling defensive, ready to strike back to prove a point. Sometimes we may snap in response, rather than taking a deep breath and answering calmly. And sometimes during a rough time when we're feeling sorry for ourselves, it's incredibly hard to get out of our own heads and feel empathic toward the person we love. All couples slip up at times and react toward each other in less-than-effective ways. The key is not to let it become a pattern, as that can start to erode the trust between you and your partner and diminish the harmonious passion in your relationship.

It's also important to watch out for this behavior in anyone you become romantically involved with, as it's a warning sign he or she could be obsessively passionate. Vallerand's research indicates that obsessively passionate people tend to be defensive, argumentative, controlling, and competitive in their relationships.[24] When a relationship is infected with these negative behaviors, it becomes very difficult to sustain. These behaviors are corrosive, undermining the respect needed to work through challenges, so it's not surprising that they can lead to maladaptive conflict between partners. In these cases, when a problem arises, couples will be unlikely to see it as a learning opportunity, as a time to be open to and curious about each other. Instead, they are more likely to end up lashing out or shutting down and drawing further apart from each other. As is to be expected, obsessively passionate relationships (like Amit and Padma's) tend to burn out quickly. Often it seems to be all or nothing when it comes to obsessive passion. Raging fire or all smoke—with insufficient stability to sustain the relationship.

Sandra Murray, leading trust researcher and professor of psychology at the State University of New York at Buffalo, notes the importance of replacing these destructive behaviors with ones that promote trust and attunement. Her research indicates that this can help free us from trying to avoid our partners out of a fear of rejection or in an effort to protect ourselves from their anger or disapproval when a conflict arises. Murray and her colleagues have found that establishing mutual trust and respect helps couples avoid these damaging reactions that can lead to relationship dissatisfaction and dissolution. Moreover, trust can help partners feel safe and allow them to approach each other with confidence.[25] But trust is not something that develops overnight. Rather, it is built slowly in brief moments and daily increments that accrue over time. At the end of this chapter, we will invite you to complete an exercise to help you build trust in your relationship.

#2: Make sure you don't lose yourself in an unhealthy way in your relationship. Beware of behaviors such as thinking constantly about your partner and struggling to concentrate on anything else; feeling unable to be apart from him; when you must be apart, needing to check in with him constantly; canceling important appointments, obligations, or plans with friends in order to be at your partner's beck and call; and sacrificing your own self-care measures to take care of your partner instead. Our advice here is to follow the airlines' wise counsel: "Put on your own oxygen mask before assisting others." If you engage in any or all of these behaviors, it may be time to restore balance by diversifying your interests and activities, making sure you maintain a sense of your own identity rather than getting swept up and lost in your relationship. We're not saying you necessarily need to take a cold-turkey approach and break off the relationship. Nor are we recommending that you stop including your partner in activities you enjoy doing together. Instead, as Vallerand suggests, spreading your attention across several interests (including but not limited to your partner) naturally combats the all-consuming thoughts and behaviors that can arise from focusing on your relationship in a way that is unhealthy for both of you.

Vallerand recommends that each partner maintain close and healthy friendships outside of the romantic relationship, and that these friendships involve activities of passionate interest.[26] This might require thinking back to activities you each used to enjoy individually before your relationship began. Did one of you like to go hiking on the weekends while the other usually spent Saturdays and Sundays browsing antique stores, visiting museums, or volunteering? Perhaps one of you loved catching sports games with friends and the other organized movie marathons with his or her pals. Whatever your distinct interests are, make a point to schedule times to explore and experience these separately with your friends on a regular basis. This doesn't mean you can never invite your sweetheart to a baseball game or brunch with friends; just don't feel that you have to invite her every time, so you don't become dependent on her being there to have a good time yourself. Strategically and judiciously including enjoyable times away from each other in your life will help pull both of you back from developing any obsessive tendencies. And even better, it'll make the times you're together even sweeter and more fun—reminiscent, perhaps, of the early stages of your romance.

#3: Finally, build harmonious passion in your relationship by taking up new and interesting activities together as a couple. Over time, it's scarily easy to get stuck in narrowing patterns of behavior that suck the excitement, interest, appeal, and romance out of your relationship. As the pressures and demands of work and home life cut more and more into our time and take up our creative energy, couples can become trapped in the same dull habits and routines day after day and find that they no longer explore new activities together. This may kill your passion (the good kind, that is!) for each other, and if you start looking for that excitement outside your relationship, it can even threaten your commitment to each other.

You can fight against this unhealthy tendency by intentionally looking for new things to experience. They should be activities both you and your partner enjoy, with the goal being to connect and cooperate, not compete with each other.[27] As Vallerand emphasized in numerous conversations with us, the point is to have fun together, not to win, so leave your egos at the door. If you're a champion swimmer, for example, and your partner can barely tread water, it may not be best to insist on waterskiing or a snorkeling expedition. Likewise, if your partner is a chess enthusiast, but you can't tell the difference between a pawn and a bishop and have no desire to learn even if your life depended on it, you may want to suggest taking up another game instead. In fact, the most enjoyable results for both of you will likely come from trying things each of you has always been interested in but has not yet done. Sometimes, you will want to engage in these activities together; at other times, you may want to experiment with being in the same room as each of you undertakes your own activity. And you don't necessarily even need to leave the house. For example, if you both enjoy reading, but you like juicy psychological thrillers and your partner is more of a historical novel buff, you can each get a book you've been wanting to delve into and sit quietly on the couch next to each other, immersed in your own reading. Or you could experiment with working quietly side by side. We have personally found that when we are both being productive on our laptops in the same room, we feel a stronger bond. Above all, by enjoying some quality time apart and some together, you can nurture that important harmonious passion to enrich all aspects of your relationship and help you develop and sustain a satisfying and long-lasting love.

And if you're not in a healthy romantic relationship and would like to be, perhaps you can take a cue from Amit, who's been working on building his own interests and his sense of self and is now actively looking to develop a harmoniously passionate relationship with someone. "I'm in a really good place right now," he told us recently. "I would like to be in a long-term relationship again."[28] And he finally knows how to go about it. With the help of a life coach, he has created a list of essential values he's looking for in a partner. He wants someone who is empathic, kind, and caring. And he's taking deliberate steps to create a habit of slowly cultivating a healthy romantic relationship with a woman rather than being swept away by magnetic obsessive passion over someone, falling for her immediately, and rushing into a serious relationship too quickly, as has been his habit in the past. He has also developed a meditation practice in an effort to help him manage his emotions, as he has become aware of how frequently they can get the best of him. As Vallerand told us in an interview, "Meditation will likely help him make better choices in the future by helping him regulate his emotions so that they don't cloud his judgment and lead to obsessive passion."[29] And just in case he needs help along the way, Amit has put together a group of friends (five women and one man) to help prescreen his dates and spot any red flags that he may be missing. Before a date, he gathers information about the woman based on his conversations with her and summarizes the key points to his friends, listing, for example, the woman's values and what she's looking for in life and in a relationship. If the opportunity arises, his friends even get to meet his prospective date. Vallerand's research shows that friends can often see red flags of obsessive passion and other warning signs in our prospective partners sooner than we can, because they're far more objective observers.

We understand this process may not be easy. It can take hard work to break deeply entrenched habits that are harmful or negative (or even addictive) and to create new ones that promote a more harmonious and healthy relationship. But when it comes to building and sustaining a satisfying and loving relationship, you've got to put in the work to reap the rewards. Since Amit did the work on himself and is continuing to do the things he enjoys (such as competing in triathlons), he's more likely to find someone to inspire him to want to become a better man. And Phoebe is real-life proof that this pays off. As she told us, "I was always waiting for a significant other before I did things on my bucket list. Then when I turned forty, I just started doing these things, and working on myself at the same time. And that's when I met my husband, Patrick. He appreciates me and brings out the best traits in me. And I want to be better for him."[30]

Now that we've established the importance of cultivating the right kind of passion in your relationship and explored ways of doing so, we'll turn in the next chapter to another critical component of being happy together: positive emotions. Newlyweds and other love-drunk couples are frequently prone to taking them for granted, thinking the positive emotions in their relationship just happen—and always will. They often do just happen, of course, especially during the honeymoon phase of a relationship. But like any sparks, they fade over time, as life and work stresses get in the way. Given how important positive emotions are to our overall health and our relationships, it's important to cultivate them. Actively. Continually. In the next chapter we'll take a look at how to do just that. Before you move on, though, be sure to complete the following exercises for cultivating harmonious passion.

HARMONIOUS PASSION EXERCISES

1. **Share Good Secrets with Each Other**
   Practice sharing with your partner important things about yourself that you have never previously revealed to him or her. Perhaps it's a childhood memory, a life-changing experience, or a vivid dream. Maybe it's a hope you have for the future. Or a line of work or a hobby you've always found strangely fascinating and wanted to try. It can be serious or lighthearted; it's just important that you authentically share

something meaningful. Start by confiding in your partner about small things, and when you feel more comfortable, work up to a bigger thing—something near and dear to your heart, such as a deep secret you've never told anyone before.

Think of at least one thing you would like to share with your partner today and do it. Explain to him that you are sharing this because you love and trust him, and ask him to refrain from judging or reading into it too much, if possible. You simply want to share a piece of yourself with him. And to help your partner learn to trust you more, remember to be fully *attuned* (as Gottman advises) when he shares his secrets with you. In general, try to be open to his points of view, even if—or especially if—you don't agree with or share his perspective. Being open to, curious about, and welcoming of new opinions, ideas, and confidences will help both you and your partner feel safe and make it easier for you to develop and deepen reciprocal trust in your relationship.

2. **Remember Yourself**
    For those of you with tendencies toward obsessive passion, you may identify with continually seeking that breathless swept-away sensation in a relationship. Although it feels good in the moment, this feeling can result in a loss of identity and sense of self, as described in this chapter. To make sure you haven't lost yourself in an unhealthy way, think back to your life before your relationship. How did you enjoy spending your time then? What were the activities that made you feel like you? Perhaps it was your daily *New York Times* crossword puzzle, weekly yoga class, or

monthly book club meeting. And whom did you enjoy doing these activities with? Are those friends still in your life?
If you find that you are no longer engaging in any of those
activities and that you are not maintaining any of those
friendships, we encourage you to take up some of them
again (as long as they are healthy). Schedule a weekly date
with a friend who also enjoys spinning, trying new restaurants, conjugating Latin verbs, or just meeting up over cof-
fee to discuss whatever is on your minds. Regardless of the
level of obsessive passion in your relationship, continuing
to engage in your individual interests and connecting with
close family and friends on your own as well as with your
partner are things you can practice to cultivate a more
healthy, harmonious type of passion to sustain and deepen
your love for and satisfaction with each other.

3. **Seek Out New Adventures Together**
   Take turns with your partner to select a special activity to
   do together. As we saw in this chapter, research shows
   that seeking out and engaging in fun, exhilarating, and
   novel activities can increase mutual attraction and promote a healthy passion in intimate relationships. The key
   is to pick things that you *both* enjoy. Remember to avoid
   serious competition. The point is to have fun together and
   connect, not to compete. So it's probably best to select
   activities for which you have roughly equal talent. And
   switch up the activity from time to time to keep it from
   becoming too routine or boring.

CHAPTER 4

The Importance of Practicing Positive Emotions

*S*EAN, *A* TALENTED *twenty-one-year-old Irish rock musician, spent his youth perfecting his craft and began booking regular gigs at local Dublin hot spots with his band. When he was suddenly discovered by a leading music label, offered a lucrative deal, and swiftly relocated to Los Angeles, his life changed dramatically. Soon he and his bandmates were touring the United States and performing at top venues throughout the country. The band's popularity spread like wildfire. Sean quickly gained notoriety and was living a life many young people only fantasize about.*

Then one of his band's singles became a smash radio hit, making the Billboard Rock chart and catapulting Sean's rock-star status to a whole new level. Along with his successful music career and newfound fame came endless invitations to top restaurants, trendy nightclubs, and hip industry parties. He reveled in the fun and the new friends he met, including Rachel, the well-connected woman who soon became his wife. The fun continued, with the two of them painting the town red most nights. And on the rare nights they opted to stay in, they'd host decadent parties, with overflowing cocktails and fabulous food, that would linger into the wee hours of the morning.

But when his band released its next album, it tanked. Soon the funding from the record label dried up. So did the fun, Rachel complained. As his marriage quickly fell apart, Sean crumbled with it. What had happened?

Sean and Rachel's marriage is an example of a relationship based on pleasure. While they had many good times together, those good times were based on fun, and when the fun came to an end, there wasn't anything else to sustain their partnership. This is a classic case of the second kind of friendship Aristotle writes about, and as he predicted of relationships based on pleasure, when the fun ended, so did the relationship.

Now let's take a look at another relationship, that of Sam and Beth. Here's their story:

A few years ago, our friend Beth told us she honestly thought her partner, Sam, was one of the most cheerful and positive people she had ever encountered. Since that time many of Sam's friends have backed up her claim. And we, too, have noticed his remarkable and consistently upbeat attitude. Regardless of the struggles Sam might be going through at work or elsewhere, he always seems to maintain a cheerful and optimistic mood. His positivity appears to be contagious not only to Beth but to all who are in his presence. We continue to hear about the positive effect he has on everyone. While Beth and Sam are also a fun couple, and their relationship is rich with pleasurable moments, fun isn't the foundation of their relationship. Rather, the bedrock of their marriage is a mutual respect for one another and a shared goal of becoming better individuals and working together to help increase the goodness in the world. This is a classic case of Aristotelian friendship, with Beth and Sam being exemplary Aristotelian lovers. Their relationship is rich in shared positive emotions and values, which is a big part of what has kept their partnership going strong for more than twenty-five years!

So what's the difference between Sean and Rachel's relationship that was based on pleasure, and Sam and Beth's relationship that is sustained by positive emotions? Aren't pleasure and positive emotions the same thing? Not according to Barbara Fredrickson, Kenan Distinguished Professor at the University of North Carolina at Chapel Hill and the leading researcher on positive emotions. She does admit that they are similar, calling them cousins and noting they often occur together.[1] And we value both of them for their own sakes and not because they lead to anything else. In our terminology, they are green-cape parts of our lives. For all their similarities, however, Fredrickson argues that they are different in significant ways. She observes that pleasure tends to narrow our attention to focus on our immediate needs and desires.[2] It brings us immediate rewards that are often short-lived. Consider the pleasures of luxuriating in a warm bath, eating a delicious meal, or drinking a fine glass of wine. These pleasures focus our attention on immediate sensations: the warmth of the water on our skin, the taste and texture of the finely prepared food, and the complex flavors and feel of the wine on our palate. To understand how these experiences differ from positive emotions, let's examine Fredrickson's work in more detail.

WHAT GOOD ARE POSITIVE EMOTIONS?

For many years, empirical researchers in psychology neglected the study of emotions. They found them hard to define and harder to measure. Even more tellingly, they considered emotions to be inconsequential for the study of human behavior, believing them to be mere by-products of our responses to stimuli. They certainly didn't see them as things we could control, let alone cultivate or grow to improve our lives and outlooks.

As perspectives changed in empirical psychology and more

evidence came in that emotions may be more malleable and useful than originally thought, researchers began to take an interest in the roles they play in our lives. Initially, most of the focus of this new research was on emotional reactions to negative aspects of our environment, to what are often referred to as "negative emotions." If you've seen the movie *Inside Out*, you will readily identify a core group of them as anger, sadness, fear, and disgust.[3] In that movie, each of these emotions understands its special job. Anger is there to protect us against threat by urging us to attack; sadness helps us adapt to our environment by urging us to withdraw and rethink when things don't go our way; fear alerts us to danger and urges us to flee; and disgust helps us avoid contamination by urging us to expel unhealthy things. Connected with each of these emotions is a strong urge to act in a specific way. Researchers call this a *specific action tendency*, and they argue that emotions play a very important role in our survival. By narrowing our attention to specific actions— and by preparing us physiologically to carry out those actions— emotions make it possible for us to act quickly and effectively in life-threatening situations. Furthermore, individuals with the greatest sensitivity to these emotions, and thus the quickest reaction times, were most likely to survive and pass along their genes to subsequent generations.[4] So this would help explain why we are so good at experiencing and responding to these emotions.

This makes a lot of sense, doesn't it? But there is one problem here. Movie buffs will realize that we've left out one of the emotions from *Inside Out*: joy. What is the specific action tendency affiliated with joy? Well, in the movie, the character did a lot of dancing around and smiling and laughing. Are these the special urges connected with joy? If so, how could they possibly be of survival value? Did our ancestors escape from hungry saber-toothed tigers by laughing at them and bouncing around in excitement? Not likely.

So what good are positive emotions, if not for survival? Not just joy but also the others that round out Fredrickson's top ten list of the most frequently experienced positive emotions: gratitude, serenity, interest, hope, pride, amusement, inspiration, awe, and love.[5] What real, fundamental use do they have in our lives? These are questions Fredrickson puzzled over and that eventually led her to create a new theory for how positive emotions work. She considered the possibility that positive emotions are just as important as negative emotions, but that they work in a different way. As a result, she developed the *broaden-and-build* theory of positive emotions,[6] which has become the most influential and best-supported explanation for the way positive emotions work. According to this theory, positive emotions affect us differently than negative emotions do, and this allows them to have a very different but equally important role in our survival.

While negative emotions narrow our attention and urge us toward specific action tendencies, Fredrickson argued, positive emotions do the opposite. They broaden our attention and increase our thought-action repertoire; that is, they increase the range of possible thoughts we might have and actions we might take in a particular context.[7] We can see this pretty easily when we consider what happens in our bodies when we feel sad and when we feel joyful. When we feel sad, we'll often say that we are "down." Indeed, when we are feeling this way, our eyes are often looking down, our shoulders are drooping, our backs are bent, we are breathing shallowly, and our minds seem blank or perhaps focused inward on what is making us sad. We're not likely to notice what's going on around us, and we're much slower to react to things.

When we feel joyful, by contrast, we say we are feeling "up." Our eyes are often looking up and around, our shoulders are back, our chests are out, our backs are straight, we are breathing deeply, and our minds are lively. We're much more likely to notice what's going on around us and much quicker to engage with things. And you'll notice that when we're not happy, people encourage us to "cheer *up*" or tell us not to worry because "things will start looking *up* soon." Positive emotions open us up, making us more receptive and more creative.

Scientific research bears this out. Studies have found that positive emotions help us take more in visually, allowing us to see more of what is in our periphery than we otherwise would. They can also make us more creative and able to solve complex problems more quickly.[8] In one study, positive emotions helped participants unlock more possibilities for action. When asked to list all the things they felt like doing in the moment, those who were in a positive mood were able to think of more things than those who were in a neutral or negative mood.[9] Researchers at Cornell University also found that physicians who were in a positive mood were able to think through complex medical cases more effectively, identifying the salient issues more quickly and coming up with more accurate diagnoses.[10] Finally, positive emotions can lead to upward spirals, in which the openness they cause can lead to greater positive emotions, and these greater positive emotions can in turn lead to more openness.[11]

If positive emotions broaden our attention and make us more open and creative in the moment, do they have any long-term effects? After all, emotional states are pretty fleeting, and no matter how positive we feel in any given moment, that particular emotion will come to an end. The second part of Fredrickson's broaden-and-build theory is that positive emotions do, indeed, have long-term consequences. Temporary as the moments themselves are, they can help us build significant long-term resources. One way they do this is by helping us get to know the world in new ways. Fredrickson points out that when we are feeling joy, we want to play and be creative; when we are feeling interest, we want to explore and learn new things; and when we are feeling serenity, we want to savor our experience and integrate it into a new view of ourselves and the world.[12] This openness allows us to get to know ourselves and our world in new ways, and the resulting new knowledge can be of great help as we encounter new situations in our lives.

Scientific research indicates that by helping us to get to know the world in new ways, positive emotions can help us build specific and enduring physical, psychological, and social resources. Fredrickson reports that people who experience more positive emotions enjoy lower levels of stress-related hormones and higher levels of beneficial hormones, resulting in lower blood pressure, less pain, fewer colds, and better sleep. Indeed, these people are less likely to have hypertension, diabetes, or a stroke and are more likely to live longer.[13] They also benefit psychologically, becoming "more optimistic, more resilient, more open, more accepting, and more driven by purpose."[14] On the social level, those who experience more positive emotions with others have stronger and more satisfying relationships, with the good times they share buffering against the tough times, and in the case of marital relationships, helping to protect against divorce.[15]

To illustrate the broadening and building effects of positive emotions on our social relations, imagine it's lunchtime and you enter a cafeteria at your school or workplace to get something to eat. It's been a tough day and you feel pretty beaten down. You're feeling a lot of negative emotions and not many positive ones. As you enter the cafeteria, you notice that people are sitting at about half the tables, but that none of your friends or close colleagues are there. When you get your food, where will you likely go to eat it? If you're like us, you'll probably try to find a spot by yourself in the corner where you can quickly finish your lunch and head to your next class or back to your office without anyone noticing you.

Let's imagine the same scenario again—but this time it's been a *great* day, and you walk into the cafeteria filled with positive emotions. You're feeling confident, excited, happy, hopeful, and inspired. When you get your food, you will be much more likely to walk over to one of the tables with people sitting at it and introduce yourself because you're feeling good about yourself and about life. Perhaps you have seen these people around, but you've not yet met them. They invite you to join them, and you spend your lunchtime getting to know them and making positive connections with your new acquaintances that may last a long time and could even lead to further positive connections and feelings in the future.

One thing to keep in mind about positive emotions is that we often consider them to be effects of good things happening in our lives. They're icing on the cake. We get a promotion at work, and we feel proud that our talents and accomplishments are being recognized. We begin reading a biography about a selfless leader, and we are filled with interest about his or her life. We go on a family vacation, and we are filled with gratitude at being able to spend time in beautiful places with people we love. We don't often consider, however, that positive emotions can also *cause* good outcomes in our lives.[16] Maybe the pride we take in our work is what motivated us to perform at the level needed for a promotion. Perhaps it was our interest that made us pick up the biography in the first place. And it could be that the gratitude we have felt toward our family over the years is a big part of what makes the vacation so enjoyable when it comes.

At this point, we can see more clearly the contrast between positive emotions, as Fredrickson understands them, and negative emotions. Negative emotions, as we have mentioned, narrow our attention and lead to specific action tendencies, which protect us from immediate threats. In these contexts, it is helpful to have our attention narrowed on the danger and to be presented with a limited range of helpful options from which we can quickly choose.

Positive emotions, on the other hand, broaden our attention and lead to expanded thought-action repertoires when we are not feeling threatened, giving us an opportunity to increase our resources. This growth is pleasant in itself and can be valuable at a later time, when that information can rescue us from danger. Thus, positive emotions are not just inconsequential distractions; across a broader time span, they can be just as helpful for our survival as negative emotions.[17]

We are also now in a position to understand better the differences between physical pleasure and positive emotions. While both draw us toward what we want, Fredrickson points out that pleasure narrows our attention and gives us immediate rewards, while positive emotions broaden our attention and in addition to immediate rewards give us even more significant long-term rewards in the future.[18]

WHAT GOOD ARE POSITIVE EMOTIONS IN ROMANTIC RELATIONSHIPS?

As important as positive emotions are for us as individuals, they may be even more important for our relationships. They help us forge strong connections with others by breaking down boundaries that separate us from each other. By broadening our attention in ways that help us see ourselves as less distinct from others, they allow us to create all kinds of relationships, including romantic ones.[19] As we mentioned in the previous chapter, when we are in romantic relationships, we desire to expand ourselves by including our partner or spouse within our self and we associate that expansion of our self with the other. This influential self-expansion model of love is based on the research of leading relationship scientist Arthur Aron, professor of psychology at Stony Brook University. Aron argues that self-expansion is a catalyst for positive emotions.

He and his colleagues use pairs of overlapping circles to ask couples about their relationship quality. On one end of their scale, the pair of circles does not overlap at all, and at the other end, the circles overlap almost completely. The researchers have asked thousands of couples to pick which pair of circles best depicts how they feel about their relationship. The more overlap an individual feels with his or her partner, the better the relationship is likely to fare. This simple measure has been more effective than more complex surveys and interviews at predicting which couples will stay together and which will break up.[20]

While self-expansion triggers positivity, Fredrickson finds it works the other way around, as well. In a variety of experiments, she has found that even lab-induced positive emotions can help people see more overlap between themselves and others.[21] These emotions can help people feel closer and more connected to their loved ones. And the more you continually kindle positive feelings in your relationships, the more connected and happy you feel overall.

Another way positive emotions can enhance relationships is through contagion. Just as we can pass colds along to our partners through physical contagion, so we can pass along our feelings to our partners through *emotional* contagion. Ever notice how when you spend time with your partner, you often wind up feeling the emotions he or she is experiencing? Emotional contagion is rather complex and often happens below the level of our consciousness. It results from the fact that we are built to mimic each other. As infants, we start mimicking our parents soon after we are born, behavior that is critical for our development and constitutes a primary pathway to learning and growing throughout our lives. Emotional contagion results from our tendency to copy or synchronize our facial expressions, vocalizations, postures, and behaviors with those around us, and as a result take on their emotional landscape.[22]

So although the underlying processes are different, we can talk about catching emotions from others, just as we can talk about catching their colds. And just as there are those who are more susceptible to catching colds from others, there are those who are more sensitive than others to their emotional environment, and thus more likely to pick up the emotions of those around them. This experience, of course, is even more common than the common cold. How many times have you found yourself in a situation in which you are doing fine, but then you spend some time with a partner who is not doing fine? Soon you begin picking up the other person's negative emotions, and before you know it, you are not doing fine, either. Your partner's negative emotions have spread to you, and you are now feeling them yourself.

Researchers have studied this phenomenon by various means and have documented ways in which emotional contagion can result in behavior change. One such researcher is Sigal Barsade, now professor of management at the Wharton School at the University of Pennsylvania. She and her colleagues conducted an experiment with ninety-two college undergraduates, bringing them into a lab and randomly assigning them to twenty-nine groups of two to four students each to simulate a managerial exercise. In some of the groups, she also included a research confederate, an actor trained to display a negative mood. Before beginning the managerial exercise, participants completed a mood questionnaire rating how they felt right at that moment. Each participant, including the confederate, took turns giving a presentation. Immediately afterward, participants completed another questionnaire with the same mood items they had rated previously. They were also independently rated by video coders trained to recognize emotion through facial expression, verbal tone, and body language. Sure enough, the groups with the research confederate became more negative over time, with lower levels of cooperation, decreased perceived performance, and more conflict as compared to the other groups in the study.[23] This indicates that negative emotions can not only spread to those around us but also negatively affect behavior and performance. This study and others like it show us how important it is to be aware of our emotional states. The negative emotions we are feeling can easily spread to our partners and this can affect not just how we feel but also how we behave.

This is the red-cape side of things. There is also a green-cape side: We can catch positive emotions from others, as well. We've all experienced occasions when we're in a neutral or even negative mood and then spend time with our partner, who is in a positive mood. Sometimes, we catch our partner's positive mood and begin feeling good ourselves. Even better, research shows that—just as with negative emotions—catching positive emotions from others can have an impact not only on our emotional states but also on our behavior and performance. Barsade demonstrated this by introducing a research confederate trained to display a positive mood in the remaining groups of students. She found that these groups became more positive over time, with higher levels of cooperation, increased perceived performance, and less conflict as compared to those in the negative-contagion groups.[24]

So emotional contagion is a complex process. In relationships, it can facilitate the spread of negative emotions or positive ones. And the emotions that are shared can have important effects both on our moods and on our long-term behaviors. Negative emotions can cause us to explode with anger, be filled with anxiety, or shrink and draw inward. In these states we often can't see or even imagine any alternatives, possibilities, or creative solutions to our problems. When we are in a bad mood, small problems seem to worsen, a domino effect occurs, and we may fall into a downward spiral of negativity. We focus on our problems and what's going wrong in our relationship. Suddenly, our annoyances magnify and seem to multiply. Soon enough we've created even more problems to deal with and are feeling even more miserable with ourselves and our significant other. As a result, we may end up feeling hopeless, perhaps desperate, and our relationship may even feel like a lost cause.

Positive emotions, on the other hand, can buoy our spirits, fill us with gratitude, and energize us with interest. These states broaden our thinking and open our hearts, enabling us to connect more closely with others. This wider-angle view of the world brings more possibilities into our focus, helping us see the bigger picture and preventing us from getting stuck and hung up on small, day-to-day problems and annoyances in our relationships. It's easier not to sweat the small stuff, and we are able to come up with more ideas that can benefit us not just in our interactions with our partners, but across all domains of our lives.[25]

Positive emotions, then, can help cultivate love. But more than that, Fredrickson argues, positive emotions are an important part of love. In her book *Love 2.0*, she refers to love as *positivity resonance*, defined as "the momentary upwelling of three tightly interwoven events: first, a sharing of one or more positive emotions between you and another; second, a synchrony between your and the other person's biochemistry and behaviors; and third, a reflected motive to invest in each other's well-being that brings mutual care."[26] On top of that, she notes that "any moment of positivity resonance that ripples through the brains and bodies of you and another can be health-and-life giving. . . ."[27] Studies of successful marriages also support this idea. Couples who regularly carve out time to do novel and exciting things together such as hiking, snowboarding, dancing, or attending musical performances and plays enjoy higher-quality marriages. Not only do these activities lead to harmonious passion, as we saw in the last chapter, but according to Fredrickson, they also provide a consistent "stream of shared micromoments of positivity resonance."[28] Like vitamins and minerals that boost our physical health, she argues, positivity resonance serves as "nutrient-rich bursts"[29] for our relationship that accrue over time to make our bond with our spouse or romantic partner even stronger.

This indicates how important positive emotions are for couples, especially those who aspire to be Aristotelian lovers. Sharing positive emotions with your partner, Fredrickson holds, can motivate you to invest in each other's well-being and engage in mutual care.[30] This goes beyond a desire for profit that underlies relationships of utility, and it moves past an interest in enjoying pleasant experiences together that forms relationships of pleasure. Instead of focusing on what we can get out of the relationship, we concentrate our attention on how we can help our partner grow and flourish, with a love of the goodness in the other person's character serving as the foundation for our desire to do so. And that kind of love—one based on virtue—is more likely to last a lifetime.

ARE POSITIVE EMOTIONS ALWAYS POSITIVE?

Now that we understand the importance of positive emotions in creating healthy relationships, there's still the question of how to cultivate them. Before we explore that practical matter, however, we need to address one more fundamental question: Are positive emotions always positive?

Let's begin by returning to the thought experiment we conducted together in chapter 1. We agreed that when confronted with the choice between a red cape with powers to help us fight against the things we don't want and a green cape to help us grow the things we do want, both are essential for well-being and that we need a reversible cape to flourish. Now we would like to pose a further question: Which side of the cape is positive? How would you answer that question?

Well, it's pretty obvious that the green side of the cape is positive, since it helps us get the things we want. But what about the red side of the cape? Is it negative?

Many of us working in positive psychology have had the experience James had one day when he was at a dinner party and was introduced to another guest. This woman asked him about the work he does, and when he briefly described his involvement with positive psychology, the woman laughed and said, "Is that as opposed to *negative* psychology?" "No, no," James explained. "It's in contrast to *mainstream* psychology, which I don't consider to be negative."

So what is mainstream psychology, then, if it's not negative? What is the red side of the cape if it's not negative? These are troubling questions, and because James is a philosopher, he has *really* been troubled by them. So he decided to try to get to the bottom of what positive psychology means by the "positive." The result was a seventy-five-page paper that has now been published as two articles in *The Journal of Positive Psychology*.[31] But don't worry, Suzie is not going to let James throw his seventy-five pages of philosophical analysis in here. Instead, we'll share four key points from James's research, which will help us address the question of whether positive emotions are always positive.

The first point is that not all positive things are optimal. Imagine waking up on your birthday and your partner singing "Happy Birthday" to you. That would certainly be positive. But now imagine your partner taking the day off work to spend it with you doing the things you enjoy most. That would be even more positive. In each of our relationships, there are things we would choose for their own sakes as being positive. Things such as cooking dinner together from scratch, staying up late and watching movies, reading novels that shaped our partners growing up, or going for long walks in the woods. And yet, there are things in our lives we consider to be more important than these activities. We would likely cut back on some of these things if one of us goes back to school for a master's degree, or if our partner is just beginning a career in a meaningful but demanding new profession, or if we have children who need our time and attention. It's important to find a balance, of course, but our point is that just because something is positive in itself, it does not necessarily mean that it is the best—or optimal—path to flourishing.

The second point we want to emphasize about the meaning of the positive addresses the question of how to characterize the red side of the cape. It's pretty easy to see that getting more of what we want in the world is positive. But what about getting less of what we don't want? Isn't that positive, too? Isn't finding a cure for a debilitating disease just as positive as discovering how to increase the yield of a particular crop? Isn't treating a mental illness just as positive as helping someone get an education? Of course it is!

Curing disease and treating mental illness are both positive—but they are *indirectly* positive. They move us in the direction we want to go by removing obstacles to well-being. Increasing crop yields and providing someone with an education are both positive, as well; but *directly* so. They move us in the direction we want to go by providing important components of well-being. So we think the red side of the cape is just as positive as the green side; it's simply positive in a different way. And we think mainstream psychology, with its emphasis on treating mental illness, is just as positive as positive psychology, with its emphasis on building human strengths. They are simply positive in different ways.

A third and related point to consider is that some things that are indirectly positive require us to undergo negative processes to arrive at the outcomes we desire. Here's a way to illustrate this point: What do you think the proper punishment should be for someone who drugs your partner, straps her down on a table, slices open her abdomen, and takes out one of her internal organs? How many years should this person spend in prison? Five? Ten? Twenty? What if he or she does this not just to your partner, but to lots of other people, too? And what if this person is paid a lot of money to do this? Can you believe some people would actually behave this way?

What if we told you that this person's victims actually consented to this practice voluntarily? And that they thanked the person afterward? What if we explained to you that this person is a doctor who specializes in removing inflamed appendices? That changes everything, doesn't it? There's no way we would consider surgery a positive process in itself, but it is something we would willingly undergo for the outcome of saving our lives.

The final point contrasts the green side of the cape with the reversible cape. We believe these perspectives represent two modes of engaging in positive psychology. From the standpoint of the green side of the cape, positive psychology is *complementary* to mainstream psychology. While mainstream psychology focuses on getting rid of the mental illnesses we don't want, positive psychology focuses on the complementary goal of building up the strengths we do want. From the standpoint of the reversible cape, on the other hand, positive psychology aims at a *comprehensive* approach to overall human flourishing. We believe that both of these perspectives are important and that we can see the complementary, green-side-of-the-cape emphasis on well-being as one part of what it takes to achieve comprehensive, reversible-cape human flourishing.[32]

So how can these four points help us answer the question of whether positive emotions are always positive? And what can this tell us about the role of positive emotions in our lives in general and in our relationships in particular?

We have been focused in this chapter on the value of positive emotions in our lives and for our relationships. Given their value not just for feeling good but also for our long-term well-being, we want to emphasize their importance and explore ways of cultivating them. At the same time, we want to make sure our approach to positive emotions takes into account our overall goals of flourishing as individuals and as couples.

Consider the fact that there are researchers all around the world investigating the benefits of vitamins in our lives. It's great to know, for example, that vitamin A can help improve our vision, that the vitamin B complex helps provide us with energy, and that vitamin C can boost our immune systems. Yet when we sit down to dinner, we don't simply put a handful of vitamin A, B, and C pills on our plates. It's important to have a balanced diet, which includes the full range of vitamins in the right amounts, as well as other essential nutrients. It's also important to make sure that the wrong things are not on our plates. In this book, we are focusing on relational vitamins such as positive emotions because so many relationships are low in these essential components. But we want to be very clear in acknowledging that this is not all we need for healthy relationships.

Our goal should not be simply to max out on positive emotions. Just as it is possible to have too many vitamins in our system, it is possible to have too many positive emotions. Mania is actually a pathological condition. And even under normal circumstances, it is possible to have too many positive emotions to function effectively. James remembers the excitement he felt when he learned how to cultivate strong positive emotions in his life. He would get up in the morning and activate those emotions until he was vibrating with positivity, then he would sit down to read philosophy—and find it all but impossible. He was too ecstatic to concentrate! So James learned to modify his morning routine to evoke emotions that would be more helpful to his goals.

It's certainly possible to cultivate levels of positive emotions that are not helpful. And there are times when it may be more helpful to focus on decreasing our negative emotions than on cultivating our positive ones. For Fredrickson, it's not just the level of positive emotions that's important, but the ratio of positive to negative ones. We can improve this ratio, she notes, by increasing positive emotions, decreasing negative emotions, or both.[33] So there are contexts in which it may be just as important to use the red side of our capes to decrease negative emotions as it is to use the green side to increase positive emotions. This is especially true, Fredrickson suggests, if your level of positive emotions is seriously low, or if you have high levels of positive emotions but they are matched by high levels of negative emotions. The goal, of course, would not be to eliminate all negative emotions from our lives, but to reduce inappropriate and unhelpful negativity.

One more important point to keep in mind is that not all negative emotions are truly bad or unhealthy. That is, there are times when negative emotions are appropriate and healthy. When we are grieving the loss of a loved one, for example, we will experience a range of negative emotions, and it is important not to short-circuit these feelings of loss since they are important parts of the healing process. Prolific psychologists Todd Kashdan and Robert Biswas-Diener have written an entire book called *The Upside of Your Dark Side* to point out the value of negative emotions for our well-being. There are times, they argue, when unpleasant emotions aren't things to be gotten rid of, but are negative processes that can lead toward something positive. Anger, for example, can be a strong motivator for justice, guilt can make us more sensitive and aware of the impact our actions have on others, and self-doubt can help us work hard to enhance our performance.[34] More recently, Susan David, a psychologist at Harvard Medical School, has published *Emotional Agility*, in which she makes similar arguments. Emotions such as sadness, anger, guilt, and fear, she writes, can lead to positive consequences, ranging from improving our memory, to raising our test scores by encouraging perseverance, to helping us form better arguments by thinking more carefully.[35]

So what can we conclude from these observations? It would be simplistic and mistaken to think that positive emotions are always positive and negative emotions are always negative. There are times when it is not appropriate to experience positive emotions, and there are times when it is healthy to feel negative emotions, especially when they lead to positive outcomes. With that said, this doesn't mean that all negative emotions are beneficial—we all know how easy it is to fall prey to unhelpful negative emotions. If you or your partner is experiencing extremely high levels of negative emotions or extremely high levels of positive emotions that are interfering with your relationship or your other life activities, we advise you to seek professional help. In the more normal ranges of emotional fluctuations, we strongly believe in the importance of being open to and learning from negative emotions as they arise. It's the positive emotions, however, that we want to actively cultivate in our daily lives, with all of their broadening and building benefits. So let's now turn to the question of how we can cultivate positive emotions effectively.

HOW CAN WE CULTIVATE POSITIVE EMOTIONS?

Oscar Wilde is said to have observed, "Some cause happiness wherever they go; others whenever they go." We suspect this rings as true in your life as it does in ours. We feel fortunate to have encountered people who, like Sam at the beginning of this chapter, seem to bring joy with them wherever they go. They seem to have a kind of Midas touch, but instead of turning everything to gold, they bring positive emotions to all those around them. By contrast, we have also come across people who routinely seem to thwart happiness in themselves and others. Like Winnie the Pooh's gloomy friend, Eeyore, they get lost in negative rumination. After an encounter with them, we feel the need for a psychological bath to rid ourselves of the negativity. Most of us probably lie somewhere between these extremes, hopefully closer to Sam than to Eeyore. One useful way to get a sense of where we stand is to take Fredrickson's Positivity Self Test.[36] Take a few minutes to answer the following questions and score your responses to determine your current positivity ratio. If possible, have your partner take the test, as well.

POSITIVITY SELF-TEST[37]

Instructions: How have you felt over the past twenty-four hours? Look back over the past day and using the 0–4 scale below, indicate the *greatest degree* that you've experienced of each of the following feelings.

0 = Not at all
1 = A little bit
2 = Moderately
3 = Quite a bit
4 = Extremely

_____ 1. What is the most amused, fun-loving, or silly you felt?

_____ 2. What is the most angry, irritated, or annoyed you felt?

_____ 3. What is the most ashamed, humiliated, or disgraced you felt?

_____ 4. What is the most awe, wonder, or amazement you felt?

_____ 5. What is the most contemptuous, scornful, or disdain-
         ful you felt?

_____ 6. What is the most disgust, distaste, or revulsion you
         felt?

_____ 7. What is the most embarrassed, self-conscious, or
         blushing you felt?

_____ 8. What is the most grateful, appreciative, or thankful
         you felt?

_____ 9. What is the most guilty, repentant, or blameworthy
         you felt?

_____ 10. What is the most hate, distrust, or suspicion you
         felt?

_____ 11. What is the most hopeful, optimistic, or encouraged
         you felt?

_____ 12. What is the most inspired, uplifted, or elevated you
         felt?

_____ 13. What is the most interested, alert, or curious you
         felt?

_____ 14. What is the most joyful, glad, or happy you felt?

_____ 15. What is the most love, closeness, or trust you felt?

_____ 16. What is the most proud, confident, or self-assured
         you felt?

_____ 17. What is the most sad, downhearted, or unhappy
         you felt?

_____ 18. What is the most scared, fearful, or afraid you felt?

_____ 19. What is the most serene, content, or peaceful you
         felt?

_____ 20. What is the most stressed, nervous, or overwhelmed
         you felt?

SCORING

Circle questions 1, 4, 8, 11, 12, 13, 14, 15, 16, 19, and underline questions 2, 3, 5, 6, 7, 9, 10, 17, 18, 20. Count the number of circled (positivity) questions you marked with a 2 or higher and the number of underlined (negativity) questions you marked with a 1 or higher. Calculate the ratio by dividing your positivity tally by your negativity tally. If your negativity tally is zero, replace it with a 1. The resulting number represents your positivity ratio for today.

The goal of this test is to determine what your balance of positive to negative emotions is. When your positive feelings significantly outnumber negative ones, you tend to be more resilient in life and in your romantic relationships, Fredrickson found. She suggests that in relationships, we want positivity scores of at least 3 and more like 5, or even higher.[38] This is consistent with world-renowned marriage expert John Gottman's research on the high levels of positive interactions between partners in healthy, flourishing, long-term relationships.[39] If your score is below 3, then like most research participants, you are likely suffering negative effects from low positivity.

So how did you do? Were you surprised at all by the results of the test? Is your positivity riding high today? Or are you closer to Eeyore than you thought you would be? If your partner also took the test, did you wind up with similar scores, or were they different? If you both had strong positivity scores, bravo! Keep practicing and spreading positivity. If one or both of you had lower scores than you would have liked, don't fret. We have included exercises at the end of this chapter that you can practice to help raise your positivity. Either way, it's important to be active in your cultivation of positive emotions. Before we turn to specific exercises to foster positivity, let's take a closer look at the positive emotions we mentioned that appear on Fredrickson's top ten list of most frequently experienced positive emotions. We'll explore them in the order Fredrickson says they often develop in a relationship.[40]

- Interest: You're drawn forward to explore and engage in something different and novel. You feel open and alive with a desire to learn more. Perhaps you're learning a new skill such as sailing or experiencing something more simple such as being intensely curious about the thrilling plot in a new book.
- Amusement: Nonserious surprises that bring on laughter in a social and safe setting. Causes an urge to share with others. Shared laughter helps us connect with others. Your spouse tells you a hysterical joke. Or after explaining to your three-year-old while bathing him how he needs to eat all his vegetables to grow tall like his Uncle Jimmy, Uncle Dan, Aunt Lisa, and Aunt Hope, he remarks with a twinkle in his eye, "Well, what about Aunt Arctica?" You erupt in uncontrollable laughter and your husband laughs so hard that he does a backward tumblesault. Amusement catches us off-guard, surprises us, happens in a safe place, and brings us closer to others.
- Joy: A brightness in demeanor and a lightness in step. You feel more alive. For heartfelt joy to occur, a safe and nurturing environment is usually required. Perhaps the birth of your child or your wedding day.
- Hope: Unlike other positive emotions, which typically occur when we are feeling safe, hope arises in exactly the opposite circumstance, when we are not feeling satisfied with how things are currently going. With hope, we see possibilities for

a better future. We see our situation as temporary and believe things can change. It motivates us to continue. Maybe we bombed an important interview, and rather than feeling despair we figure out how to prepare better the next time and envision ourselves succeeding. Or perhaps it's something more serious such as a difficult medical diagnosis, and we courageously follow through on the treatment protocol with an eye toward a better tomorrow.

- Serenity: Similar to joy but in a more laid-back way. Safety is required. You feel utter comfort. Fredrickson calls serenity the "afterglow emotion," in that it often follows other positive emotions such as joy, awe, or amusement. It's sitting on the beach and listening to the waves crash along the shore. Or walking on a fresh spring morning and taking in the beautiful sweet fragrances of flowers in bloom.

- Gratitude: With an open heart you feel authentic appreciation for something that has been bestowed upon you. You feel a strong desire to freely give back and do good in return. It could be a response to a huge favor someone did for you or simply appreciation for waking up to a glorious day.

- Pride: This positive emotion is triggered when you feel good about—or are praised for—something good that you did or achieved. These accomplishments are socially valued. Pride helps motivate us further to achieve more. It can result from a job well done at work that merits a promotion, distinction in school that earns a scholarship, or hard work at home that results in a flourishing rose garden.

- Inspiration: A self-transcendent emotion that occurs when we respond to human excellence. It's uplifting and heartwarming. Perhaps we witness our partner's generosity in taking time to help a struggling student despite his own tight academic deadlines. Or we see a homeless person give the few cents he or she has to someone else who is even less fortunate.

- Awe: This positive emotion is like inspiration taken up a notch. We feel awe when we witness extreme levels of goodness. Perhaps we see our partner do something so good that we feel overwhelmed by greatness and momentarily suspended in time. We experience a sense of oneness. Awe can happen when we witness arresting beauty in nature, such as a breathtaking sunset on the beach or a marvelous snowfall in the mountains. Awe makes us feel connected to something larger than ourselves, such as God or an ultimate purpose.

- Love: This is the supreme or ultimate positive emotion. Fredrickson says it's all of the previously described positive emotions transformed into love by the context in which they occur. As she puts it, "When these good feelings stir our hearts within a safe, often close relationship, we call it love."[41] Fredrickson observes that our love usually progresses in stages. In the beginning it might be triggered by interest, then move into amusement and build into joy. We then start to share our hopes with each other and the relationship brings serenity. Feelings of gratitude and pride toward each other develop. Inspired by our partner's qualities and good character, we may experience a sense of awe for the natural forces that brought us together. For Fredrickson, each of these moments can be accurately described as love.[42]

This is quite the list, isn't it? Simply reading through it can be uplifting. And examining each in turn is much richer than just lumping them all under one umbrella term such as *happiness* or *joy*. So let's look at some things we can do to experience more of these emotions in our lives. Not all methods of cultivating them are equally effective, so here are a few things to keep in mind as you work on promoting more positivity in your life.

The first thing to remember is that positive emotions are not the simple opposites of negative emotions. This means merely ridding ourselves of unhelpful negative emotions is insufficient for cultivating positive emotions.

Also, simply willing ourselves to feel positive emotions is unlikely to work. In fact, such efforts can actually backfire and make us less likely to feel the positive emotions we desire. One study demonstrating this involved sixty-nine women who were brought into a lab and told they would be taking part in an experiment about TV programming. Participants were randomly assigned to read one of two articles. The first article indicated that those who report high levels of happiness have better relationships, more successful careers, and better health. It also claimed that the happier people can make themselves feel, the more likely they are to experience these positive outcomes. The second article was neutral, with no reference to happiness. Next, some of the women who had read each article were randomly assigned to watch a happy scene from a movie and then asked to rate how much they experienced two positive emotions (joy and happiness) and seven negative emotions (anxiety, sadness, shame, worry, nervousness, frustration, and tension). Participants also rated to what extent they tried to feel more positive while watching the film clip, felt disappointed while watching it, and felt they should have enjoyed it more. Tellingly, those who tried to increase their happiness while watching the film felt worse afterward than the others, and they felt worse because of feelings of disappointment and self-blame. When they weren't able to improve their level of happiness, they thought of it as their fault, and this made them feel even worse.[43]

The key is in how you go about trying to make yourself happier. It's not a good idea to try to will yourself into it and then beat yourself up when you don't succeed. Nor is it helpful to focus on how you are feeling at each moment. Instead, here are some better approaches.

STRATEGIES FOR CULTIVATING POSITIVE EMOTIONS

#1: Prioritize positive emotions. The first approach is based on research conducted by Fredrickson and her colleagues on what they call *prioritizing positivity.*[44] The key here is not simply to value happiness. As we found in the studies we just examined, valuing happiness too much can actually get us into trouble by encouraging us to undertake actions that, paradoxically, make us *less* happy. As a matter of fact, research indicates that valuing happiness is inversely associated with positive emotions and satisfaction with life and positively associated with negative emotions and depression.[45] Prioritizing positivity, by contrast, predicts just the opposite: more positive emotions and fewer symptoms of depression. And as a result of experiencing more positive emotions, people who prioritize positivity have greater psychological resources such as resilience and self-compassion.

As defined by Fredrickson and her colleagues, prioritizing positivity means making decisions and organizing our lives in ways that are likely to result in the experience of positive emotions. Instead of a fixation on how we are feeling at each moment of the day and feeling frustrated if our levels of happiness are not as high as we wish them to be, we plan our days in ways that are more likely to result in the natural experiencing of positive emotions. Perhaps for you checking out a new exercise class at the gym is really fun, or completing do-it-yourself home repair projects fills you with pride, or reading historical novels stimulates great interest. Noticing what those activities are and making sure to include them in your life is likely to result in higher levels of positive emotions.

While some people seem to naturally exude consistently high levels of positive emotions on a regular basis, they may actually be able to do so precisely because they prioritize positivity. Take our friend Sam as an example. We discovered that even for him positive emotions didn't just happen all the time. Positivity takes work. In Sam's case, we learned that positivity is something he practices with his partner every day. Rather than just let life happen to them, they help direct their future by focusing on what they want and taking steps to make it happen. For example, they have worked thoughtfully together to create a bucket list of places they want to visit, goals they want to achieve, and experiences they want to have. This helps guide them in prioritizing positivity in their lives.

#2: By acting out how we want to feel, we can indirectly influence ourselves to feel that way. American philosopher and psychologist William James observed that although it seems like our emotions precede and cause our actions, they really go together, with our actions often causing or at least augmenting our emotional reactions. He added that although our emotions aren't under the direct control of our will, our actions often are. From these observations, he concluded that by regulating our actions we can indirectly influence our emotions.[46] This is why we may observe that striking a sassy pose when our partner is taking our picture may actually make us feel playful. And if we add to these physical actions the mental perspectives that come with certain emotions, this can make the effect all the stronger.

Have you ever been amazed by the control actors have over their emotions, able to cry on command on the stage or in front of a camera? Thespians know the secrets of being able to regulate their emotional states by means of their facial expressions, bodily poses, breathing patterns, and mental focus. With practice and time, we, too, can develop to a surprising degree the ability to manage our emotional states through exercising voluntary control over our bodies and our minds.

#3: The more we cultivate positive emotions in our own lives, the more likely we are to pass them along to our partners, magnifying their

beneficial effects in our relationships. This approach is particularly important for creating healthy, happy relationships long-term. Earlier
in this chapter, we discussed emotional contagion and the fact that
we can catch both positive and negative moods from others. This
fact is particularly salient with couples, who typically spend more
time with each other than with anyone else in their lives. Again, we
want to emphasize that we need to be open to what we can learn
with the help of negative emotions. There are certainly times in a
relationship when we need to be with those emotions and let them
work themselves out. But most people experience significantly
more negative emotions than necessary and significantly fewer positive emotions than optimal. So the more we cultivate positive
emotions in our individual lives, the more likely we are to pass
them along to our partners, magnifying their effects in our relationship.

What happens, though, when one partner is in a negative mood
and the other is in a positive mood? Does the negative mood get
passed along to the other person, or is it the positive mood that
wins out? How does it typically work in your relationship? Negative
emotions often have an advantage here because they are typically
stronger than positive ones.[47] It would be tempting to suggest that
the partner with the positive mood should work really hard to pass
along his or her emotions to the other. Be so positive that your mate
can't help being positive, too. When that works we are all for it, but
we're also mindful that this puts pressure on one person to "make"
the other one happy. And we're also mindful that when you're feeling negative emotions, it can often be quite annoying to have someone try to cheer you up. So we would like to challenge the partner
who's in the negative mood to experiment with opening him- or
herself up to being infected with the other's positive emotions.
Again, assuming this is a case of unhelpful negative emotions, then
it is to both partners' advantage for the positive emotions to win

out, and the more aware we are of the value of opening ourselves up to positive emotional contagion and letting go of our negative emotions, the more likely it is that the right emotions will win out. The key here is to think of this as an experiment. If it works, great! If not, try to avoid blaming yourself or feeling like you've failed. Just move on and give it a try again the next time.

Now let's turn to a specific exercise to go with each of these three approaches to cultivating positive emotions. Take some time to practice these approaches before moving on to the next chapter. Once you are finished, we will explore a topic that is closely connected to positive emotions. Savoring, which has to do with the way we respond to good events in our lives, will open up further practical ways for cultivating positive emotions in our relationships.

POSITIVE EMOTIONS PRACTICE EXERCISES

1. **Prioritize Positivity**

   What are the things you and your partner do to prioritize positivity? What things did you do in the past that have now fallen by the wayside, perhaps because things have gotten so busy that you don't seem to have time for them anymore? We invite you to make one significant change in your schedule to prioritize positivity. This could be planning a day—or at least a significant part of the day—when you engage in activities that bring positive emotions to both of you. Or you may want to schedule regular daily or weekly time for connecting through watching the sunset or listening to music together, taking up dance classes, or trying out new restaurants. The point here is not to force positive emotions but rather to put yourself in contexts where they naturally tend to arise.

2. **Be an Actor and "Act As If"**

   Look back at the list of Fredrickson's top ten positive emotions. Choose one you would like to practice by means of exercising voluntary control over your body and your mind. For the emotion you choose, what are your physical and mental triggers for experiencing that emotion? Practice cultivating the emotion by adopting the positive gestures, facial expressions, and breathing style you typically have in that emotional state. What kinds of things do you think about that trigger that emotion? It can be helpful to consider a particular time in the past when you felt that emotion in a powerful way, and to imagine you are back at that point in your life, focusing on reproducing the physical positions and mental focus you had then. This may take some practice, but if you approach this with some openness and perhaps a bit of playfulness, its effectiveness may surprise you.

3. **Be a Positive Emotion Conductor**

   Take a few minutes to write down ways in which you and your partner catch each other's positive and negative emotions. What, specifically, can you do to be a positivity conductor and help your partner catch your positive emotions? What, specifically, can you do to be open to catching your partner's positive emotions, even when you are in a negative emotional space?

CHAPTER 5

Slowing Down to Savor

*U*RSULA, *A* SUCCESSFUL *makeup artist and entrepreneur, operates a thriving professional beauty and makeup studio named Ursula's About Phace, located in the heart of Philadelphia. Her client list runs the gamut from brides-to-be to celebrities to professional women and men seeking some serious sprucing up or a quick touch-up before a big event. Most days, she's booked in back-to-back appointments, on her feet all day, with little time to answer her phone. Out of a desire to prevent any unnecessary interruptions while interacting with her loyal clients, she regularly relinquishes her smartphone to her assistant, giving her full permission to answer any calls and texts. On one such day, after hearing a succession of phone rings followed by an influx of text alert beeps, Ursula stopped what she was doing and approached her assistant to inquire if there was an urgent matter. Rather than immediately responding, her assistant silently stared at the phone in disbelief. A stunned expression crossed her face. Fearing the worst, Ursula pressed on to ask what was wrong. Hesitantly, her assistant meekly handed over the phone, pointing out the myriad sexy texts from some man complimenting Ursula and thanking her for their morning "endeavors." Her assistant then asked if*

*Ursula was having an affair. Ursula smiled and revealed that the myste-
rious man was Joe. Her husband, Joe. To whom she has been married for
more than twenty-five years!*

Her assistant may well have found this situation even more stunning than what she had suspected was going on. For Ursula, though,
it's a normal part of her relationship with Joe, a relationship for
which she is profoundly grateful. During their more than two dozen
years of marriage, Joe has continued to savor their relationship,
valuing it like he did on the day he asked for her hand in marriage.
Whether it's whispering sweet things in her ear at five a.m. or spontaneously embracing her from behind and affectionately kissing her
neck in the kitchen at five p.m., he continues to express his love for
her. Just recently, he told her he was so happy he had asked her to
marry him more than twenty-five years ago.

If only we could all be like Joe! The good news is that even if we
can't be exactly like him, we can at least learn some great lessons in
how to savor our relationships. It's so important to savor our partners and our time with them, rather than take them for granted and
risk losing them. Consider the case of Marco and Tonya, whose
marriage ended after more than twenty years. Well liked in the
community, they had many friends and appeared to be a happy
couple. Marco worked in a midsize finance company and because of
his strong affinity for numbers was quite good at his job. Admired
by colleagues and clients alike for his ability to get right down to
business, he was able to plow through work without becoming side-
tracked by unnecessary details. His pragmatic approach in the office garnered him accolades and led to success in his career.

Unfortunately, his no-nonsense approach didn't work so well in
his personal life. Tonya was irritated by the overly logical way
Marco interacted with her. When she would ask for some much-
needed attention to tell him about her long day with the kids or
suggest they hang out on the couch for a while to connect, he would

say he didn't have time to chat, that he was tired and had a lot of work to get done. After all, he had a lot of responsibilities at work, needed to focus, and couldn't afford to get off track. Sure, if there was a task that needed to be done for the kids, he'd do it. Or if there was a specific matter, he was game to listen (as long as it didn't take too long!). And on those occasions, he was quick to offer a solution. But just to talk about nothing, with no specific objective or goal, wasn't what he wanted. As he told her many times, "I'm a very sensible guy."

However, when it came to their romantic relationship, what Tonya was looking for during these moments was sensitivity, not sensibility. And it wasn't something necessarily tangible she was looking for. It wasn't a specific matter, but rather a matter of the heart. As Helen Keller is said to have observed: "The best and most beautiful things in the world cannot be seen or even touched—they must be felt with the heart." Not only did Tonya feel she wasn't heard or seen, she felt unloved. "He didn't value me beyond the children," she told us. Rarely did Marco touch her, compliment her, tell her he loved her, or express how much he appreciated her.[1]

When they did have some free time on their hands, he'd focus on his work, working out, and his own needs rather than reaching out to her to take advantage of these available moments to spend time together. Fun ideas and activities that Tonya would often excitedly suggest as ways for the two of them to connect would regularly be met with rejection. After repeatedly being turned down in her many bids for attention over the years, Tonya finally couldn't bear the emotional toll Marco's constant neglect took on her.

"I felt like I was withering," she said.[2] She knew she had to get out of the relationship to preserve what remaining strength she had. When she told him she was leaving him, after twenty-two years, he was shocked. He didn't understand what he had done, what could possibly have been so awful that she felt she had to leave. There weren't any affairs or big fights. But there was "a slow boil over the years that caused irreparable damage to the relationship," she explained.[3] Only later, once he began dating again, did Marco realize how good he'd had it with Tonya and begin conveying that to her. For Tonya, however, it was too little, too late.

It's been several years now since their divorce and Tonya feels like she is finally healing and giving herself all the nurturing that was absent in her marriage. One of the things that has helped her feel like herself again was returning to her childhood passion of dancing.

"Latin dance class has reconnected me to my emotions after they were bottled up for many, many years. My dad was disconnected from his emotions, and I realize now that I learned from him to be disconnected from my emotions, as well. For a time, my dad was my boss, and I actually used to get the hiccups when I worked for him. I think it was because I literally had to hold in my emotions around him. I wasn't free to express myself. He was very controlling (as was my husband). It's interesting that my parents ended up divorcing, as well. It also took my mom, who was very much like me, more than twenty years to leave my dad. I'm now working on myself so that I don't attract the same sort of guy. Marco was very much like *his* father, who wasn't the best role model when it came to marriage. Marco's dad often shamed his wife. And Marco shamed me a lot. I only now see how similar our behavior was to that of each of our parents. Dancing has helped me learn how to access my emotions again, rediscover myself, and express myself. All of me. My integrated whole, not just the parts of me that Marco allowed me to show."[4] While Tonya is not currently dating anyone, she enjoys the attention she gets from her male dance partners, who freely express their platonic positive appreciation toward her through dance.

THE SCIENCE OF SAVORING

Our response to the events in our lives is just as important as the events themselves. On the red-cape side of things, difficult things happen to all of us. Sometimes we experience big adversities, such as the loss of a job or the death of a loved one. At other times we experience smaller adversities, such as missing a plane or getting stuck in a traffic jam. We have a broad range of ways of responding to those things, and the way we choose to respond has a huge influence on our experience of the events themselves and on the effects the events have on our lives. Psychologists call the way we respond to adverse effects *coping*.[5]

Imagine you have an appointment with your doctor, who informs you that you are at risk for a heart attack. There are different ways of coping with this difficult medical diagnosis. How would you respond? You could treat it as a problem to be solved, learning all you can about your condition and what you can do to keep your heart healthy. You could seek social support, telling your family and friends about the diagnosis and drawing strength from their loving attention. You could, of course, remain in denial, refusing to tell anyone about the diagnosis and pretending it never happened. Or you could turn to alcohol or drugs to take your mind off the significance of what the doctor told you. More than one of these responses is possible, as are others. How you choose to respond will likely make a big impact on your health and your life. If you do all you can to take care of your heart, you will be less likely to experience the heart attack. Connecting with your family and friends will help you have a strong support system even if you do have a heart attack. Trying to stay in denial about what the doctor told you may help you feel good in the short term, and drinking or taking drugs might do the same. But denial does nothing good for you in the long run, and substance abuse actually compounds your problem.

On the green-cape side of things, we experience a variety of positive events in our lives. Some are big, such as landing a dream job or getting married, and some are small, such as watching the sunset or getting help from a friend on a home-improvement project. The way we respond to these events has a huge impact on our experience and our lives. Sometimes we just forget them, and sometimes we allow our lives to be transformed as a result of them. In the 1980s, two psychologists, Fred Bryant and Joseph Veroff, realized that much psychological work had been done on coping, how we respond to negative events, but that very little had been done on the flip side, how we respond to positive events. Perhaps this is because it's obvious that we need to know how to respond effectively to adversity but not so evident that any response is needed when something goes well. Bryant and Veroff recognized the importance of responding to good events and eventually cowrote a book on this topic, which they have come to call *savoring*.[6]

In their book, *Savoring: A New Model of Positive Experience*, they define savoring as the processes underlying our capacities to attend to, appreciate, and enhance positive experiences.[7] They do a masterful job laying out the conceptual and scientific case for savoring, and we will be exploring some of the highlights of their work in this chapter.

The first thing we want to clarify is the difference between positive emotions and savoring. In our terminology, they are both green-cape events, and Bryant and Veroff hold that they are closely allied.[8] But the authors also claim that they are distinct parts of our experience, since savoring involves some sort of mindfulness or meta-awareness that goes beyond our initial experience itself.[9] Savoring, they point out, is not just the reality of having positive feelings, but the process of attending to those feelings in some way. At whatever level of experience we may encounter a positive emotion, savoring requires that we attend to it with some level of conscious awareness.

In the previous chapter, we explored Barbara Fredrickson's broaden-and-build theory of positive emotions, and in this chapter, we will investigate what we like to call the *lengthen-and-strengthen* theory of savoring. Fredrickson argues that positive emotions broaden our attention and enable us to build up our physical, psychological, and social resources. Bryant and Veroff explore ways savoring can help us lengthen the duration and strengthen the level of the positive emotions we experience. And lengthening and strengthening the positive emotions themselves can help lengthen and strengthen their impact on our lives. Furthermore, as we will see shortly, they can also help lengthen and strengthen our romantic relationships. Before we turn to the specific effects of savoring on relationships, let's explore in more detail some of the important distinctions Bryant and Veroff make about savoring itself. We'll start by looking at a set of key factors they identify that affect the level of enjoyment of any experience we have.

To do this, we would like you to join us in imagining a very special evening in which we take you and your Aristotelian lover to dinner at a French restaurant so we can enjoy great food, wine, and conversation together. What are the things we can all do to make sure we savor the experience and get the most out of it? The first thing, no doubt, is to clear our schedules of anything else before or after it. Since it's a French restaurant, we expect the pace of the evening to be calm and leisurely, with plenty of time to chat and get to know each other between courses and to share thoughts about nurturing positive relationships. To make sure we have plenty of time to enjoy the experience and no one has to rush off before the dinner is done, let's all be sure to clear the entire evening, making whatever plans are necessary to ensure we are not interrupted. And how about if we make the reservation for a Friday night? That will be a great way to unwind from the stresses of the meaningful but challenging activities we are engaged in during the week.

When the day arrives, we meet each other at the entrance to the restaurant. Inside, the ambience is one of sophisticated serenity, and we all take in the decor appreciatively. We attend as completely as we can to the experience of being at the dinner together. We deeply enjoy the conversation but temporarily put it on pause at each stage of the meal so we can savor the complexity of the wine, the smooth texture of the soup, the exotic herbs in the entrées, the fresh simplicity of the sorbet, and the delicate balance of flavors in the cheese plate we enjoy together at the end. When we first open the menus, and again at the end of the evening, we remind ourselves how fortunate we are to be able to enjoy this special cuisine and to spend an evening sharing insights about things that deeply matter to all of us. Thank you so much for having joined us! Let's be sure to do it again sometime soon.

In this very special, if imaginary, evening, we can identify a number of factors that affected our level of enjoyment of the experience. Following Bryant and Veroff, let's pay particular attention to six of them. First is the duration of the experience. This refers to both the length and the pace of the event. Because the dinner lasted the entire evening, and because we had all planned in advance to be available without interruption, we had plenty of time to enter into the experience together. And because the courses were paced well, we never had the feeling of being rushed, but rather had a chance to savor each one of them deeply.

Second, Bryant and Veroff point out that savoring typically happens at times of low stress, but that it may be more intense if the time of low stress follows a time of high stress. By scheduling the dinner at the end of a hectic week and the beginning of the weekend, we made it very likely that we would be able to come together at a time of low stress for all of us, made all the sweeter by the stressful challenges of the week just past.

Complexity is another factor affecting the level of our enjoyment. Sometimes a lack of complexity allows us to savor an experience more effectively, as we found with the sorbet. At other times, greater complexity allows us to integrate two or more factors to strengthen the intensity of the experience, as we found when we combined the fig compote with the Camembert at the end of the meal.

This takes us to the importance of the fourth factor: the degree of attentional focus. During the dinner, we found we naturally paused our conversation to enjoy the fullness of the wine and savor as deeply as we could the first bites of our entrées. This is because we know that the more we can attend to an experience, the more deeply we can savor it.

We also paused a couple of times during the meal to remind ourselves how fortunate we were to be spending the evening in this way. These moments added to our savoring of the experience. But we didn't go overboard with this, trying to force ourselves to enjoy the evening or continually rating how happy we were. As we saw with positive emotions in the previous chapter, trying too hard can actually backfire and decrease our well-being.[10] The case is similar here: Balanced self-monitoring can deepen savoring, but extreme self-monitoring can dampen it.

The final factor we want to mention is how much we enjoyed spending the evening with the two of you. If any one of us had gone to the restaurant alone, we could have taken in the very same ambience, imbibed the very same wine, and dined on the very same food, but we wouldn't have enjoyed it nearly as much. Savoring an experience with the right person or persons can greatly strengthen our enjoyment.

With these key factors in mind, let's turn to the temporal dimension of savoring. If savoring is about attending mindfully to what is going on in and around you, it may seem that it could only be about the present. Indeed, Bryant and Veroff hold that savoring is about the here and now. But they also point out that the past and the future can play important roles in savoring—and even more, that savoring can be *about* the past or the future. Indeed, the analysis of our evening at the French restaurant is closely connected to reminiscence, or savoring the past, and our feelings between the time of scheduling our dinner and the evening in which we experienced it no doubt involved what Bryant and Veroff call *anticipatory savoring*, or savoring the future.[11] Let's examine more closely what these researchers have to say about reminiscence and anticipatory savoring.

Reminiscing can be a powerful way to continue the enjoyment of positive experiences long after they are gone. Taking the time to enter as fully as we can into the memories of those experiences can actually allow us to feel all over again some of the positive emotions they originally created in us. Bryant and Veroff point out, however, that there are more and less adaptive ways of savoring the past. Some participants in their studies reported being motivated to reminisce by a desire to escape the difficulties of the present. By thinking back to a happier time in their lives, they could take a break from their current problems and experience some of the positive emotions from their past. Unfortunately, though, a return to the present brought a return of their problems. And the contrast between the joys of the past and the troubles of the present actually made them feel worse than before they had engaged in the reminiscing. This may motivate some people not to want to return to the present at all and instead live their lives as much as possible in the past. Bryant and Veroff have found that in contrast to these maladaptive approaches to savoring, many people reminisce in order to gain perspective and self-insight and to strengthen their identity. By reliving past positive experiences, we can learn from them about what helps us thrive, and we can bring what we learn into the present to help improve our current situation. Reminiscing can also reconnect us with who we are—with where we came from, who has been important in our lives, and what our values are.

Instead of an escape *from* reality, this type of reminiscing is an escape *to* reality. It is not only pleasant in itself, but it can also bring lasting benefits.[12]

According to Bryant and Veroff, savoring the future is more difficult than savoring the present or the past.[13] In savoring the present, we simply have to be aware of our sensory experience or our current thoughts and feelings, and in savoring the past, we can avail ourselves of a rich repository of memories to attend to. But in savoring the future, the objects of our savoring don't yet exist; we have to create them using our imagination. For most of us, this is a much more difficult process. Still, anticipatory savoring can be a very powerful way to connect to events we are expecting in the future. As with reminiscing, Bryant and Veroff have found that anticipatory savoring can be practiced in more and less adaptive ways. Attending too much to the future, they observe, can actually interfere with our savoring of the present. And too much anticipatory savoring of an event can interfere with our savoring of the event when it actually occurs. This can happen because, having imagined the future event in great detail, we may be less likely to be pleasantly surprised by various aspects of it when it finally arrives. Or worse, we may have built up the event so powerfully in our minds that when it actually occurs, we are bound to be disappointed. To avoid some of these negative consequences of anticipatory savoring, we are advised not to allow ourselves to turn anticipation into expectation. We can enjoy imagining what an event will be like in the future, but when it arrives we can let those imaginations go and savor the actual event as it unfolds. In general, Bryant and Veroff recommend maintaining a good balance between savoring the future and savoring the present.[14]

Whether we are savoring the past, the present, or the future, Bryant and Veroff identify something that can seriously undermine our efforts: kill-joy thinking. Instead of focusing us on the present moment, kill-joy thinking takes us elsewhere, to the other places we think we really should be and the other things we think we really should be doing. It may also include considerations of how the present event could have been better. During our evening out, if we had been focused on a concert we were missing that night or on all the work we were not getting done by taking an entire evening off, or if we had compared the French restaurant with a Michelin-rated restaurant we had once visited in Paris—with its superior decor, food, wine, and service—that would clearly have dampened our enjoyment of the occasion. And kill-joy thinking can do more than dampen enjoyment; if unchecked, it can eventually lead to depression.[15]

Up to this point in this chapter, we have been exploring the nature of savoring and how to practice it in our lives in general. Now let's turn to its role in relationships.

HOW TO PRACTICE SAVORING IN ROMANTIC RELATIONSHIPS

Savoring can be a powerful way to enhance long-term happiness and satisfaction in romantic relationships. You may not find this surprising, given that positive emotions, as we saw in the previous chapter, are vital in a relationship and that savoring, as we have seen in this chapter, can lengthen and strengthen these good feelings. What may be surprising is Bryant and Veroff's conclusion that savoring may actually be more effective at communicating love to one's romantic partner than a variety of other means for doing so. They acknowledge that helping out with chores, doing favors, showing physical affection, sharing passion, and giving gifts can certainly be important parts of a relationship. But they point out that some of these methods of communication have potential downsides. Although giving gifts on anniversaries, birthdays, and

Valentine's Day, for example, can be an effective way of communicating our love for our partners, it can also, as they observe, become routine, a duty that must be fulfilled, regardless of the way either person in the relationship is feeling at the time. Although under these circumstances, special days can present opportunities for getting a relationship back on track, we suspect they more often lead to a sense of obligation and behaviors that lack deep meaning. In these cases, our partners are extra nice not because they *want* to be, but because they feel they *have* to be.

In contrast with gift giving, Bryant and Veroff emphasize that savoring is not dictated by the calendar. Rather, they argue, it is an indication of the presence of several relationship-affirming factors. First, since it's spontaneous, it is likely to be communicated at a time when positive emotions are deeply felt. Second, savoring, by definition, indicates that a person is free of a variety of social needs,[16] so it follows that the partner doing the savoring is not likely to be concerned about his or her own social status, about whether his or her love is approved by other people, or about feelings of insecurity in the relationship. Since the savoring is not governed by the calendar or other kinds of social expectations, it is likely to be intrinsically motivated. Finally, savoring carries with it a focus on the present moment and a conscious awareness of what one is focusing on. This full and mindful attention to one's partner allows for a powerful communication of love and care.

In light of this, Bryant and Veroff conclude there is no stronger way than savoring to express your love for your partner.[17] Ursula agrees. She says that having her husband, Joe, tell her on a regular basis how much he savors the joy of having her in his life is beyond wonderful. When he communicates to Ursula how much he savors the joy of loving her, he clearly lets her know that he is attending to her, and Ursula basks in his undivided attention.

It is not enough, of course, just to feel an appreciation for your partner, no matter how focused and intense it may be. Your partner is not a mind reader. So you need to express that appreciation directly. Ursula recounts many, many moments when her partner has spontaneously expressed his appreciation to her. Tonya, by contrast, can cite just two or three incidents in their twenty-two years of marriage! The difference savoring made for these two relationships is abundantly clear.

To be most effective, these expressions of appreciation must be reciprocal. Just as Joe savors Ursula, she savors him and makes it a point to regularly express her appreciation to him, as well. This leads to upward spirals of positivity in their relationship and enhanced well-being for them individually and as a couple.[18] Their relationship continues to flourish, with savoring as a core component.

According to Bryant and Veroff, when Joe and Ursula savor their love and communicate it to each other, this leads to a key component of healthy romantic relationships, a feeling of being deeply cared for and respected, which they call *affective affirmation*.[19] Veroff and his colleagues have created a way to assess the level of affective affirmation in a relationship. Their measure consists of just four items. Take a moment now to answer the questions in the following box.

THE AFFECTIVE AFFIRMATION TEST[20]

During the past month, how often did you:
1. Feel that your spouse (or romantic partner) felt especially caring toward you?

   Often   Sometimes   Rarely   Never
2. Feel that your spouse (or romantic partner) made your life especially interesting or exciting?

Often   Sometimes   Rarely   Never

3. Feel that your spouse (or romantic partner) made you feel good about having your own ideas and ways of doing things?

Often   Sometimes   Rarely   Never

4. Feel that your spouse (or romantic partner) made you feel good about the kind of person you are?

Often   Sometimes   Rarely   Never

Spend a few moments considering your answers to this test. Hopefully, they are more toward the "often" side than the "never" side, as this brief questionnaire is intended to measure how cherished you feel in your relationship. Ask your partner to take the test as well and then compare your individual answers (or, if your partner is unavailable, compare your answers with those you imagine your partner would give). Think about what you could you do in your relationship to help each other feel more deeply valued or affectively affirmed.

In a longitudinal study of married couples using this questionnaire, spouses who felt especially affirmed by their partners reported having thriving marriages. Across a wide variety of demographic differences, husbands who felt affectively affirmed by their spouses in their first year of marriage were more likely to remain in a stable marriage over time,[21] and wives who reported being affectively affirmed by their spouses in their first year of marriage felt the strongest commitment to remaining in their marriages seven years later.[22] This research indicates what a powerful impact the communication of relational savoring can have on the length and strength of a marriage.

So what are the processes through which this savoring can occur and be communicated to one's partner? Bryant and Veroff identify five interrelated savoring processes that can help strengthen a relationship. These processes are all connected to the single most dominant form of savoring reported by participants in their studies: sharing with others. Sharing an experience with someone else—either while it is happening or after it has happened—can greatly increase our enjoyment of that experience.

1. *Appreciative sharing and mutuality.* When partners have interests in common and are mutually engaged in activities around those interests, they report more affective affirmation. In one study, appreciative sharing between partners as they told the story of their relationship was actually indicative of the health of their marriage. Couples who weren't very expansive as they told the story of how they met, when they decided to get married, and some of the ups and downs of their relationship had less healthy marriages that eventually ended.[23] So something as basic as being open to sharing and savoring the details of the story of the relationship can be an important factor in the health of a marriage.

2. *Self-disclosure.* We often keep our inner world hidden, but being willing to share this world with our partner can open the door—not only to harmonious passion, as we saw in chapter 3—but also to a deep savoring of the relationship. Research shows that women tend to be more willing to openly discuss memories from their past, while men tend to resist doing so—at least directly. But carefully listening to what men say about past events and activities can reveal emotional content that they are sharing indirectly. Whether your disclosure is direct or indirect, making your inner world available to your partner can greatly strengthen your relationship.

3. *Minding.* A third process is what researchers refer to as *minding*, or consciously attending to your partner and what he is like.[24] As you carefully observe your partner, you get

to know him better and better, learning things about him you would be likely to miss in normal, everyday life. Minding can give you more and more nuanced information over time for how to savor your partner and strengthen your relationship.

4. *Collaboration*. Can you think of a time when you and your partner were truly in sync, working on something together? Maybe it was making music together, planning a family vacation, or cooking a special dinner. When you fully enter into these shared experiences and neither you nor your partner is approaching them as an opportunity to dominate or impress the other, they can be magical moments of connection in which you enjoy the moment and savor your partner. Meaningful collaboration can even take place when telling the story of your relationship. In a study similar to the one showing the value of appreciative sharing, Veroff and his colleagues found that many couples did not collaborate with each other while recounting the history of their relationship and imagining its future— some disagreed with each other, others merely laughed, and still others simply agreed with what their partners said. Some couples, however, did truly collaborate by cooperatively building on what their partners expressed. And the more collaboratively these couples told their stories, the more they reported feeling affectively affirmed in their relationship.[25]

5. *Sexual empathy*. Another outcome of the study we just mentioned is that both men and women who felt affectively affirmed also reported more enjoyment of sex in their relationship. This makes sense, since mutually satisfying sexual relationships require empathy with your partner's feelings and awareness of your own. This empathy can make it easier for you to savor your partner and your relationship.

These green-cape processes Bryant and Veroff identified for strengthening a relationship through savoring are closely related to processes identified by other researchers as also being key to healthy relationships. John Gottman, for example, in his book *The Seven Principles for Making Marriage Work*, urges couples to "nurture their fondness and admiration" for each other.[26] He recommends we do this by intentionally thinking and talking about positive aspects we appreciate and value in our partner and our relationship. This is especially important because these things can easily slip out of our awareness in the frustrations of everyday life. When you find this happening to you, it is vital to spend time reconnecting to the good things in your partner and your relationship. If even this becomes too difficult, Gottman suggests thinking back to the things you valued in your partner in the past. This can be a way of reminding yourself of the good things in your partner and helping you know where to look for them in the present. In essence, he is saying that savoring the past in your relationship can be a way of sparking your savoring of the present.

Research by Shelly Gable at the University of California, Santa Barbara, sheds further light on the importance of the green-cape approach of focusing on what goes well in our relationships and our lives. While it's important for couples to cope during the tough times and work to fix problems that arise, Gable has found that the way couples respond to each other's good news may be more important to their relationship quality than their response to negative situations. Flourishing couples do well at acknowledging, calling out, and savoring things that are going well in their relationship and with each other. Be it something small, such as a good deed their partner has done for them, or something big such as a promotion, those couples who respond supportively to good news (practicing what Gable calls "active, constructive responding," or ACR) increase their chances of having a healthier and more lasting and fulfilling relationship. Additionally, Gable found that a passive and unengaged response to a romantic partner's good news, with a comment such as "That's nice, sweetheart," and then returning to the newspaper or whatever you were previously doing, is almost as detrimental to a relationship as ignoring or directly criticizing a partner's good news.[27]

As we mentioned in chapter 1, we have evolved to be especially sensitive to problems. When we have a problem, we typically know it, because problems scream at us. Opportunities and other good things typically just whisper and often fade into the background. Even though people report having far more positive than negative things happen to them (as many as three times more, according to one study[28]), we often tend to focus more on the negative things. For this reason, it can be easy to lose sight of the many good things in our relationship. This is why Gable recommends making sure to celebrate the good times and the good things our partners do. If we don't, we can lose sight of them, making our partners feel unappreciated and even taken advantage of.

Savoring can be a powerful way of balancing the score, making sure the negative things in our lives don't count as more than they actually should, and making sure the positive things remain in our consciousness. And the good news is that no matter how unfamiliar or awkward it may seem to use our savoring skills, Bryant reassures us that "Like any cognitive-behavioral skill, we get better at it with practice."[29]

Once you complete the important savoring exercises that follow, you will be finished with part 1. In this section of the book, we have focused on what it means to have a healthy relationship by exploring the ideal of Aristotelian love and the significance of harmonious passion, positive emotions, and effective savoring, key elements positive psychology research has revealed as essential to building long-lasting, happy, and fulfilling partnerships. In part 2, we will focus on character, exploring how to change our habits to improve our relationships by identifying and building on our individual and relational strengths.

SAVORING EXERCISES

1. **Your Savoring Style**

   Think of a positive event that happened to you in the past week. Write down what happened, along with your answers to the following questions: How did you respond to that event? Did you forget about it and move on? Did it automatically come back into your consciousness later? Did you intentionally do something to savor it (whether or not you thought of it as savoring)? Did you write about it in a journal? Look at a picture you had taken of it? Share the experience with someone else in person or on social media? Savor it in some other way? If you did savor it, what was the effect of your savoring on the overall amount of enjoyment that came from the experience? If you didn't savor it, how might you have done so, and how might that have changed your experience?

2. **Developing Savoring Practices**

   Of the specific practices identified by Bryant and Veroff (appreciative sharing and mutuality, self-disclosure, minding, collaboration, and sexual empathy), which do you think would be most powerful to work on in your relationship? What specific steps can you take to put it into practice?

3. **Positive Relationship Portfolio**

   Gather into one place some of the mementos, music, pictures, cards, letters, and movie clips that remind you how special your partner is and how important your relationship is. Spend fifteen minutes every day for a week savoring the emotions connected to these items and the experiences, realities, and possibilities they represent.

4. **ACR**

   The next time your partner shares good news with you, be sure to engage in what Gable calls "active, constructive responding." Stop what you are doing and focus your attention completely on your partner. Help her savor the moment by asking her questions and actively celebrating the news. For you analytic or strategic types, if you can see potential problems that may arise because of the good news, as long as there is no immediate danger, wait until a later time to discuss these things. In the moment, help your partner savor the good news as deeply as she can.

PART 2

Why Cultivating
Character Matters
for Committed
Relationships

CHAPTER 6

Know Thyself: Identifying Your Strengths

So far in this book, we have argued that being happy together is not something that just happens to a couple, as it seems to in most fairy tales. But it also isn't an elusive dream, as many skeptics and cynics claim. Rather, it is something we can cultivate through concerted effort. For our efforts to be effective, though, they need to be directed properly. And we have looked to age-old wisdom and contemporary scientific research, integrated with some of our own ideas, as sources for this needed direction.

Turning to age-old wisdom, we have explored Aristotelian love as an ideal in which partners are attracted by the good they see in the other person and are motivated by it to become better themselves. As we have seen, this is what happens to Melvin in the movie *As Good as It Gets*, when he sees the good in Carol and tells her, "You make me want to be a better man." It can certainly be flattering to hear "You complete me!" from a Jerry McGuire, or to have a Mariah Carey sing, "I can't live without you!" But we have pointed out that these may actually be red flags for relationships. If someone needs you to complete her or to make her life worth living, this may be a sign of obsessive passion and an indication that she believes she is missing something that only you can magically provide. This attitude is often one of storybook romances, in which Prince (or Princess) Charming swoops in and makes everything all right. This approach may make for entertaining stories, but it doesn't hold up in real life and in mature relationships. That's because this perspective can take away personal responsibility and lead to an overreliance on others. While partners do need each other, as we noted in chapter 2, it's interdependence—and not codependence—that is crucial for healthy romantic relationships.

So Melvin definitely had the right idea. But it's important to keep in mind that *wanting* to be a better man (or woman) is just the first step. If that's as far as it goes, it doesn't bode well for a relationship. As we all know, the road to hell is paved with good intentions. Wants and wishes are not sufficient for becoming a better person. For that we need action. In particular, we need to cultivate our character. And this is what we will turn to in part 2.

As we will soon see, the cultivation of character is not a quick fix. Rather, it's a lifelong process that requires continual practice. The key is to continue to work at it. As with a muscle, we need to exercise our character in challenging ways to keep it strong. The active cultivation of our character is important for our own growth and development, as well as for that of our partner. As our character develops, we will begin to interact with our partner differently, supporting her in the development of her own character. The more we focus on the identification and cultivation of our individual and collective character strengths, the more we can support each other in our quest to become better versions of ourselves. This doesn't mean losing ourselves or becoming different people, but rather realizing more of our potential, developing more fully into the unique and wonderful individuals we already are.

This is not to say cultivating our character is easy. Particularly within the context of a romantic relationship, in which your partner has his own set of strengths he is struggling to develop, there will be setbacks, and times when you seem to have forgotten everything you have learned. But the overarching goal of becoming a better person and supporting your partner in the same endeavor provides a powerful and meaningful approach to relationships. And we are fortunate to be able to rely not just on philosophical wisdom but also on a growing body of scientific research. Positive psychology gives us a wealth of evidence-based approaches for helping us to appreciate the good in our partners and to work to become better ourselves. This research helps us define in great detail the kind of goodness that can occur in human beings, offers us specific ways in which we can find the particular goodness in our partners and in ourselves, and suggests concrete steps we can take to feed and grow that goodness.

In part 1, we focused specifically on how we can define the good in our relationships in the context of passion, emotions, and savoring. And you completed exercises to help you cultivate harmonious passion, positive emotions, and effective savoring. In part 2, we will focus on the good within the individuals in the relationship. How can we define, find, and feed good character in our partners and in ourselves? And what effect does this have on our relationships? In this chapter, we will look to Aristotle, William James, and contemporary work in positive psychology to understand what character is and why it is so important for happiness. In subsequent chapters, we will discuss the importance of good character for healthy relationships and explore ways of cultivating it in ourselves and our partners.

ARISTOTLE'S TAKE ON CHARACTER

Aristotle observed that we all experience a common set of emotions (such as fear and anger) and desires (for things such as pleasure, wealth, and honor). Yet we respond to these emotions and desires in very different ways. And it is our response to these common human experiences, he argued, that constitutes our character.

Consider the emotion of fear, for example. Aristotle noted that there is a continuum of ways we can respond to this emotion, from not being sensitive enough to it to being too sensitive. At one end of the continuum, insensitivity to fear leads to recklessness; at the other, oversensitivity leads to cowardice. Somewhere in between these extremes is courage, which is marked by just the right sensitivity to fear.

Now consider the desire for pleasure. If we don't give in to the desire enough, we may be something of a bore; if we give in to it too much, we may be out of control. It's best if our response to desire is somewhere in the middle, where we can take enjoyment in pleasure without it dominating (and perhaps devastating) our lives.

Aristotle noted that many of the emotions, desires, and actions we experience are similar to fear and pleasure. We can respond to them on a continuum, from deficiency to excess, with the proper response being somewhere in the middle. In Aristotle's terms, the proper response is a virtue, which is the mean between two vices. And good character is choosing virtues across the spectrum of emotions, desires, and actions.[1]

When you think of it this way, character is likely to seem pretty easy. All you have to do is avoid extremes. But that's only part of it. For Aristotle, knowing where on the continuum the virtue lies is crucial. And this varies with the context. What counts as courageous self-disclosure when a relationship gets serious might well be recklessness on a first date or cowardice if it takes us twenty years to bring up the topic. With regard to anger, Aristotle writes that getting angry is easy. The hard part is being angry with the right person, to the right degree, at the right time, for the right purpose, and in the right way.[2] He argues that in order to determine the right form of anger—and in general, to identify where on the continuum a virtue lies in a particular situation—we need to use a special human power: practical wisdom. When Aristotle visited us back in chapter 2, he helped us identify practical wisdom as a function unique to human beings. And human happiness, he held, lies in using this power well. Identifying the virtuous response in a given situation is often quite difficult and can require the careful cultivation of practical wisdom over a lifetime.

So how do we cultivate practical wisdom effectively? For Aristotle, we do so like we cultivate any other practical ability. To become good at playing the trumpet, for example, you actually have to play the trumpet. A lot. To become good at relationships, you have to work at relating with people over the course of many years. Mastery in these domains involves action of the right sort. And this action must be more than just occasional; it must be repeated action that results in the development of good habits. So for Aristotle, virtue can be understood as good moral habits, and the way we develop those habits is through repeated moral actions. The way to become virtuous is to act virtuously.

Virtuous action, Aristotle points out, begins with the informal education we get from our parents. As soon as we can speak, we are taught to say please and thank you. These actions are the beginnings of our habits of politeness and civility. Our parents teach us moral lessons directly, by instructing us on what to say and how to act across various situations. More powerfully, no doubt, they teach us moral lessons *indirectly*, through the words and actions they model in front of us. These lessons have a tremendous impact on our relational lives. As we have seen from the stories of couples we have recounted earlier in this book, so many of the habits we bring to relationships are ones we model from our parents. When these habits are good, they can help us forge strong romantic relationships of our own. When these habits are not good, however, they can stand in the way of developing the healthy relationships we desire.

Given what we now know about neuroplasticity, it is clear that character formation is not something that happens only in children, but rather is an ongoing process throughout our lives. So it is crucial for us to understand how, at every stage of our development, we can make choices for adopting and maintaining the habits that constitute good character and that support healthy relationships. To explore these ideas further, let's turn to a thinker who in many ways bridges Aristotle and positive psychology.

WILLIAM JAMES AND THE STREAM OF CONSCIOUSNESS

William James (1842–1910) was an eminent American philosopher and psychologist. A Harvard professor for more than thirty years, he was also the older brother of the novelist Henry James. As a philosopher, he was one of the founders of American pragmatism, and as a psychologist he is known as the father of American psychology. He has also been referred to as America's first positive psychologist.[3] He was deeply interested in where actions come from and how they develop into habits. Delving into his views on these matters will provide us with some foundational insights on how to develop good habits of character to support our relationships.

James believed in the importance of introspection in psychology. Sensitive to the nuances of our feelings and thoughts, he coined the term *stream of consciousness* to describe the dynamic realities of our inner lives.[4] One characteristic he observed about this stream of consciousness is that it is always changing. And the change is much more extensive than we tend to realize. We speak of experiences by putting them in verbal categories: We lump the ocean, the sky, and our favorite suit together as being "blue," for example, and that makes us think that when we see them we are repeating a single visual experience. But it turns out that the experiences we have when we see "blue" are not the same, at all. The blue of the sky changes throughout the day and varies at any given moment depending on what part of the sky we are observing. And the particular hue of our suit is different in different lights and changes with the color of the clothes worn by those around us. In the same way, we tend to use broad verbal categories and cognitive shortcuts to describe our life with our partner. We might label as "fun," for example, activities as varied as a night out on the town, an afternoon bike ride, or a late-night movie. Digging deeper into the nuances of our experiences allows us to understand more clearly what we value in them. This knowledge is important for the savoring processes we discussed in the previous chapter and, as we will soon see, for choosing activities that can lead to relationship-enhancing habits.

This leads us to the second characteristic James observed about the stream of consciousness: It is selective. Given the limited range of visible light and the narrow band of audible sounds, for example, our senses limit the kinds of stimuli that can make it into the stream of consciousness. And given the complexity of the stream itself, we can't attend to the entire stream all at once. If you were attending to all the background noises in your environment right now, and to the feel of the chair as it supports your body, and to the color of the walls in the room you are sitting in, you would not be able to concentrate on what you are reading.

How do we select what portions of the stream of consciousness to focus on? Often, our attention is involuntary, meaning we don't exercise any intentional control over it at all. Rather, our attention is attracted by movement, sounds, what we find interesting, or things we're just used to focusing on. We do, however, have the ability to focus our attention voluntarily and thus to influence our perception intentionally. For example, in the famous figure-ground vase drawing by Dutch psychologist Edgar Rubin, the picture that emerges—either two faces or a vase—depends upon where we focus our attention.[5] Intentional focus may also help us notice particular things in our environment. We may focus on trying to find a friend in a crowded restaurant or, once we have found that friend, on listening to what she has to say over the sounds of the other conversations taking place around us. Sometimes we must exert great effort to keep our attention voluntarily focused, as when we are listening to a difficult lecture, learning to play a complex piece of music, or sitting in a bird blind watching for the appearance of a rare bird. James held that "the faculty of voluntarily bringing back a wandering attention, over and over again, is the very root of judgment, character, and will."[6]

In the context of relationships, it's crucial to know what portion of the stream of consciousness we should focus on. It can be all too easy to focus on our partner's shortcomings, or on the ways in which our relationship is leaving us unfulfilled. There are certainly times when it is important to use the red side of our reversible cape to focus on problems in a relationship so we can try to fix them. In cases of physical or emotional abuse, for example, being honest about the situation can motivate us to get help, or to leave the relationship if necessary. In most cases, however, using the green side of our reversible cape to focus in detail on the good in our partner and in our relationship can be a very effective way to improve the quality of that relationship. Noticing and appreciating our partner's strengths, as we will see, can help a relationship flourish. Even better is taking action on what we notice.

Indeed, one of the reasons James emphasizes voluntary attention so much is that it is a precursor to voluntary action. And when we turn our thoughts into actions, our actions may, with time, become habits. And thoughtfully cultivated habits help our character grow as Aristotelian lovers.

James points out that there are some great practical effects of habits. First is increased competence. When we have practiced something like tying our shoes, typing, or driving a car with a manual transmission so much that the behavior becomes habitual, we are able to do it much more smoothly and effectively than if we are constantly paying attention to what we are doing. A second practical effect of habits is that they decrease effort. When we first learn to tie our shoes, type, or use a stick shift, we have to concentrate all of our attention on what we are doing. But once the activity becomes habitual, it seems almost effortless, and we can carry on a conversation, listen to music, or plan our day while doing it.

James likened habit to financial capital. Without financial capital, anytime we need money, we need to exert effort to earn it first. Saving money is the key to getting out of this cycle. And if we can save enough money, it begins to work for us, and we are able to benefit from the interest. Similarly, without habits, any action requires effort. But if we develop the right habits, eventually they begin to work for us, and we can benefit from the actions without having to exert effort.

This is the value of good character. It involves the establishment of good habits that are beneficial to us and to those around us, including our partner. It is the quintessential pathway for becoming a better person through your relationship.

SNAP

Of course, developing good habits in our relationships is far easier said than done. William James presents four maxims to help us in this endeavor. And James Pawelski has created an acronym to make them easy to remember: SNAP.

1. *Start strong.* The more highly motivated we are to start a new habit, the more likely we are to be successful. One way to

increase our motivation is to make a public announcement of what we are going to do. That makes it easy for our friends to support us in achieving our goal and hard for us to go back on our intentions.

2. *No exceptions.* We may think that once we have acted in accordance with the new behavior for a few days, we can give ourselves a break. But James argues that this is likely to make us have to start the process all over again.

3. *Always act.* Whenever we have an urge to act in accordance with the new habit, we should follow that urge, no matter how annoying it may seem.

4. *Practice exercising the will.* James suggests doing something hard every day, for no reason but that it is hard. Doing so, he says, can strengthen the will, making it ready for our use when we need it.[7]

These maxims, along with William James's insights into the roles of awareness, selection, action, and habit, will be helpful as we deepen our exploration of the importance that character plays in romantic partnerships. It's worth pointing out that these insights also apply to the earlier chapters on harmonious passion, positive emotions, and effective savoring. Each of these components of good relationships requires an awareness of our feelings, thoughts, and behaviors, an intentional choice to attend to certain ones, and a commitment to take action and develop healthy habits. Now you can see why we emphasize so strongly the importance of completing the exercises in each chapter. Without action, we can't develop good habits. It's interesting to note how many of the people we interviewed for this book referred back to their childhoods as times when they picked up relational habits from their parents. Many of the habits they picked up were good ones, but some have been destructive to their relationships. These bad habits are ones that in adulthood they have had to work hard to break.

When we think about the habits that form good character, it's important to realize that we are not talking about mere routinization. That is, good habits are more than just automatic ways of behaving under all circumstances. Harmonious passion, for example, involves more than just picking an activity you and your partner enjoy and committing to doing it every Friday night for the rest of your lives. Cultivating positive emotions doesn't mean simply practicing being joyful on Tuesday and Thursday mornings. Nor does effective savoring mean we think back to the same positive childhood memory every day at noon. Activities and memories can become stale. And positive emotions don't just appear on command. The kinds of habits we're talking about here are more skills than knee-jerk reactions.

These are the kinds of habits we must develop if we are to avoid what is known as the *hedonic treadmill*, where we take action but then become habituated to it so quickly that we don't get anywhere.[8] Let's see how this works with savoring. If we think back to a wonderful childhood memory one day, we are likely to get a positive boost from reminiscing about what happened to us. If we think back to the same memory the next day, we may still get something of a boost, but it's likely to be smaller. If we think back to the same memory every day for a month, we're likely to be totally acclimated to it and not get any boost whatsoever out of the experience. If, on the other hand, we think of savoring as a skill and develop the habit of spending time savoring on a daily basis—but vary the things we savor and the way we go about doing the savoring—we are more likely to thwart the hedonic treadmill and continue to benefit from savoring. In fact, as we gain mastery over the skills of savoring, we are likely to get even more benefit from exercising these habits than when we first started.

THE SCIENCE OF CHARACTER

In chapter 1, we mentioned that James (Pawelski, that is) met Martin Seligman at the first public meeting on positive psychology, in 2000. At that meeting, Seligman invited James to a subsequent, by-invitation-only gathering, where a small group of scholars would be working to develop a science of character. There were about twenty-five people at the meeting, including the members of the Positive Psychology Steering Committee, the core group of scientists responsible for the strategic development of the field. Led by Seligman, the committee included four other esteemed members. Mihaly Csikszentmihalyi, a longtime professor at the University of Chicago, was best known for his research on flow, a psychological state we experience when we are fully immersed in an absorbing task. Ed Diener, a well-known researcher at the University of Illinois, was famous for his pioneering work on subjective well-being, a psychological formulation for happiness. Chris Peterson, of the University of Michigan, was a world-class expert on optimism. And George Vaillant, a renowned Harvard professor and research psychiatrist, was director of the Grant Study of Adult Development, a groundbreaking, long-term investigation of flourishing across the lifespan.

The meeting was sponsored by the Mayerson Foundation, which had donated the funds to create a classification of character strengths and a scientifically validated way to measure the range of specific strengths in individuals. The head of the foundation, Neal Mayerson, was there with his wife, Donna, both of them psychologists committed to using social science to help make the world a better place. Seligman announced that Peterson had just taken a three-year leave of absence from the University of Michigan to join him at the University of Pennsylvania to head up the project.

One of the presenters at the gathering was Barbara Fredrickson, who gave a spellbinding account of her work on positive emotions, leading to a rich discussion of the connections between emotions and strengths. Another presenter was Katherine Dahlsgaard, a graduate student at the University of Pennsylvania, who had carried out an extensive review to identify core virtues that were valued across time in cultures around the world. She had looked at lists, for example, from Confucius, Plato, Aristotle, Thomas Aquinas, and Benjamin Franklin. She divided the items she encountered into three groups: virtues that had shown up regularly across the lists she had examined (bravery, kindness, and the like), virtues that seemed to be much more strongly connected to specific cultures and not others (cleanliness and punctuality, for example), and strengths (such as humor) that were not typically included on historical lists of virtues but that are important for flourishing. Given James's philosophical background, this presentation was of particular interest, and Seligman asked him to lead the group in its discussion.[9]

What eventually emerged from that meeting and much subsequent work by a large network of researchers was Peterson and Seligman's hefty volume, *Character Strengths and Virtues: A Handbook and Classification*.[10] Its authors viewed the book as a bridge connecting Aristotelian virtue theory with contemporary psychology. As we have already seen, Aristotle believed the best way to make sound ethical decisions is to become a good person by cultivating the virtues. Philosophers today call this view *virtue ethics*. Peterson and Seligman wrote, "We can describe our classification as the social science equivalent of virtue ethics, using the scientific method to inform philosophical pronouncements about the traits of a good person."[11] Thus, positive psychology is about more than just the science of well-being. It's also about the cultivation of human flourishing through the development of good character.

The work led by Peterson and Seligman resulted in the creation of the VIA Classification of Character Strengths and Virtues, often referred to simply as the VIA.[12] This classification is an important complement to the *Diagnostic and Statistical Manual of Mental Disorders* (DSM), published by the American Psychiatric Association. The DSM is an important diagnostic tool, listing hundreds of mental illnesses with their symptoms, and aiding psychiatrists and psychologists in the recognition of these illnesses in their patients. What's missing from the DSM is the green-cape side of things: methods for positively identifying good mental health. The VIA is a green-cape approach that can be used to help diagnose what is going right with people. Peterson used to like to call it the "un-DSM" or the "manual of the sanities."

The VIA contains twenty-four character strengths, ranged under the six virtues of wisdom, courage, humanity, justice, temperance, and transcendence. Specific criteria were developed to identify the strengths that would be included in the classification. Just as with the virtues, for example, these strengths are valued across time and culture. In addition, they are different from talents, which tend to be fixed and automatic (think of perfect pitch, for example). Character strengths, by contrast, are traits that involve the will and can be cultivated. They contribute to well-being and are morally valued as ends in themselves and not just as a means to other things we want. They are something in their own right, and not merely the absence of a particular negative trait. Finally, since this is a classification in empirical psychology, the character strengths need to be measurable.

With all this in mind, let's take a look at each of the virtues in turn, along with the character strengths listed under them.[13] We'll just look briefly at them now to get acquainted with the classification. In the next few chapters, we will spend more time digging into what they mean and the value they have for relationships.

The first category in the classification is strengths of wisdom and knowledge. They focus on the cognitive aspects of good character, on how we can acquire and use information effectively to support well-being. There are five character strengths in this category. *Creativity* involves coming up with new ideas, behaviors, or products that are useful in some way. *Curiosity* is being interested in things and wanting to find out more about them. *Judgment* (or *open-mindedness*) implies not rushing to conclusions, but rather maintaining an openness to all the evidence and a willingness to go where the evidence leads. *Love of learning* is characterized by a motivation to master skills or domains of knowledge. It is similar to curiosity, but more systematic. Think of becoming fluent in a foreign language, and not merely being curious about what a particular word in that language means. Finally, having *perspective* is being able to understand situations deeply and provide good advice to others.

The second category in the classification is strengths of courage. These strengths emphasize the exertion of effort when things are difficult. When we think of courage, we probably immediately think of *bravery*. And that, indeed, is the first strength in this category. This includes the classical meaning of standing strong on the battlefield, but it can also mean speaking up for what is right in other kinds of contexts, as well. In addition, we can also demonstrate courage through *honesty*, the second strength in this category, which involves being authentic no matter what the situation. The third strength is *perseverance*, which is about getting things done—not just starting them, but finishing them. (This, by the way, was one of the strengths Peterson himself was particularly good at. He and Seligman called it "out-the-doorness," and it was clearly one of the key strengths needed to complete the classification itself.) Finally is *zest*, which is about living life fully and with energy, entering into things completely.

This brings us to the third category: strengths of humanity.

These strengths can be seen in caring relationships with others, specifically in one-on-one interactions. They include *kindness*, being helpful to others; *love*, having close relationships in which there is mutual sharing and caring; and *social intelligence*, knowing what makes people tick and how to fit in to social situations.

The fourth category, strengths of justice, also consists of strengths involving relationships with others. Whereas strengths of humanity involve one-on-one relationships, though, strengths of justice involve relationships between an individual and a group or community. So while strengths of humanity occur *between* people, strengths of justice occur *among* people. There are also three strengths in this category. *Fairness* involves treating everyone as they deserve to be treated, regardless of the way you may feel about them; *leadership* is helping a group of people be productive, while at the same time being on good terms with them; and *teamwork* involves being a good member of a group, including doing your part well and sticking up for the group.

More than a quarter of the character strengths are in the final two categories of the classification. Strengths of temperance help us with balance in our lives, keeping us from harmful extremes. The first of these strengths is *forgiveness*, which keeps us from the extreme of hatred. The second is *humility*, which keeps us from the extreme of arrogance. The third is *prudence*, which involves being careful about what we do and not taking unnecessary risks. This strength keeps us from the extreme consequences of pleasures that are not good for us in the long run. And the fourth is *self-regulation*, the kind of discipline that keeps us from all sorts of damaging emotional extremes.

The final category is transcendence. The five strengths in this category help us find meaning by connecting with the world outside ourselves. First is *appreciation of beauty and excellence*, noticing and valuing these qualities in a variety of contexts, including nature, the arts, intellectual pursuits, sports, and simple elements of our everyday lives. Second is *gratitude*, which involves being thankful for the good things that happen to you, and taking the time to express that thanks. Third is *hope*, defined in terms of believing in a good future and working hard to make it happen. Fourth is *humor*, seeing the light side of things, and liking to smile, joke, and laugh with others. And finally, *spirituality* is about having a sense of a higher purpose and meaning in the universe and living your life in accordance with this larger reality.

Peterson and his colleagues argued that having good character doesn't mean we have to be paragons of each of these strengths. But it does involve having strengths across all six virtues. One way we might approach developing our character would be to use the red side of our reversible cape to identify and fix our character flaws. Indeed, many of us are all too aware of these flaws and have been working for years to try to fix them. What we may not have spent as much time on, and what we want to emphasize in this book, is the green-cape approach of focusing on what we're good at and trying to develop *more* of it. Using the green side of our cape more frequently and effectively can yield beneficial results that are astonishing. It can help us flourish in ways we never thought possible, and it can sometimes be even more effective than the red side of the cape at solving problems. The good news about cultivating our character using this approach is that we don't have to start from scratch. We each have strengths we are naturally good at. These are called our *signature strengths*. To find out what your signature strengths are, be sure to complete the following exercises. At the end of this chapter, we provide a list of the character strengths with the definitions currently used by the VIA Institute on Character, led by Neal Mayerson. In the next chapter, we'll explore the meaning and value of signature strengths, and why knowing our own and our partner's signature strengths can be so helpful in building love that lasts.

SIGNATURE STRENGTHS EXERCISES

1. **Strengths Survey**
   Identify your signature strengths by taking the VIA Survey of Character Strengths. The survey is free, and you can find the link on our website, at buildhappytogether.com. Once you've completed your survey and printed out the results, take some time to reflect on your top strengths. Do they seem to fit you well? Are you surprised by any of them?

2. **Strengths Video**
   Popular filmmaker Tiffany Shlain has created a great video introduction to character strengths and virtues, called "The Science of Character." Watch it by following the link on our website, at buildhappytogether.com. Be sure not to miss it!

THE VIA CLASSIFICATION OF CHARACTER STRENGTHS AND VIRTUES
(from the VIA Institute on Character)[14]

1. Strengths of Wisdom and Knowledge
   - CREATIVITY: Thinking of new ways to do things is a crucial part of who you are.
   - CURIOSITY: You like exploration and discovery.
   - JUDGMENT: You think things through and examine them from all sides.
   - LOVE OF LEARNING: You have a passion for mastering new skills, topics, and bodies of knowledge.

- ◆ PERSPECTIVE: People who know you consider you wise.

2. Strengths of Courage
   - ◆ BRAVERY: You do not shrink from threat, challenge, difficulty, or pain.
   - ◆ HONESTY: You live your life in a genuine and authentic way.
   - ◆ PERSEVERANCE: You work hard to finish what you start.
   - ◆ ZEST: You approach everything you do with excitement and energy.

3. Strengths of Humanity
   - ◆ KINDNESS: You are kind and generous to others.
   - ◆ LOVE: You value close relations with others.
   - ◆ SOCIAL INTELLIGENCE: You know how to fit in to different social situations.

4. Strengths of Justice
   - ◆ FAIRNESS: One of your abiding principles is to treat all people fairly.
   - ◆ LEADERSHIP: You excel at encouraging a group to get things done.
   - ◆ TEAMWORK: You excel as a member of a group.

5. Strengths of Temperance
   - ◆ FORGIVENESS: You forgive those who have done you wrong.
   - ◆ HUMILITY: You do not seek the spotlight, and others recognize and value your modesty.
   - ◆ PRUDENCE: You are a careful person.
   - ◆ SELF-REGULATION: You are a disciplined person.

6. Strengths of Transcendence

- ◆ APPRECIATION OF BEAUTY AND EXCELLENCE: You notice and appreciate beauty and excellence in all domains of life.
- ◆ GRATITUDE: You are aware of good things that happen and don't take them for granted.
- ◆ HOPE: You expect the best in the future, and you work to achieve it.
- ◆ HUMOR: Bringing smiles to other people is important to you.
- ◆ SPIRITUALITY: Your beliefs shape your actions and are a source of comfort to you.

CHAPTER 7

Know Your Partner: Applying Your Strengths in Your Relationship

IN THE PREVIOUS chapter, we discussed the importance of good character for romantic relationships. In particular, as we think about the ideal of Aristotelian love, in which relationships are built on the appreciation of the good in our partners and the consequent motivation to want to become better ourselves, the cultivation of character is crucial. We noted that for Aristotle, good character is the habit of choosing the virtuous mean between two vices. And we explored William James's emphasis on attention, selection, action, and habit in the development of good character. Finally, we discussed positive psychology's VIA Classification of Character Strengths and Virtues, emphasizing the green-cape approach to cultivating character through our signature strengths, those strengths we just naturally seem to be good at.

In this chapter we will explore our signature strengths in greater detail. Initially, we will focus on understanding and developing the strengths of each person in the relationship, then we will focus on integrating both partners' strengths so that the whole becomes more than the sum of its parts. This is particularly important because research suggests that when you recognize and appreciate your partner's character strengths you are more likely to be happy in your relationship, have your psychological needs met, and be more sexually satisfied.[1] (That got your attention, didn't it?) You'll want to make sure you know your own signature strengths, as identified by the VIA Survey. And if you're reading this book with your partner, you will want to know each other's, as well. So if you haven't yet taken the survey, we invite you to pause right now and do so. The link to the survey is posted on our website, at buildhappytogether.com. Once you've taken the survey, we encourage you to print out the results and keep them handy as you read this chapter.

So what are the results of your survey? What are your signature strengths? The great thing about character strengths is that you can't go wrong. Whenever we hear a person's top five strengths, we think, "Wow! What a great set of strengths!" And it's true. Each collection of five strengths is a powerful asset to have in our lives and our relationships. Although it takes just a few minutes to identify our signature strengths, it takes a lifetime to develop the potential they represent. The list may seem simple, but each strength in the classification is a rich and complex trait with a long history and a plethora of nuances. Identification of our strengths is a great first step on the journey toward their mastery.

As you take a look at the strengths that have come up for you, is their meaning clear? Do they seem to fit you well? Were you surprised by any of them? When you first get your survey results, it's important to understand the strengths on your list and to think about the various ways in which they are already a part of your life. That's what we want to focus on now.

Signature strengths are often strengths we just can't help exercising. They seem to be a natural part of us. For example, do you have a friend with the strength of kindness? We hope so! Kind people make great friends—and can be wonderful mentors. They are naturally helpful and great to be around. But sometimes people take advantage of kind people in very unkind ways. Maybe they take them for granted, or exploit them in some way. When people with the strength of kindness are taken advantage of, they don't say, "That's it! I'm never being kind again!" Instead, they just keep on being kind. It's as if it's in their DNA, and a few negative encounters are not going to keep them from being kind.

Sometimes when we look at our list of signature strengths, one or more of them can seem surprising. We may not realize we have a particular strength until it comes up in our survey results. As we reflect on it or talk with our family and friends, we may realize it is a strength we just didn't know we had. Sometimes this is because we assume everyone thinks and acts the way we do and we're surprised that our perspectives and behaviors are considered unusual. Sometimes this is because we have an unnecessarily limited understanding of what a particular strength is. That was the case for each of us.

When James was in high school, he was convinced he had zero creativity. This was because he equated creativity with artistic ability. Because he couldn't draw well at all, he thought he had no creativity whatsoever. It took James many years to realize that there are lots of ways to be creative beyond being artistic. You can be creative with language, for example. Like with poetry. And he really likes writing poetry. Or you can be creative with ideas. And he loves brainstorming and coming up with new and creative perspectives on things. As it turns out, creativity is James's top signature strength!

Suzie has had a similar experience with creativity. Like James, growing up she didn't realize she was creative, since she clearly was not a budding Rumi, Renoir, or Rachmaninoff. Although she appreciated poetry, art, and music, she was not particularly talented at creating any of it. So when she took the VIA Survey, she was surprised when it identified creativity as one of her signature strengths. As she thought about it, though, she began to realize that much of the fulfillment and meaning in her life was due to this strength of creativity. So, too, was much of her professional success. In her work in the media and public relations, she relied heavily on her strength of creativity to write and produce television programs and to pitch new ideas. The surprising results of the VIA Survey helped her understand herself more deeply and enabled her to tell the story of her life with greater insight.

As our personal stories demonstrate, it's not unusual to be surprised by one or more of our signature strengths. Less frequently, we might actually be disappointed by them. When that happens, it's important to look carefully at why we are responding in this way. Is it because one of the strengths on the list isn't one of our signature strengths, after all? Is it because we are still not clear on what the strength really means? Is it because we have certain assumptions about how these strengths may limit us?

Imagine a young man or woman who aspires to attend the West Point military academy. Taking the VIA Survey, that person might hope for strengths such as bravery, leadership, and perseverance. Yet what if she finds her top strength is love? She might well be disappointed, thinking this indicates she would be more suited for a career as a social worker than for a place in the military. But believe it or not, the number one signature strength among the cadets at West Point—among those training for careers in military leadership—is love. Although these cadets surely are brave and perseverant leaders, their most important strength is being able to care deeply for the others in their unit—even being willing to die for them, if necessary.[2]

So thinking through any disappointment we may initially feel when viewing our list of strengths is important. Getting clearer about the strengths and what they entail can help us understand their potential more deeply and overcome our sense that they might limit us somehow. Another thing to keep in mind here is the possibility that a strength you expected to see in your top five may actually be your sixth or seventh strength. There is nothing magical about limiting signature strengths to your top five, and you should feel free to focus on six or seven, if you would like. The key is just to avoid trying to focus on so many at once that it becomes overwhelming.

A final thing to keep in mind is that, although the results of the VIA Survey are fairly stable over time, it is possible for some of the strengths to go in and out of your top five as circumstances in your life change. And cultivating a particular strength intentionally over time can result in its eventual appearance among your top five. So if there is a particular strength you value that is not currently among your signature strengths, feel free to work on cultivating it. Keep in mind that the VIA Survey is not like a test for blood type, identifying some permanent biological fact about us. Rather, it is intended to be a helpful guide to aid us in understanding ourselves and realizing more of our potential.

Although we can initially be surprised or disappointed by one or more of our signature strengths, more frequently they seem to fit us quite well. They may even seem obvious. But again, each of the strengths is a rich and important trait that takes a lifetime to master. And identification of our signature strengths is just the first step. Whatever our initial feeling about our list of strengths, further reflection on them can sometimes yield important insights about ourselves and the life choices we have made. Our strengths can really explain a lot. They can help us understand ourselves better, and they can help our partner understand us better, as well.

In James's case, his top two strengths feel to him like the story of his life. We mentioned that his top signature strength is creativity. His second signature strength is judgment, or open-mindedness, which involves seeing things from all sides, not jumping to conclusions. It's also sometimes called critical thinking. He has used this strength throughout his life, and it helps him understand why he chose to be a philosopher. He loves trying to get to the bottom of things, seeing things from all angles, trying to understand people and ideas, no matter how strange or difficult they might at first seem.

Sometimes, he feels torn between these two strengths of creativity and judgment. With creativity, he wants to jump on a great idea and go with it. But with judgment, he wants to think about the idea from a variety of perspectives to make sure it really is a good one. This is like having an internal editor checking everything to make sure it's just right. But he's also learned that the strengths of creativity and judgment can work very well together. When the creative brainstormer comes up with great ideas, the internal editor works hard to develop them and make sure they are well thought out. This kind of collaboration yields far better results than he could achieve by using just one of the strengths in isolation. So the VIA Classification has given him a language he can use to understand himself better.

This same language of strengths also helps *Suzie* understand him better. Sometimes, James seems to be excited to move forward with an idea, but at other times, he seems to hesitate and hold back. Instead of merely feeling frustrated by this seeming inconsistency, Suzie can now see that James's behavior is due to a balance between two of his signature strengths. Depending on the context, she may want to support his creativity and encourage James to go for it, or she may choose to benefit from the fuller consideration brought by his judgment.

With all this in mind, take a look again at your list of signature strengths. Are there any on this list you find surprising? If they seem disappointing, can you understand why? If they seem fitting, is there a way they can help you understand your life more deeply? As you think about these questions, it can be helpful to talk them over with your partner, too. It's important for your partner to understand your strengths and how you feel about them. And he or she may be able to help you gain new insights about your strengths, as well.

Let's pause here for a powerful exercise, developed by Martin Seligman, that can help you and your partner connect more deeply to the role your signature strengths have already played in your lives to this point.

STRENGTHS STORIES EXERCISE

1. Choose one of your signature strengths and think about how you have used it in the past. Think about a particular occasion on which you used it effectively and write down the story of how you did so. (Keep in mind that this story is less about talents and achievements and more about you at your best.) What were the circumstances? Who else was involved? How, specifically, did you use your strength? What was the outcome? Take time right now to write a page or two on what happened.

As you look over what you wrote, what stands out for you? Are there aspects of this story you had forgotten? Was it awkward for you to write any of it down? Did it seem at all like bragging? It's interesting that many of us have no problem remembering our failures. Our brains just seem to keep reminding us of them over and over. And because in many contexts it is socially acceptable—and even socially desirable—to talk about our failures, we may find ourselves frequently sharing with others times when we screwed things up. This focus on failure can affect our self-perception, narrowing our sense of what we are capable of and limiting the activities we undertake. So it's especially important to remember that our lives are also filled with successes—big and little triumphs resulting from decisions we have made and effective actions we have taken; times when, using our signature strengths, we were able to save the day, help someone in need, or advance an important project. But it's easy to forget these occasions, and when we do talk about them, it can feel like we are tooting our own horns. The tendency to focus more on failure than on success, although natural, is not balanced. And we can restore the balance and be more fair to ourselves by intentionally cultivating green-cape approaches. Making it a point to remember times when you did something right, and taking the time to write about them, can be a very effective way to do so.

2. Now share your story with your romantic partner. (If you're not in a relationship right now, feel free to complete this exercise with a close friend or family member.) Both you and your partner will want to have identified your VIA signature strengths and thought about a particular time when you used one of these strengths successfully.

Take turns sharing your stories with each other. When you are the speaker, tell (or read, whichever you prefer) your story to your partner, but don't say what the strength is that you're describing. When you are the listener, make sure to be attentive to what your partner is saying. In many cases, being a good listener is actually a lot harder than being a good speaker. Good listening means not interrupting with your own thoughts or stories, but rather putting aside your ideas to pay attention to your partner. It means listening actively, with plenty of interest, eye contact, and nodding. It means listening for the strengths in your partner's story.

When your partner has finished his story, help him savor it. A good way to do this is by asking questions that give him a chance to elaborate on different parts of the story. You can ask him to share more about how he felt at key times, or what motivated him to respond as he did. As we noted in chapter 5, savoring is a very important part of relationships, and yet with our busy lives and our externally imposed modesty, we often don't take the time to celebrate and enjoy deeply the times in the past when we have used our strengths to do the right thing. After helping your partner savor the story, tell him what strengths you heard in it. The point here is not just to guess the signature strength he had in mind. Rather, mention and discuss with him all the strengths you heard, even if they are not listed formally in the VIA Classification.

We hope you enjoyed thinking, writing, and talking about a specific time in the past when you used one of your signature strengths in a meaningful way. Writing down our strengths stories and then sharing them can be a very empowering experience and can help us connect deeply with our partner. Couples who have taken the VIA have told us it has helped them see their partners in a completely different light. Instead of continuing to be annoyed by something they saw as one of their partner's character flaws, they began to appreciate the positive value of the behavior. This allowed them to understand their partner's strengths more deeply and interact with them more effectively.

Sometimes these connections and insights can happen within the context of a rich set of family relationships, in which the sharing of strengths stories seems to have an emotional contagion factor that can spread throughout an entire family.[3] Not long ago, we went into our son's school and led sessions on strengths for parents, teachers, and students. Upon learning their signature strengths, students mentioned to us similarities they saw with their parents' strengths, in some cases identifying particular strengths they had learned from their mothers or fathers. It's true that our parents can have a huge influence on the development of our strengths, teaching us healthy psychological and relational habits that can last a lifetime. This truth helps balance out some of the stories we shared in part 1 about the negative perspectives and relationship habits we can sometimes pick up from our parents.

When the students went home at the end of the day, some of them brought up the subject of character strengths with their families, further spreading the positive impact of the session. One mother recounted to us later how her daughter had helped the family have a conversation about strengths, exploring in particular a strength the daughter had in common with her father. And it got the mother talking to her husband about each of their strengths and how they applied them in their marriage. She told us that it has helped her and her husband understand each other better by giving them a new language to discuss some of their similarities and differences. Another mother told us that the dinner conversation in her family that evening had also been about strengths. The conversation drew all three of her children into an animated conversation, in which each member of the family was deeply engaged. This mother, her husband, and their children all greatly enjoyed identifying and discussing their strengths and sharing their strengths stories with one another.

Both mothers reported that these strengths conversations had been one of the best conversations they had ever had together as a family, helping them connect in a new and powerful way. Where the talk at dinner habitually consists of light chatter or idle banter—or even heavy discussions about problems and the vices that lead to them—it can be a welcome change to have a deeply meaningful conversation about strengths. And involving our families in our strengths discussions can help us understand ourselves and our partners in new ways by learning from the insights of those around us.

USING YOUR STRENGTHS IN NEW WAYS

As we can see by reflecting on the role of our signature strengths in our lives, putting them into action can energize us and bring about a whole lot of positive results for ourselves and for those around us. Now let's turn from an examination of the role these strengths have played in our lives in the past to a consideration of the role they might play in the future. What can we do to use our strengths even more frequently and effectively?

One key thing to keep in mind as we consider how to hone the use of our signature strengths is the importance of using them in a wise and balanced way. As we have already seen, Aristotle made a similar point about virtue, understanding it as the mean between two vices. What he said about anger, we can say about character strengths: Using our signature strengths may be easy, but using them in the right degree, at the right time, for the right purpose, and in the right way is not. That takes a lifetime of practice.

When discussing how to optimize our use of character strengths, we often talk about overusing or underusing them. Think again about the strength of kindness. If someone isn't very sensitive at all to the needs of others and rarely or never helps them, we can say that person is underusing the strength of kindness. On the other hand, if someone is overly sensitive to the needs of others and is not taking proper care of herself because she is continually helping those around her, we can say that person is overusing the strength of kindness.[4] Using a strength so that it works both for you and for others is one indication you are using the strength in a balanced, healthy way. Finding this balance can be a challenge and often requires practice and asking for advice from others, including our partner, to make sure we're using our strength well.

Have your signature strengths ever gotten you into trouble? This is a question Peterson often used to ask. It points to the difficulty of using our strengths well. And thinking about times when our strengths have gotten us into trouble can bring some amusing stories to our minds. Sometimes, though, the stories aren't so amusing.

One of the graduates of our Master of Applied Positive Psychology (MAPP) program at the University of Pennsylvania, who is a teacher, told James the story of a meeting he had with a student athlete who was in trouble over a hazing incident. The student had done something he thought was funny to another player, but it had been mean and inappropriate, and the student was now being suspended from the team. Because the student had taken the VIA Survey, both he and his teacher knew that one of his signature strengths was humor and playfulness. So instead of simply giving him a scolding and then kicking him off the team, the teacher was able to talk with him about the very real strength he had. The problem, his teacher suggested, was that he had used the "dark side" of his strength, and the teacher challenged him to think about how he might use his strength to better ends. This was a much more helpful conversation for the student to have. He was able to see the situation without becoming defensive, and that led to a much quicker path back to good behavior and rejoining the team. This story can help us see the important difference between strong character and good character. Using our signature strengths in our lives can easily lead to *strong* character, but we must also use those strengths to healthy ends to ensure we develop *good* character.

Before we turn to an exercise to help us use our strengths more in our lives, we'd like to address one more very important question:

Is it more effective for us to focus on developing our signature strengths, or to work on our lesser strengths?

Psychologist Jonathan Haidt tested this question in a series of studies comparing results from two groups of students. He asked one group to engage in an activity every day that used one of their top five strengths, and he asked the other group to engage in an activity every day that used one of their bottom five strengths. After two weeks, both groups increased their well-being, with no differences in well-being between the two groups. It was only in the long run that the differences began to appear. From this time perspective, the students who focused on their top strengths had an advantage. Their boosts in well-being persisted, while those of the group that focused on their bottom strengths did not. It seems that those who were working on their lesser strengths were relieved to be able to stop at the end of the two weeks and so didn't maintain positive effects from their efforts. By contrast, those who worked on their signature strengths enjoyed the activities more and were more likely to continue them on their own. They were thus better able to maintain the well-being benefits over the long run.[5]

Haidt's studies suggest that the better approach seems to be to focus on your signature strengths. This is because it is more likely that you will keep doing things you find enjoyable, and the more you keep doing them, the more likely you are to benefit from them. But where does that leave us with respect to our lesser strengths? What if kindness is in your bottom five? Can you just say it's not something you're good at and leave it to others, while you focus on strengths you excel in, such as curiosity, let's say, and zest? Well . . . no. Kindness is not something we can just outsource to others. It's important for all of us to have at least a basic level of kindness. Peterson's recommendation in this case would be to use your signature strengths to shore up your weaknesses. If curiosity and zest are signature strengths for you, you will likely really enjoy using them. So you might ask yourself how you could use those strengths to be kinder. Perhaps you could be curious about the effects of your kind acts on others, or maybe you could note how practicing kindness can help increase the level of energy and vitality in both you and others.

There is another group of strengths we should also mention. There are five strengths that have been found to be most closely connected to flourishing. Can you guess which ones they are? If these strengths aren't already among your top five, we recommend spending some effort cultivating them, since they seem to be especially important for well-being. The five strengths are love, gratitude, zest, hope, and curiosity.[6] Captain Obvious would no doubt point out that love is of particular importance in romantic relationships. Indeed, this entire book is about love. In the next chapter, we will focus specifically on another one of these strengths—gratitude—and examine its huge importance for romantic relationships.

So what happens when we intentionally try to use our signature strengths more? Seligman and his colleagues asked research participants to use their signature strengths in new ways each day for a week. They then compared them to a group who were asked to write down childhood memories every day for a week to see if there were any differences in well-being. Using their strengths in new ways increased participants' happiness levels for up to six months![7] This is an astonishing result for a one-week exercise. Given how powerful this activity can be, let's stop right now and try it out for ourselves.

USING YOUR STRENGTHS IN NEW WAYS EXERCISE

Choose one of your signature strengths. It can be the same one you chose for your strengths story or a different one. Brainstorm a list of ways you could use this strength more in your life, and write down a list of specific actions you could take for applying it in healthy and balanced ways. Use this strength in a new way every day for the next week. Each day, you can choose a different activity from your list, or you can come up with something else. But the point is to experiment with seven new ways you can use this strength over the course of the coming week.

USING YOUR STRENGTHS IN ROMANTIC RELATIONSHIPS

Earlier in this chapter, we discussed ways in which we can understand our own strengths more deeply and use them more frequently and effectively in our lives. In the context of a romantic relationship and especially one in which the partners aspire to be Aristotelian lovers, it is important not only to know and use your own strengths but also to know and enable your partner's strengths. Your combined group of strengths is an asset of your relationship and is a key part of what will keep both of you growing—and growing *together*. Let's now explore three green-cape activities to help you work on your combined group of strengths. The first activity is a variation of the Strengths Stories exercise.

STRENGTHS STORIES ABOUT YOUR PARTNER EXERCISE

Earlier in this chapter, we asked you and your partner to tell each other a story about when you used one of your signature strengths successfully. For this exercise, you will reverse the process and tell each other a story about when you observed the *other* using one of his or her signature strengths successfully. Take turns sharing your stories, savoring them together, and discussing the various strengths your partner demonstrated in the story you told. For some of you, this may be even more effective than the first exercise, as it can be incredibly powerful to hear your partner tell you a story of you at your best. It can help you feel clearly seen, deeply understood, and profoundly loved.

It can be fun to have help in telling strengths stories about your partner. Friends or family members can be good sources of information. Birthday celebrations, get-togethers with friends, or holidays with family can be good times to ask others to chime in with stories about your partner.

This is something we decided to include in our wedding celebration. When we got married we wanted to incorporate the science of positive psychology into our wedding. From the rehearsal dinner to the wedding ceremony to the reception, we wanted our special two days to best reflect who we are as unique individuals and as a couple. One thing we did was to create a "rehearsal dinner of strengths," in which we invited Suzie's family and friends to tell stories about her that illustrated the strengths she would bring to the marriage and James's family and friends to tell stories about him that illustrated the strengths he would bring to the marriage. It was a moving experience for all who were present to hear first-person accounts from many of the most important people in our lives about the range of strengths each of us would bring to our union.

Of the many stories and insights that were shared that evening, we'll mention one special observation made by Suzie's father. It resonated deeply with us then, and still does to this day. He remarked that Suzie has always been very quick, noting that she thinks fast, speaks fast, and even moves fast. Her father told the assembled guests that her energy has served her very well in life,

allowing her to accomplish many things personally and profession-
ally. Sometimes, though, she can tend to go too fast, and he often
tells her to slow down. He then turned his attention to James and
commented that, in contrast to Suzie, James tends to do things at a
slower, more deliberate pace. He noted that James could help her
slow down when she was going too fast, adding that sometimes
James's philosophical nature could lead him to move too slowly,
and on those occasions she could help him speed up.

When Suzie's father finished speaking, we knew what he had
said was exactly right. And indeed, it has proved prescient. One of
the main themes of our relationship since that day has been working to find the right balance between slowing down and speeding
up. There have been many occasions when James's calm approach
and broad perspective are exactly what is needed to help Suzie slow
down. By the same token, there have been many times when her
energetic approach and emphasis on taking action has been what
James has needed to help him move something forward. Sometimes it's not clear whether a faster approach or a slower one is
likely to be more effective, and our tendency is to go with what each
of us is more comfortable with. That's part of the creative tension at
the core of our marriage. It can sometimes feel exasperating. Yet
the resulting compromises often save each of us from ourselves.
And one thing is clear: Our complementary strengths and the continual need to look for the mean between the extremes in this area
helps us develop our potential as individuals and as Aristotelian
lovers.

Suzie's father's insight about how we can use our signature
strengths collaboratively illustrates how important it is for anyone
in a relationship not only to know his own strengths and those of
his partner but also to consider ways in which they can integrate
these into their partnership and use them in complementary ways.

This is key for making both individuals feel valued, and for ensuring that the relationship is functioning at its best. One way you can practice combining your strengths in your relationship is by planning and going on a "strengths date."

This activity, developed by Seligman, provides a way for you and your partner to use your signature strengths in new ways—and to do so in tandem. The key is to design a single event in which each of you can use one of your signature strengths. For example, if you have the strength of humor and your partner has the strength of kindness, do something together that helps people while making them laugh. Or if you have the strength of creativity and your partner has the strength of zest, you might pick something a little crazy you've always wanted to do and really go full out with it!

Here's an example of a strengths date the two of us went on. One of James's top strengths is love of learning, and most nights, he'd be happy staying home reading a philosophy book and gaining new insights into life and the world. Although Suzie enjoys evenings at home learning as well, she also immensely enjoys going out to dinner to sample international cuisines. So she decided to combine her strength of creativity with James's love of learning for a night out they could both enjoy. She made reservations at Chifa, a local restaurant inspired by the unique hybrid of Peruvian and Cantonese cuisine. Before dinner, she researched the menu's Latino and Asian culinary influences, printed out the information, and brought it to dinner to discuss with James. By the end of dinner, Suzie's and James's palates were sated, as was James's intense hunger for knowledge. The evening was mutually satisfying, and their bond was strengthened.

Now it's your turn!

STRENGTHS DATES EXERCISE

Select one of your signature strengths and one of your partner's signature strengths and plan a single activity that will let each of you put that strength into practice. After the activity, discuss how it went. In what ways did it work well for each of you? What can you learn from this occasion to help you plan your next strengths date?

To aid us in the understanding and application of our strengths, it can be very helpful to have conversations with others to explore more deeply what the strengths mean and how they can be used. This is especially true in romantic relationships. Becoming a bit nerdy about strengths can be quite valuable. Including your strengths in the vocabulary of your relationship and discussing them frequently can help you keep a balanced focus on the good things in your life together.

Oftentimes couples have conversations about fixing things in the relationship or in the other person. And it can be important to address those things. But it can be just as important to put aside the red side of the cape in favor of the green side and spend time discussing what's going well. Strengths conversations can be occasions in which partners can discuss who they really are at their core. They can help each partner better understand the other and feel more deeply understood. In the excitement of early romance most couples spend a lot of time asking questions, being detectives of sorts, and trying to understand what makes their partner tick. As relationships develop and turn into marriages, we tend to engage in these activities less frequently and begin to assume we know all we need to know about our partner. To counteract this unfortunate tendency, it's critical for couples to exercise their strength of curiosity to keep their relationship moving forward and to help their partner feel truly listened to, cared for, and understood.

Instead of merely talking about strengths conversations in relationships, we thought it would be more fun to give you an example of the way strengths conversations sometimes go in our own relationship. So here goes!

> JAMES: How interesting that we each have creativity as a signature strength, and yet neither one of us would have guessed that in high school.
>
> SUZIE: That's true! One of the things I really like about our relationship is that we are both energized by ideas and how much fun it is to brainstorm together to come up with cool ways to advance our various interests and projects, as well as the opportunities that come our way.
>
> JAMES: Definitely! Yet it's also interesting how different our creativity looks in practice. Do you remember the Crossword Puzzle Fiasco?
>
> SUZIE: [*laughing*] How could I possibly forget that?!
>
> JAMES: [*laughing*] After much cajoling, you finally convinced me to join you in one of your favorite hobbies: doing the *New York Times* crossword puzzle. If I had only known what awaited me! As soon as we began, you started talking, and you never stopped! You jumped all over the place, from clue to clue. How was I supposed to keep up, let alone make any contribution toward solving the puzzle? Makes me dizzy just thinking about it!
>
> SUZIE: [*teasing*] Couldn't handle the Big Apple pace, could you? Lighten up! The NYT crossword is not the GRE. You don't have to be silent, somber, and systematic when you solve it.

How can you possibly be creative sitting still with your mouth shut? Half the fun of solving the puzzle is calling out potential answers aloud and letting your intuition—or even a whim—guide you to the clue you want to take up next.

JAMES: Are you kidding me?! How can you possibly think with someone talking in your ear?

SUZIE: My dad sure hit the nail on the head with what he said at our wedding rehearsal dinner, didn't he?

JAMES: You mean his insight about me slowing you down and you speeding me up? How could he have known how impossible it would be for us to try to solve a crossword together?

SUZIE: [*laughing*] My dad's a wise man! But seriously, it's interesting how my zestful creativity is similar but also quite different from your open-minded creativity.

JAMES: It sure is! And we've been really good together when we've been able to follow your dad's advice. Do you remember that time when we were on our honeymoon at Sandals when they had the contest for the best engagement story?

SUZIE: Yes! When they asked for volunteers, I knew you would tell the best story, but you were just sitting there.

JAMES: Well, I was considering things from all angles.

SUZIE: That wasn't the time to consider things! That was the time to get up there and win us a free dinner on the beach.

JAMES: True. And thanks to you that's exactly what I did.

SUZIE: Yup! You were the last guy to go up front, but you did a great job telling our engagement story, and you won us the dinner. You know, when you're on stage, your creativity seems to be a lot more like mine. A lot more zestful!

JAMES: That's an interesting insight. I hadn't thought of it that way before, but you're right.

SUZIE: But I really needed your open-minded creativity that time I shattered the screen on my smartphone.

JAMES: That was freaky! You had your phone in your back pocket and hit it just wrong on a doorknob when you were heading out to the gym.

SUZIE: I was in such shock—I didn't know what to do. But you were very calm, and step-by-step you walked me through what I had to do. You saw that the phone was still functioning a bit, and you knew the first thing I had to do was back it up to save all the pictures I had just taken of Liam's first day of kindergarten. Then you told me to put everything else on hold and go to the phone store right away to get it replaced. That is exactly what I did, and everything turned out just fine. Being slow and deliberate in that case was definitely better than trying to be quick.

JAMES: Thanks, Suzie. It's great that we can rely on you when quick action and connections are needed.

SUZIE: And it's great that we can rely on you when we need to be strategic and focused.

NOW IT'S TIME for *you* to practice having a strengths conversation with *your* partner.

STRENGTHS CONVERSATION EXERCISE

Have a strengths conversation with your partner (or with a friend or family member). Here are some questions you might discuss:

What do you notice about your lists of signature strengths? How are they similar? How are they different? How do your strengths interact with one another in your relationship?

Does a focus on strengths help you understand more deeply your attraction for each other? What makes the two of you such a great team? How could you integrate your strengths even more so you can be an even better team in the future?

Does a focus on strengths help you gain new insights on some of the frictions in your relationship? Can you think of new, strengths-based ways of addressing them?

Make a point to continue to discuss these matters in the days ahead. What works best for you and your partner in terms of timing and setting for strengths conversations? How will you put to use in your relationship the insights that emerge from your discussions?

In the next two chapters, we will build on these ideas and practices and explore other exciting and fun ways you and your partner can use your strengths effectively to enrich your relationship further as you aspire to become Aristotelian lovers.

RECAPPING STRENGTHS EXERCISES

For this chapter, we gave you exercises to do along the way. If you've been doing them as you read the chapter, you are now ready to go on to chapter 8. But if there are any exercises you haven't already completed from this chapter, take time to do them now.

- Strengths Stories (see p. 151)
- Using Your Strengths in New Ways (see p. 158)
- Strengths Stories About Your Partner (see p. 159)
- Strengths Dates (see p. 163)
- Strengths Conversation (see p. 166)

CHAPTER 8

The Gratitude Dance

*B*Y THE TIME *he noticed what was happening, he was in trouble. He was having difficulty moving his legs and would soon lose his balance and topple over. Which would be utterly mortifying, given the momentousness of the occasion. He had to do something right away to avert disaster, and with all the people watching, he had to do it while keeping a smile on his face. As Etta James crooned, "At last, my love has come along," he slowly realized what the problem was: His feet were entangled in cloth . . . a long, white lace cloth.*

It was our first dance at our wedding reception, and James, having circled in the same direction too long, was getting wound up like a top in Suzie's veil! What to do? Fortunately, he figured out that if he just moved in the opposite direction for a while, he would get unwound, and we would avoid the ignominious fate of starting our married life sprawled on the floor in front of the people who mattered most to us.

If that experience wasn't enough to convince James he really needed help with his dancing skills, what happened next certainly was. His new father-in-law masterfully took James's place, and easily avoiding all danger of getting entangled in Suzie's veil, he gracefully floated her around the dance floor.

After this experience, James shouldn't have been too surprised when, for his birthday the next year, Suzie gave him a gift card for dance lessons at the Society Hill Dance Academy, in Philadelphia. Shana, the owner of the dance studio, was a patient and supportive teacher. In just a few lessons, James was making good progress on posture, timing, and steps. It was much easier, he found, without the veil!

Suzie thought she would make rapid progress, too. Although James had not grown up dancing, she had. Her parents are excellent dancers, and she'd enjoyed taking lessons in tap, ballet, toe, and modern dance during her childhood. She quickly realized, however, that ballroom dancing is very different from the kind of dance she'd studied as a child. Not only did she need to learn the dance steps, but she needed to interact well with James, to learn to slow down and follow his lead. Initially, she got a bit frustrated when Shana would point out that she was keeping her shoulder too rigid or that she was trying to lead the dance. But then she began to get the hang of it, learning not to rush the dance but rather to respond sensitively to James's improvisational moves. Learning to dance together was fun but also challenging for both of us. We had to work in tandem. If James forced a move, we would either trip over each other's toes or Suzie would be flung across the room. And if Suzie resisted his gentle guidance, we'd be stuck in place. Thanks to Shana's patience and our persistence, we learned a few things about dance through those lessons—and a lot about ourselves!

Dance, we realized, is a great way to learn about relationships. In this chapter we will focus specifically on the dance of gratitude and its importance for romantic relationships. Not sure what dance has to do with gratitude? Read on! The connection will be abundantly clear by the time you finish reading this chapter.

THE POWER OF GRATITUDE IN ROMANTIC RELATIONSHIPS

Let's begin by deepening our understanding of gratitude and its role in our lives and relationships. Gratitude is an important and complex part of human experience. As we saw in chapter 4, Fredrickson identifies it as one of the key positive emotions. She describes it as a feeling of authentic appreciation for something that has been bestowed upon you. And as we saw in chapter 6, it is one of the twenty-four character strengths in the VIA Classification. In that context, Peterson and Seligman define gratitude as "a sense of thankfulness and joy in response to receiving a gift, whether the gift be a tangible benefit from a specific other or a moment of peaceful bliss evoked by natural beauty."[1] Robert Emmons, a gratitude researcher at the University of California, Davis, has pointed out that gratitude has also been defined as "a mood, a moral virtue, a habit, a motive, a personality trait, a coping response, and even a way of life."[2] Cicero, the great Roman orator, argued that "gratitude is not only the greatest of virtues, but the parent of all the others."[3]

As we have already indicated, research suggests gratitude is one of the most important of the character strengths for overall well-being. If it's not already one of your top five strengths, we recommend you put special effort into developing it. It's so powerful in part because it focuses our attention on what we already have, rather than on what we lack. As a result, Emmons finds, we tend to feel happier and "experience an upward spiral of positive outcomes."[4] We can cultivate gratitude with the green side of our reversible cape by focusing on our gifts and celebrating the good in life. We can also cultivate it with the red side by comparing our present circumstances to times in our lives when things weren't going so well—or to what our lives could be like if we weren't so fortunate.

In a recent review of gratitude research, Emmons and his

colleagues concluded, "Gratitude is foundational to well-being and mental health throughout the life span."[5] For one thing, grateful people tend to have more positive interactions with those around them. Not surprisingly, this helps them get along better with others and boosts their own well-being. Grateful people also tend to be better at empathy and forgiveness, and more willing to help others. Among the physical benefits of gratitude are more and better sleep and more exercise. Additionally, gratitude tends to breed gratitude, so feeling grateful in the present is likely to make us feel grateful in the future—and to experience more of its benefits moving forward.

Although gratitude is something we all feel from time to time, most of us could no doubt benefit from experiencing much more of it. And the good news is that it is possible to cultivate gratitude intentionally. Gratitude interventions have been shown to lead to greater life satisfaction, optimism, and prosocial behavior. They have also led to increased positive emotions and decreased negative emotions. And these effects have been documented to last for up to six months.[6]

Some of the most common and powerful exercises in positive psychology focus on the cultivation of gratitude. The effects of the age-old advice to "count your blessings" has been tested in experimental studies in which Emmons and his colleagues compared people who were asked to write about what was going well in their lives to individuals who were instructed to write about their daily annoyances. Those who counted their blessings experienced emotional, physical, and interpersonal benefits. They exercised more regularly, enjoyed more robust health, were more satisfied with their overall life, and displayed more optimism about the future. And these effects were both immediate and long-term.[7]

Perhaps the most well-known exercise in all of positive psychology is one connected with gratitude. Created by Seligman, it is known as the Three Good Things Exercise. In this exercise, participants are asked at the end of each day to write down three good things that happened to them that day and why they happened. In a study to measure the effectiveness of this intervention, participants were asked to engage in this exercise for a week. Compared to other participants in a control group, who were asked to write down childhood memories every night for a week, those who completed the Three Good Things Exercise were happier and less depressed up to six months later. Astonished by this long-term effect of such a short exercise, the researchers followed up with the participants to see what had happened. It turned out that those who had experienced these long-term effects had not stopped the exercise after one week. They had found it so helpful that they kept it up and benefited from its effects long term.[8]

Another common gratitude exercise in positive psychology, also developed by Seligman, is the Gratitude Visit. In this exercise, you think of someone who has helped you out in your life, but whom you have never properly thanked. You write a letter detailing the thoughtful things this person has done, taking time to write and polish the letter carefully. Then you go see the person, without telling him about the letter. At some point during your visit, you read the letter to him. In terms of the degree of change in the participants, this is one of the most powerful gratitude exercises to be tested so far. In the individuals participating in the study, there was a significant increase in happiness and decrease in depression, and these benefits showed up immediately and lasted for up to a month.[9]

If you have not done the Three Good Things Exercise or the Gratitude Visit, you'll want to try them out. Gratitude exercises help us reconnect with the good things that have happened in our lives and the good people who have been responsible for so many of them. Unfortunately, our awareness and appreciation of these good things often get buried under memories of difficult things we have endured in the past, mounds of unfinished tasks we face in the present, and fears of problems to come in the future. Gratitude can help balance all of this out, enabling us to see life itself as a gift.

It's not surprising, then, that gratitude is such an important part of healthy relationships. It helps us move beyond ourselves to reconnect with those around us. It helps us focus less on *me* and more on *we*. And it allows us to take a break from focusing on what we can get so that we can appreciate what we have been given. Gratitude is associated with higher levels of joy, love, and optimism, and it can help protect us from envy, greed, and resentment. It also tends to come with increased feelings of connectedness and higher levels of altruism. All of this can enable us to be more resilient and forge closer bonds with our loved ones.[10]

Emmons (2007) points out that people "high on dispositional gratitude . . . have better relationships . . . are more securely attached, and are less lonely."[11] And when it comes to thriving relationships, Fredrickson argues that gratitude may be one of the most important positive emotions. As we discussed in chapter 4, positive emotions such as gratitude, while fleeting, can broaden our attention and allow us to build enduring physical, psychological, and relational resources. Gratitude can help us appreciate our partner, rather than taking him or her for granted. As Fredrickson told us, by helping us attune to the things our loved ones do, gratitude can help us avoid adapting to our partner's kindness and in this way keep him or her from fading into the background like wallpaper.[12]

Sadly, many marriages and relationships often flounder and ultimately fail because, over time, people forget the reasons they were attracted to their partners in the first place and start to take them for granted. This, of course, leads couples to feel underappreciated by their partners and disconnected from each other. In contrast, research suggests that continually showing appreciation builds intimacy and strengthens bonds over time. One study, led by social psychologist Sara Algoe at the University of North Carolina at

Chapel Hill, showed that on days people felt more grateful toward their spouse or significant other they also felt more connected to him or her and better about their relationship in general. They also experienced enhanced relationship satisfaction on the *following* day. Further, the benefits of the gratitude flowed in the other direction, as well: Their partners felt more connected to them and better about the relationship. Based on these findings, the researchers concluded that moments of gratitude may act like booster shots for relationships, benefiting both the giver and the receiver.[13]

THE IMPORTANCE OF EXPRESSING GRATITUDE WELL

As crucial as it is to *feel* grateful toward your loved one, though, this alone is not enough to create a mutually satisfying relationship. You need to *express* your gratitude, as well. As we have already discussed, it's *doing* that cultivates healthy habits and flourishing relationships. So while it's important to feel grateful toward your partner, it's also essential to communicate that gratitude to him or her effectively. Research shows that *expressing* appreciation to your partner on a regular basis can increase relationship satisfaction for *both* of you—in the moment and in the long run.[14]

In order to enjoy the full benefits of gratitude in a relationship, however, you need to know how to express your thankfulness to your partner in a way that works well for him or her. One important study, led by Algoe, found that people who expressed gratitude to their partners were much more likely still to be together six months later. The key, though, was that the gratitude had to be communicated in such a way that their partners felt "cared for, understood, and validated."[15]

So how can we go about communicating our gratitude effectively in a relationship? To answer this question, we will model two different interactions between us. See what you observe about them. Here is the first example:

> JAMES: Suzie, I want to thank you for the exercise, diet, and nutrition advice you have given me since we've been married. As you know, I try to eat healthy, but in the last few years, I had put on a few unnecessary pounds. You never nagged me about it, but you thoughtfully bought me a bicycle for my birthday so I could get good exercise riding it to work. And when I came to you asking for nutritional advice, you gave me very good tips based on what you had learned at the Institute for Integrative Nutrition, about how to moderate my carbohydrate intake and increase my consumption of vegetables. I followed your advice, and over the course of a few months lost the extra weight. As a result, I have gotten healthier, I feel younger, and I fit into my clothes better. Overall, I am more pleased about the care I am taking of my body. And I have also gotten numerous compliments about my trimmer look—which make me feel great, too!
>
> SUZIE: No need to thank me, James. It was no big deal.

What did you notice in James's expression of gratitude? He thanked Suzie, of course. But look again at what he said. What did he focus on? Whom did he focus on? Overall, how would you rate his expression of gratitude? If someone expressed appreciation to you in this way, how "cared for, understood, and validated" would you feel?

Now consider a second example:

> SUZIE: James, I really want to thank you for helping me recently when I was stuck on an article I was writing. I had so many ideas and didn't know how to proceed. You used your strength of analytical thinking to help me develop an outline to

organize my thoughts. Your logical mind and your ability to lay out an argument are incredible. And you seem to do it with such ease. You've used your logic and calm composure effectively time and time again in our relationship. And you bring these same abilities to the classroom, which is part of what makes you an award-winning teacher. Not to mention how effective you are when you use it in our family, especially with Liam. Thank you, James.

JAMES: You're welcome, Suzie—and you know something you're good at? You're such a great connector in so many ways. You collect friends like I collect books! Until we got married and you moved in, I didn't know anyone in my hallway. And now you have us friends not just with our floor mates, but with the entire building. You help bring people together by connecting them with others, which is really an extraordinary ability.

What did you notice about Suzie's expression of gratitude toward James? What did she focus on? Whom did she focus on? How was it different from the first example? Overall, how would you rate her expression of gratitude? If someone expressed appreciation to you in this way, how "cared for, understood, and validated" would you feel?

To help us answer these questions, let's turn to three characteristics Algoe identifies for the effective expression of gratitude. First, the best kind of expressed appreciation is other-focused rather than self-focused. Self-focused appreciation emphasizes the benefits you enjoyed because of something your partner did. Other-focused appreciation concentrates on praising aspects of your partner's actions or personality, on praising her inherent strengths and how she is using them. In other words, gratitude done well emphasizes the giver, not the gift; the benefactor, not the beneficiary. For example,

"*You're* so wonderful," and "*You* always know what I need," rather than "It's the best *present* ever," or "*I* just love it!"

So how did James do in the first example? Was his expression of appreciation focused on himself, or on Suzie? Although he was thanking her, his expression was really all about him. He used *I*, *me*, and *my* a lot more than *you* and *your*. We're not suggesting it's never appropriate to thank your spouse for the benefits you have received from his or her actions. But doing this in an unbalanced way is a sign of a relationship of utility—in which you value the relationship for what you can get out of it—rather than a deeper relationship of Aristotelian love, in which you see the good in each other and are each dedicated to becoming better people.

Now let's consider the second example. As you can see, Suzie's expression is very much focused on James. She acknowledges the positive benefits of his logical mind, but the emphasis here is on the appreciation of one of James's qualities and an observation of his implementation of it in different areas, including with Suzie, his students, and his son, Liam. Again, it's not wrong to thank your partner for the benefits you enjoy as a result of his actions, but we suspect you will agree that focusing your appreciation on his qualities and strengths is more likely to make him feel "cared for, understood, and validated." And it will also likely inspire your partner to practice those qualities and strengths even more.

Algoe identifies a second characteristic of effective expression of appreciation: authenticity. If it feels like your partner is expressing appreciation in a flip way, or out of a sense of obligation, it's likely to fall flat. If, on the other hand, it is clear that your partner feels deeply the appreciation he or she is expressing, and that it's coming from the heart, you are much more likely to be moved by it, and the chances are much greater that it will have a healthy effect on your relationship.

Third, effective expression of appreciation, according to Algoe, is sensitive to context. In this area, it is definitely not the case that one size fits all. Well aware of this, greeting card companies offer a broad range of messages on cards intended to help us express appreciation to others. Really knowing your partner and thinking carefully about her unique likes and needs is crucial for determining the type of expression most likely to be effective. Expressing thanks publicly is probably a good way to go—unless your partner doesn't enjoy the limelight. So before throwing that surprise party to thank your loved one, think carefully whether that's what he or she would want. It often turns out that your first thought on how to express gratitude may be just the thing that would work well—for you. But maybe not so well for the person you want to thank. For some people, parties are great; others would put celebrating with throngs of people in the same category as getting their teeth drilled. Expressing your thanks verbally works especially well for some people. But if your partner would prefer written thanks, then a letter of gratitude might be particularly effective.

When considering the expression of appreciation, Algoe reminds us that it's *whether* you do it and *how* you do it that seems to matter for relationship satisfaction.[16] And Fredrickson adds that we don't need to wait for momentous occasions to do so. She suggests making a habit of noticing our partner's everyday thoughtfulness and expressing our appreciation for it.[17] Although these daily moments of kindness may seem small, they add up over time and can produce upward spirals in our relationship.[18]

EXPRESSING GRATITUDE EXERCISE

Algoe has found that expressions of appreciation that are other-focused, authentic, and context sensitive are especially effective in helping partners feel cared for, understood, and validated. This, in turn, helps optimize the effects of gratitude in the relationship. This exercise is intended to help you become more aware of the way you express appreciation and consider ways you might do it more effectively. Think about a recent time when you expressed gratitude to your partner and answer the following questions:

- How *other-focused* was your expression? Did you focus mostly on your partner or on yourself? If you focused on yourself, how could you reframe what you said to be more focused on your partner?
- How *authentic* was your expression? Did you take the time to feel the appreciation deeply before sharing it with your partner? If you expressed it verbally, how could you use things such as eye contact, tone of voice, body language, and choice of words to express your gratitude even more sincerely?
- How *context sensitive* was your expression? Did you thank your partner in a way that is more effective for you than for him? Considering your partner's personality and preferred communication style, how might you share your gratitude in a way that would be even more fitting in the context of your particular relationship?

THE IMPORTANCE OF RECEIVING GRATITUDE WELL

Have you ever been on the highway and seen another driver do something unbelievably stupid, reckless, or dangerous? If you're like the participants in our Romance and Research™ workshops, you will answer this question with a resounding "Yes!" Have you ever been on the highway and done something unbelievably stupid, reckless, or dangerous *yourself*? Again, if you are like the participants in our workshops, you will answer affirmatively, only now rather sheepishly. Interestingly, although we have all observed—and committed—reckless mistakes while driving, we rarely think of these as we merge onto the highway. This is because those mistakes belong to other days and were made when we were in the company of a different set of cars. Merging onto the highway is a new experience each time, and we are surrounded by a set of cars we have never seen before. But imagine how we would feel if every time we got on the highway, we drove with the same group of cars. We would remember with anger that red car that cut us off yesterday and with shame the yellow car we nearly ran off the road the day before. Knowing that our driving would be observed and remembered by the same drivers day after day, we would no doubt behave quite differently behind the wheel.

Relationships are like driving on the highway with the same set of cars every day. The way we interact with those around us is important both in the moment and down the road (pun intended). Our choices in relationships matter in the present, but we also need to consider the effects they will have on our future interactions with these same people.

To this point, interventions in the field of positive psychology have tended to focus on actions individuals can initiate to change their own lives and the lives of those around them. Think, for example, of the interventions we described earlier in this chapter: counting your blessings, the Three Good Things Exercise, and the Gratitude Visit. In relationships, though, it's important to consider not only how we can initiate change but also how to respond to the changes initiated by others. It's not just our actions that are important, but our reactions and our interactions.

In some versions of the VIA Classification, the strength of love is listed as "the capacity to love and be loved." This is an acknowledgment of the difference between initiating and responding, between giving and receiving. This is a very important distinction, resulting from Harvard psychiatrist George Vaillant's insistence on including "the capacity to be loved" in the classification.[19] Indeed, the ability to love others is very different from the ability to accept love from them. We can easily imagine a person who is very loving but less able to receive love. Perhaps you know someone like that, or maybe you yourself struggle with accepting love from others. In contrast, we probably all know someone who enjoys receiving love but is hard-pressed to give it.

The receiving side, in general, often seems to be related to vulnerability. We need to be open to receive. Think again of Melvin in *As Good as It Gets*. Melvin valued Carol because she was a good person and made him want to be a better man. It was only when he was open, honest, and vulnerable to Carol that he was able to absorb her warm displays of affection. Like Melvin, we show our true selves to others by being vulnerable and allowing them to love us as we are, including our failings and foibles.

For some people, that is especially difficult. This is a theme Vaillant addresses in his book *Aging Well*, which reports on the men of the Grant Study of Adult Development, the longest-running study ever conducted on aging and well-being. Vaillant describes a retired doctor whose wife lovingly collected a box of nearly one hundred letters of gratitude from his patients for his commendable service over the years. She was excited to deliver the collective appreciation to her husband on his seventieth birthday. Sadly, though, he couldn't receive the gratitude; he never opened the box of letters.[20] As Vaillant observes, "It doesn't help to be loved, if you can't let yourself feel it."[21]

Love is not the only one of the strengths that has a giving and a receiving side. Consider the strength of forgiveness. It is one thing to forgive someone, and quite another to accept someone else's for-giveness. The same holds true for gratitude. Expressing thanks to others is very different from accepting the thanks expressed by oth-ers. And the strength of kindness is similar. Being kind to others is not at all the same as being open to receiving the kindness of oth-ers. In fact, we believe there is a giving and receiving side to each of the strengths. In relationships, both aspects are important because they are two sides of our interactions with others. And because this distinction is so important for relationships, we want to explore it in much more detail. In the next chapter, we will look at the two sides of kindness. But here we want to consider this duality in the context of gratitude.

Though there is a substantial body of research on giving grati-tude, there is virtually none on receiving it. This is remarkable, con-sidering that gratitude is such a critical building block for successful relationships. And yet this imbalance matches what we often find in our culture. Although it can be tough to express gratitude as frequently and as effectively as we should, many of us find it even harder to accept it well. Our culture encourages us to develop many bad habits that tend to shut down acts of gratitude and brush them off more than cultivate and acknowledge them.

Let's go back to the two examples of the gratitude interactions between Suzie and James we looked at earlier (pages 175–76) and now look at the way the gratitude was *received*. In the first example, when James thanks Suzie for helping him get healthier, she says, "No need to thank me, James. It was no big deal." What do you notice about this response? It's dismissive rather than supportive, isn't it? Suzie barely even acknowledges James's appreciation for her help. Her response actually shuts the conversation down, and it's hard to see where James could go from there besides moving on to another topic. If you were thanking your partner for something she did that really mattered to you and she replied in this way, how would you feel?

Now consider the second example. James responds to the appreciation Suzie expresses for his logical mind and clear thinking by saying, "You're welcome, Suzie." And then he launches right away into something he appreciates about her. What do you notice about this response? It seems that James acknowledges the appreciation more than he accepts it, doesn't it? And the appreciation he expresses for Suzie's ability to connect with people isn't wrong (it's even other-focused!), but the timing of his response doesn't really give him a chance to take in, let alone savor, the compliment Suzie just gave him.

These responses illustrate two different ways we can react to gratitude. We'd like to elaborate a bit on these, as well as on four others we think are fairly common, noting the likely effects of each response for promoting healthy relationships.

The first kind of response is what we call *deflection*. This is the response Suzie gave in the first example. Deflection happens when you brush off the gratitude, like you might a crumb from your shirt or even a pesky fly. Although it's not necessarily intended, the message you often give with deflection is one of indifference or even annoyance, perhaps communicating that there was no ground for the appreciation in the first place. Some participants in our workshops have communicated to us that they are often guilty of deflecting their spouse's thanks. This is especially likely to occur when they're not paying attention and not really engaged, but rather making a passive comment while their eyes are still glued to their smartphone or newspaper.

A second common reaction to gratitude in relationships is what we call *reciprocation*. This response is illustrated in the second gratitude example. James quickly acknowledges the gratitude Suzie expresses to him and then immediately launches into his own expression of gratitude for Suzie. The way he responds reminds us of the popular childhood game "hot potato," in which the goal of the game is to catch a ball and throw it to someone else as quickly as you can, as though you had just caught a hot potato with your bare hands.

This response to gratitude feels very transactional. If someone *pays* you a compliment, you now feel like you owe them something, and you want to *pay them back* just as soon as you can. We mentioned earlier how closely receiving is tied to vulnerability. There is a kind of vulnerability we often feel when we find ourselves in someone's debt. If we are not comfortable with the vulnerability, we may try to repay the debt as quickly as possible.

When our partner expresses sincere gratitude toward us, he or she means to acknowledge some good in us. This is an indication of the best kind of love we can aspire to: Aristotelian love. But if we treat the expression like a hot potato and toss it back as quickly as we can, we reduce the exchange to a relationship of utility. It is now in the domain of what's in it for each person, paying the compliment back as though it were part of a transaction.

So deep-seated in some of us is the aversion to receiving gratitude that we feel guilty if we don't immediately pass it back. We feel as though it is the last cookie on the plate, and if we take it, we're being selfish and keeping someone else from having it. Given the number of participants in our workshops who say they resonate with this feeling, it is clearly a very common obstacle to receiving gratitude well.

We want to be clear here that what we mean by "reciprocation" is the quick and often shallow passing back of appreciation. We are certainly not against a balanced expression of gratitude between partners, and in fact we believe it is very important for each Aristotelian lover in a relationship to express genuine appreciation for the other. But again, we would call that balance, not reciprocation.

A third common type of response is *discounting*. This can be seen in the following real-life example from our own relationship:

JAMES: Suzie, this is such a wonderful dinner you made tonight. It's really good! I can taste a variety of flavorful ingredients. I truly appreciate your taking the time to make this meal.

SUZIE: Thanks, but it should have been better. The potatoes were dried out because I had to stop to take a call and accidentally overcooked them. And the reason the sauce tastes strange is that I ran out of one of the spices and had to substitute with another. And the rice is so watery! I used a different brand than I normally do, but next time, I'll be sure to go back to the old one. . . .

JAMES: *(note to self) You've got to be kidding me! I was just trying to express my gratitude, and I was met with a tidal wave of negativity. Remember never to thank Suzie for dinner again!*

Suzie is certainly not the only person to respond like this when her partner expresses genuine praise or gratitude for something she did. And no doubt we've all been on the other side of a similar conversation. How does that make you feel? Pretty crummy, right? Not only is our expression not taken in, but it's systematically shredded by a litany of shortcomings, complaints, and negativity. All the good we pointed out is discounted and replaced by problems we didn't mention—and very likely didn't even notice. It's as though the other person is afraid we are going to mention all the bad things she is thinking about in the situation and feels the need to come clean and mention them first. And sometimes it's more than just a mention. In those cases, the discounting can get quite detailed. Whatever the motivation, if this response becomes habitual, the effect can be to shut down positive conversations and train us to stop complimenting our partners.

Deflecting, reciprocating, and discounting are ways of responding without receiving. We're not truly taking in what is being offered. Not surprisingly, this puts a damper on the gratitude interaction. The next three ways of responding we will consider are ways of receiving, of taking in the gratitude.

The fourth response is simply *acceptance*. This may seem straightforward, but it is actually quite difficult for many of us to do gracefully. We must remind ourselves to focus on an expression of gratitude, stopping to genuinely receive it rather than brushing it off, automatically reacting with praise of our own, or launching into excuses for why something isn't better. These kinds of responses may be routine habits we have picked up from our parents or other role models, or they may be a sign of insecurity, a feeling that we don't deserve to be acknowledged. Regardless of the motivation, if we can resist the temptation to respond in one of these ways and instead pause and truly take the gratitude in, that can make a huge difference to us and to those who are expressing the gratitude. Often, just a heartfelt "Thank you," said calmly while looking the other person in the eye, is all it takes. Again, people who express gratitude authentically to us are doing so because they want us to feel their appreciation. It is an offer to enter into a moment of genuine human interaction. By accepting this offer and receiving the gratitude, we affirm the human connection, allow ourselves to be vulnerable in a positive way, and carry the relationship forward.

An even more powerful way to carry the relationship forward is *amplification*, the fifth response to gratitude. This is where you don't just accept the gratitude, but you take it in deeply and savor it, absorbing all of its rich qualities and letting it permeate your being. It is at this point that you are fully receiving what your partner is offering you. Communicating that to your partner can be an important step in amplification. Expressing the effects of his gratitude in a self-focused way signals to your loved one that you have deeply absorbed what he has said, communicating to him the positive effect it has had on you. This, in turn, can help him feel good about having been able to give you a meaningful gift, which can result in a positive, upward spiral between you.

Consider the example of a back rub to illustrate how important amplification can be. Imagine you walk over to your partner and begin to massage her back. After a few seconds, she jumps up, thanks you, and says it's your turn. How would you feel? Probably not very good. This would be an example of reciprocation instead of reception. What you want your partner to do is to accept the back rub. More than that, you want her to relax and really take it in—to bask in it, and through it, to feel your love for her. And you want to know that what you are doing is having its intended effect. Your partner can communicate this to you in any number of ways: by arching her back appreciatively, visibly relaxing, letting out a deep sigh, or telling you how great it feels. We like it if our partner tells us we are really great at giving back rubs, of course, or that we have the gentlest hands. But we also very much want her communication to be self-focused. We want to know that what we are doing is having a deeply positive effect. And when we get this communication from our partner, it makes us, in turn, feel great—and want to continue the massage.

A sixth and final response is *advancement*. This occurs when we take the expression of gratitude or appreciation as an opportunity to connect more deeply about something that is important to both of us. To illustrate this kind of response, we'll share with you what happened when Suzie expressed appreciation to James on a particular occasion. He had just finished a talk describing his research on the well-being effects of the arts and humanities, exploring ways in which participation in music, art, literature, and film can increase our flourishing. Suzie congratulated him on the talk, and James began by receiving her compliment with a heartfelt "Thank you!" He then amplified the appreciation by taking it in and savoring it, letting Suzie know that her words were deeply appreciated and made him feel great about the talk. Then he moved into advancement, by asking her if she could tell him one thing that she thought was particularly effective. As they talked about what went well in the presentation, James asked how he might bring out those points even more effectively in the future. This naturally led into a very helpful conversation in which Suzie suggested ways he could capitalize on the strengths of his presentation and make it even better the next time. This turned into an exciting time of brainstorming together about the most effective ways of presenting this work. James took the advice, and his next presentation benefited tremendously from the conversation he'd had with Suzie. This, in turn, led to an upward spiral of gratitude, in which James was thankful for the initial expression of appreciation, and also for the subsequent insights. This whole situation resulted in growth, mutual appreciation, and deeper bonding for us as a couple.

As you consider how best to apply these insights about the reception of gratitude in your own relationship, you will, of course, want to be mindful of context. Just as there are busy days or hurried encounters in which all you have time for is a quick kiss in passing, there are times when a brief expression of gratitude or appreciation is completely appropriate. But just as every couple needs time to go beyond a hurried kiss in their physical affections, so you will want to make time to go deeper with your initiations and responses to gratitude. In these cases, practicing acceptance, amplification, and advancement will be crucial. Just how you do that will be influenced by the particular situation, your individual personalities, and the unique history of your relationship, as well as the norms of the culture in which you have grown up and the society in which you live.

With these contextual caveats in mind, responding to gratitude with acceptance, amplification, and advancement can provide powerful ways of strengthening your relationship, and we encourage you to take their cultivation seriously. Acceptance is opening a door to genuine connection with another person, amplification is taking in and appreciating the view it affords, and advancement is walking through the door and exploring new possibilities for deeper communication and greater insights. Each of these three kinds of responses to appreciation can be profound ways of growing a relationship.

At the beginning of this chapter, we promised to make clear the connection between dance and gratitude. We want to do that explicitly now. As the two of us learned in our classes, for a dance between two people to go well, both the initiation and the response are crucial. The dance will be just as surely disrupted by a poor response as by a poor initiation. And as challenging as initiation can be, we believe the response may actually be more difficult. Most of us have heard Bob Thaves's quote about the famous dance partners Ginger Rogers and Fred Astaire: She did everything he did—only backward and in high heels! Just like dancing, gratitude involves an initiation and a response. And for the dance of gratitude to go smoothly, both roles need to be played well.

In many types of partner dancing, it's up to one partner to do the initiating. For Aristotelian lovers, the situation is a bit more complicated, as it's crucial for each partner to be adept at both initiating and responding well. And this applies more broadly, of course, than just to the expression and reception of gratitude. We see marriage itself as a dance, with myriad opportunities for initiating and responding on both sides. To try to understand the complexity of this interaction and to emphasize its importance for the ideal of Aristotelian love, we have developed an Interaction Model of Relationships, which we will present in the next chapter. But before moving on, be sure to complete the following exercise on receiving gratitude well.

RECEIVING GRATITUDE EXERCISES

1. **Responding to Gratitiude**
   Spend a few minutes thinking about a recent time your partner expressed gratitude to you. How did you respond? What might you have done to accept the gratitude more genuinely, amplify it more strongly, and advance your connection with your partner more effectively?

2. **Examining Your Habits**
   Is there a typical way you receive gratitude? Do you tend to deflect, reciprocate, or discount? Or do you typically accept, amplify, or advance? Are there particular situations in which you tend toward one type of response and others in which you tend toward another? How might you modify your responses to be a better partner in the dance of gratitude?

CHAPTER 9

"It Takes Two to Make a Thing Go Right"

IN THE PREVIOUS chapter, we examined the role of gratitude in well-being. Gratitude can help us remember the good things in our lives—and the good things about the special people in our lives—and keep us from simply taking them for granted. We also noted that gratitude is like a dance, in which each partner has a key role to play. If a dance is to go well, both initiation and response must be carried out successfully. Expressing gratitude is certainly important, but unless it is received well, its full value will not be felt.

More broadly, we observed, it's not just gratitude that's like a dance. A romantic relationship itself resembles a dance, an ongoing interaction involving a complex network of initiations and responses. The work of marriage expert John Gottman supports this view. In his long-standing scientific research he has identified the importance of what he calls "bids" in a marital relationship.[1] He defines a bid as an attempt a spouse makes to establish a positive connection with his or her partner. When we make a bid, we are looking for things such as attention, acknowledgment, affirmation, and affection. And bids can take on a variety of forms. They can be verbal, as when we make a statement or a passing comment, or when we ask for help around the house or with putting the kids to bed. They can also be nonverbal, as with gestures, laughter, facial expressions (such as a smile or a come-hither look), or actions (such as an affectionate hug or playful wrestling). Women tend to make more bids than men, Gottman has found, but in flourishing relationships both partners are equally adept at making them. In one of his studies, Gottman monitored 130 newlyweds in their day-to-day life and found that the happiest couples made bids for each other's attention regularly throughout the day.[2]

Gottman's studies have demonstrated that it's not only the bids that are important but also the way partners respond to them. In the study of 130 newlyweds, the happiest couples not only made regular bids to each other throughout the day, but they also responded with interest to their partners when their own attention was sought. Gottman found, in fact, that the couples who were still together six years later responded positively to each other's bids on average a whopping 86 percent of the time, whereas those who divorced turned toward their partners on average only 33 percent of the time. This interplay of initiation and response is so important in marital relationships that observing these interactions in another one of his studies allowed Gottman to predict with a stunning 94 percent accuracy which couples would stay together and which would divorce.[3]

To help couples practice initiation and response effectively, we have developed an Interaction Model of Relationships. This Interaction Model aims to clarify the various steps involved in successful initiation and response. Think of it as our attempt to break down a complex dance into basic steps, much like our instructor Shana did for us in our dance classes. Since we are focusing on the VIA strengths here, we will present our model as it applies to character strengths.

THE INTERACTION MODEL APPLIED TO CHARACTER STRENGTHS

Not surprisingly, there are two parts to this model: *initiation* and *response*. From the outset, we want to emphasize that this is an attempt to break down complex interactions into basic steps. Real-life situations can get quite complicated, but keeping these basic steps in mind can help those situations go well. We also want to emphasize that the roles of initiator and responder shift between Aristotelian lovers. Sometimes one partner will initiate and the other will respond. At other times, the other partner will do the initiating, and then it's important for the first partner to respond well. Although in some relationships, one partner or the other may tend to do more of the initiation, particularly in certain domains, the healthiest relationships are ones in which there is a good balance of initiation between the two partners, and in which each partner is adept at both roles.

Each of the two roles of initiation and response has three steps. Beginning with the role of initiation, the first step is *cultivation*. This is where you identify a particular strength and practice it in your own life. For the sake of illustration, let's use the strength of gratitude. Perhaps this is one of your signature strengths, or maybe you have decided to focus on it because you know it's so important for well-being and relationships. Perhaps you choose to work on developing gratitude by spending time counting your blessings every day. Maybe you incorporate the Three Good Things Exercise into your life and every night before you go to bed you write down three positive things that happened to you that day and why they happened. And you might decide to have regular Gratitude Visits with the people you are closest to in your life. Actively cultivating a strength yourself helps you understand it more deeply and see its potential more clearly, which will allow you to use it more effectively in your relationship.

The second step in the initiation role is *contextualization*. In this step, you think specifically about your romantic relationship and consider how you can best use a strength to support your partner and grow the relationship. In the case of gratitude, you want to examine the role it is currently playing in your relationship. What are some ways you are already using gratitude well? How might you strengthen those good habits and even extend your actions in positive ways? What are some areas in which it might be helpful to inject more gratitude into your relationship? This is where you take into account the uniqueness of your relationship and spend time carefully thinking about what might work best for you and your partner. Maybe you realize you have not been consistent in expressing appreciation to your partner for his calm demeanor and careful attention to detail, or for his great energy and creative ideas, or for his recognition of what's most important in life. More concretely, you may realize you need to acknowledge him more for the work he does balancing the checkbook and keeping track of your finances. Or doing the grocery shopping every week.

The third and final step of initiation is *construction*. This is where you are ready to implement what you have identified in the second step, intentionally using the strength to build your relationship. In the case of gratitude, you express your appreciation to your partner for various aspects of the good you see in him, doing so in a way that is most appropriate in the context of your particular relationship.

Now let's shift our attention from initiation to response, the second role in the Interaction Model. Notice that the name of this role is "response," and not "reaction." Reacting is something we tend to do when we're on automatic pilot, and it implies much less conscious awareness and intentional control of our actions than responding. Like the role of initiation, response also has three steps for optimizing the way we interact with our partner. The first step is *awareness*. This is where you notice that the other person is using a particular strength. It may take you a while to realize, for example, that your partner is expressing more gratitude to you than she has in the past. But if you are intentionally looking for ways your partner is using her strengths, you are much more likely to pick up on this. Practicing awareness can be particularly difficult in the fast pace of our lives, when we're often distracted by a myriad of pressing things and not really paying attention to or actively looking for good things in our interactions with our partner. Taking the time to notice and be aware of the good in your partner, however, is crucial to being an Aristotelian lover.

The second step in responding is *assessment*. This is where you carefully consider the effect your partner's initiation of a specific strength is having on you and your relationship. You may note, for example, that as your partner expresses more appreciation for the good she sees in you, it raises your level of well-being and motivates you to cultivate your strengths more. You may observe that as your partner takes more specific note of the big and little things you do around the house and in the relationship, some of the household chores become less boring. Taking out the trash, for example, feels less like a waste of your precious time and more like your contribution to a healthy living environment for you and your loved ones to share.

The third step in responding is *action*. What can you do to carry forward what your partner has initiated in a way that honors the spirit of the initiation? This might mean responding in a more sensitive way to your partner's initiation. In the case of gratitude, it might mean thinking carefully about the six different ways of responding that we discussed in the previous chapter. Maybe you spend less time deflecting, reciprocating, and discounting your partner's appreciation and instead focus on accepting, amplifying, and advancing it. Instead of deflecting her thanks when you take out the trash, you savor it as you fill the bags and wrestle with trash cans. Perhaps you tell your partner directly how much you appreciate her acknowledgment. Maybe you also begin initiating your own expressions of gratitude to balance what your partner is doing. This does not mean reciprocation, of course, coming up with something you can use right away to "pay back" your partner for what she has expressed to you. That would not carry forward the spirit of the initiation. Instead, it means watching for other occasions, such as when she cleans the bathroom, for you to express appreciation for her efforts. Additionally, you might choose to honor the spirit of your partner's initiation by cultivating a strength of your own to use more effectively in the relationship. Maybe you have the strength of humor, but you've gotten so busy lately that you really haven't been using it much. Maybe your partner's initiation of gratitude can inspire you to think of ways you can be more playful to help her remember the light side of things and get her laughing again.

THE INTERACTION MODEL OF CHARACTER STRENGTHS

1. Initiation
   - CULTIVATION: Identify and practice a strength.
   - CONTEXTUALIZATION: Consider how that strength can best be put to use in your relationship.
   - CONSTRUCTION: Use the strength to build your relationship.
2. Response
   - AWARENESS: Notice your partner's use of a strength.
   - ASSESSMENT: Consider the effectiveness of your partner's initiation on you and your relationship.

◆ ACTION: Behave in such a way that it continues the
spirit of the initiation.

THE CASE FOR KINDNESS

Now that we have described the basic steps of the Interaction
Model, it's time to kick things up a notch and make them a little
more complex and challenging. (Don't blame us for this; we're just
channeling our inner Shana!) Let's see how the Interaction Model
might work with another strength that's crucial for healthy relationships: kindness.

Kindness is critical for cultivating compassionate relationships.
Imagine a relationship with someone who isn't kind—probably not
a relationship you'd want to be involved in. Kindness is a sort of
emotional tie that binds us together. When we talk to people who've
spent years together in marriages or other committed relationships
and ask them what they like about their partners, one of the things
they identify most frequently is how kind their partners are.

As we mentioned in chapter 6, kindness is one of the twenty-
four VIA strengths. In their book on the VIA Classification,
Peterson and Seligman observe that kindness involves an "orienta-
tion of the self toward the other."[4] They go on to argue that kindness
is not just something we practice to fulfill a duty or show our prin-
cipled respect for others. Nor is it something we engage in for the
purpose of eliciting kindness in return, burnishing our reputation,
or guaranteeing some other benefit for ourselves. Although these
may be by-products of our kind actions, kindness itself is motivated
by an emotional connection, a sense of common humanity we feel
with others, making us see that they are worthy of attention and
care for their own sakes. True kindness, in other words, is not what
drives relationships of mere utility, but it is at the core of relationships of goodness.

Gottman reports that happy couples in his studies overwhelmingly prioritize kindness and build it into their relationships. They make five times as many positive as negative comments to each other. And they make an effort to be kind in their daily interactions. This is true even when they are arguing. In disputes, they lead with kindness and gentleness, truly seeking to understand their partners. Couples in troubled marriages, by contrast, often belittle and degrade their partners, behaviors that can lead to the development of contempt for each other and even to the dissolution of their relationship.[5]

It's important to keep in mind here that kindness doesn't have to be momentous to be effective. While grand overtures of kindness, such as surprising your spouse with expensive jewelry or exotic vacations, can be nice on occasion, kindness counts in the mundane moments of life together, as well. It is here that our unions are built and sustained on a daily basis. Initiating this type of kindness in a relationship is important, in part, because it can evoke similar behavior from one's partner. And this can lead to upward spirals of positivity and increased levels of satisfaction with the relationship.

As we've noted, kindness is motivated by a concern for others. But it can result in beneficial effects for those practicing it, as well. Sonja Lyubomirsky, social psychologist at the University of California, Riverside, notes that practicing kindness can help us see ourselves as more compassionate, enhancing our self-perception. Furthermore, it can make us feel more optimistic and confident, making it easier for us to connect well with others. It can also help us perceive others more positively and more charitably, and help us build an increased sense of interdependence and cooperation in our social network.[6]

Depending on how it is practiced, kindness can also boost our happiness levels. Lyubomirsky conducted a six-week intervention in which participants performed either one act of kindness during each weekday or five acts of kindness on a single day each week. The type of kind acts performed ranged from small, simple ones to more involved ones and included things like washing someone else's dishes, visiting a nursing home, giving a homeless man twenty dollars, and thanking a professor for his or her hard work. Although participants in each group carried out the same number of acts of kindness over the course of the study, only those who did five acts of kindness on a single day each week reported higher levels of happiness. Based on this study, Lyubomirsky recommends concentrating our acts of kindness. She points out that doing one act of kindness per day can lead to a rut of repetition. Choosing one day each week on which we do more than usual, by contrast, can make the practice of kindness special, presenting us with an occasion to choose a range of fresh activities we value and enjoy, resulting in enhanced well-being.[7]

In a follow-up study, participants were given the choice either to do the same three acts of kindness every week for ten weeks or to vary the three kind acts they performed weekly by choosing from a list of activities they had created. Again, this study confirmed that doing acts of kindness on a regular basis can increase well-being for an extended period of time. The catch, however, is that the extent to which participants varied their kindness made a huge difference. Those participants who had to repeat the same activity actually experienced a drop in well-being at the middle of the study, before returning to their baseline levels. Lyubomirsky explains that this plummet in happiness was likely due to the tedium that can come from doing the same things repeatedly and the tendency to think of them as yet another item on a to-do list. She adds, "If an activity is meant to enhance well-being, it needs to remain fresh and meaningful."[8] So the key thing to keep in mind here is the importance of developing healthy habits in our relationships, but then varying how we carry them out to keep things fresh.

Kindness can have powerful benefits not just for those who practice it, but for those who receive it, as well. We can all no doubt recall times when we were the recipients of kindness from our partner—or from other family members, friends, or even strangers—and how powerful that was. Especially, perhaps, in situations in which we clearly didn't deserve it. Receiving kindness can affect us in a variety of ways, from making our day to transforming our lives. As Vaillant reports of participants in the Grant Study of Adult Development, receiving kindness and love from others can help heal wounds, and it can also unlock our capacity to be kind and loving in return. Receiving kindness and love can help move us from egoism to altruism.[9]

In his novel *Les Misérables*, Victor Hugo tells a compelling story that illustrates the transformative power of kindness. At the beginning of the novel, we meet Jean Valjean, a convict who has just been released from nineteen years of imprisonment. Valjean's prison record keeps him from finding work, and even a place to stay. A Catholic bishop takes pity on him and invites him to stay with him. But during the night, Valjean steals the bishop's silverware. Caught by the police the next morning, he is dragged in front of the bishop. But the bishop claims he gave the silverware to Valjean and says he is surprised he did not take the two silver candlesticks he gave him, as well. This stunning act of kindness is transformative for Valjean. A changed man, he lives the rest of his life doing good and helping others, including the workers in a factory he founds, the residents of a city of which he becomes mayor, and Cosette, a poor girl he adopts. Key to this story, of course, is the way Valjean receives the kindness of the bishop. He allows the experience to enter his heart and then builds his entire life around that redemptive act.[10]

As is the case with gratitude, there is more research on *giving* kindness than on *receiving* it. But also as with gratitude, it is clear that the way kindness is received is just as important as the way it is given.

Mindful of the importance of kindness for relationships, let's now consider how you might apply the Interaction Model to increase the use of this character strength. The first role in the Interaction Model is initiation. How might you initiate more kindness in your relationship? As we have already seen, the first step is *cultivation*. This is where you practice kindness more in your life. A good way to start would be to benefit from the results of Lyubomirsky's research and commit to doing five intentional acts of kindness one day each week. Also based on Lyubomirsky's work, be sure to vary what you do, choosing new things to do each week.

Step two, *contextualization*, involves considering how you might best incorporate your practice of kindness into your romantic relationship given your specific partner. Of course, taking into account your partner's likes and dislikes and then thinking of things you could do to help her feel good would certainly be welcome. It's important not to stop there, though. Moving beyond pleasure, think about your partner's passions and strengths: What could you do to help her grow, develop her character, become a better person? For example, if your partner takes her health seriously and works hard to keep her mind and body fit, what might you do to encourage and support her in these pursuits? If she has gotten bogged down lately with work, domestic chores, and taking care of the kids and has found it difficult to make it to the gym, you could consider rearranging your schedule so she can get back on a regular workout schedule.

Step three is *construction*, in which you actually implement your ideas and use kindness toward your partner to help her grow and to strengthen your relationship. Practicing kindness in your relationship can show your partner that you understand her deeply, respect what she values, and truly care about her. Finding ways for using kindness to help her become her best self speaks volumes. And acting altruistically can help you become a better person, as well.

Now that we have gone through each of the steps of initiation, let's turn to the role of response. This is where things can get a little complicated. To demonstrate our point, we'd like to share a personal story with you from our own relationship, told from Suzie's perspective.

I am an avid chocolate lover. So I usually carry some bite-size pieces of it with me to enjoy whenever I'd like. Early in my relationship with James, I would regularly put an extra few in my purse to share with him. After meals, I'd enjoy my piece of chocolate and give him one. He would thank me politely and put the chocolate in his pocket. I never paid much attention to the fact that he didn't eat it, assuming he was full from his dinner and was saving it for another time. After we were married, I rummaged through the pockets of his leather jacket in search of the car keys one day and was astonished to find—not the keys, but a handful of old chocolates! I also found a pile of decaying chocolates when cleaning out a dresser drawer. I looked at the frayed, discolored wrappers, and was baffled as to why James had stashed them away without eating them. Was he a chocolate hoarder? Saving them all up to binge on at some future occasion? Had he forgotten about them? Confused and concerned, I approached him about his odd behavior. "Why on earth did you never eat all those chocolates I gave you? What were you saving them for? They're now spoiled, and you wasted perfectly good chocolates!" His response was disappointingly simple: He just wasn't a huge fan of chocolate. But he didn't want to be impolite or hurt my feelings by refusing these unsolicited gifts each time I gave him one. So he would simply accept the chocolates and stuff them in his pocket.

So what should you do if you're in James's role and the initiation from your partner doesn't land well? Situations of this sort could range from actions that are harmless (as in this example), to those that are somewhat annoying, to those that are actually painful or damaging in some way. One possible response is to look past the outcome to the intention, and value the action for what your partner is trying to communicate rather than what actually comes across. This often may be the gracious thing to do, as it allows you to keep the peace and avoid hurting your partner's feelings. But this type of response passes up an opportunity for partners to get to know each other better and can actually lead to resentment on both sides. The recipient may resent having something unwelcome forced upon him, and the initiator may resent her partner's ingratitude— or worse, his inauthenticity in not telling her how he really feels about the unwanted behavior.

So are we suggesting that in all cases in which the outcome doesn't land well, you confront your partner and bluntly tell her that what she is doing isn't helpful? Of course not! Although there may be times when something like this needs to be communicated quickly and firmly to avert some kind of disaster, it's more likely that a response of this sort would be deflating to your partner, making it less likely that she will initiate positive things in the future and resulting in a chilling effect on your relationship. With the realization that there may well be times when politely accepting or strongly rejecting your partner's initiation is the way to go, let's explore an alternative way of responding that will no doubt be more effective in most circumstances.

Recall that the first step in responding is *awareness*. This step may well be the simplest, yet many times it's also the most neglected. In this case, it involves just noticing the kindness initiated by your partner. Often, the kindness may not be obvious, especially if you are not emotionally available to your partner for some reason. This may be because you are busily focused on other things, because you are taking your partner for granted, or because you have shut your eyes or your heart to him or her. Sometimes, you don't notice an action at all; other times, you may notice the action but not be truly aware of the kindness behind it. In the case of our story, it was easy for James to notice Suzie giving him chocolate, since it involved the presentation of something tangible. What wasn't as obvious to him was to consider these actions as a pattern of behavior Suzie had developed to be kind to him.

The second step in responding is *assessment*. This is where you stop to consider the effects of your partner's initiation of a specific strength on you and on the relationship. In most cases, the effects are likely to be quite positive. Your partner's actions make you feel good and help you grow, and they strengthen the relationship. In some cases, though, the results are bound to be neutral or even negative. In cases like our preceding example, assessing the situation honestly is of great importance. It was crucial for James to be clear about what was happening. Suzie's intentions were very good; she wanted to share a small kindness with him. The problem was that she lacked the information that James doesn't share her taste for chocolate. So what Suzie perceived as a kindness came across to James as well intentioned but ineffective.

Accurate assessment is so important because it sets you up for the third step of response, which is *action*. Again, in most cases, the effects of your partner's initiation are likely to be quite positive. So the action step is likely to involve an expression of gratitude. In cases in which the results are neutral or negative, however, two of the most common ways of responding are polite acceptance and strong rejection. In our example, James responded by politely accepting the chocolates. Alternatively, he could have reacted by saying, "Why the heck do you keep on giving me chocolates? I hate chocolates! Don't you know that by now?!" That, of course, would have been an ill-advised overreaction. Is there a middle way James could have followed that would have been respectful of Suzie and that wouldn't have resulted in the waste of so much chocolate?

Note that the goal of the action step is behaving in such a way that it continues the spirit of the initiation. The spirit of Suzie's initiating these chocolate gifts was clearly her desire to do something kind for James by presenting him with something he would enjoy. James's polite acceptance of the chocolates actually stood in the way of Suzie's intention, because it made her think she was achieving her objective when she actually wasn't. Of course, if James had overreacted and expressed frustration at being given something he did not like, that would not have continued the spirit of the initiation, either. A better course of action for James would have been to express appreciation for the thoughtful intention behind Suzie's actions, and then to explain to her that his taste for chocolate is not as keen as hers, so it would actually be better if she kept them and enjoyed them herself. He might have kept the moment light by telling her the story of an early experience he had with chocolate. When James was eight years old, someone gave his family a ten-pound bar of chocolate. His mother would cut off chunks of the chocolate bar for each family member to enjoy for dessert after dinner. Not crazy about chocolate even then, James saved his chunks. When his older sister—who loved chocolate—had a birthday about that time, he presented her with the chocolate he had saved up. She was delighted!

This is a way in which James could have been direct while still being kind. It would have given them both a good laugh, helped Suzie get to know him better, and prevented the stockpiles of spoiled chocolates. This was exactly the approach taken by a participant in one of our recent workshops. Early in his marriage, his wife gave him something for his birthday. It was nice, but not really something he wanted or could use. Instead of politely accepting it—and dooming himself to a lifetime of such gifts—he spoke with her directly about it. He explained that he deeply appreciated her intention of getting him something for his birthday that he liked, and that instead of receiving *things* for his birthday, he preferred gifts that would enable them to have new and meaningful experiences together. Because he approached the situation with such care and clarity, his wife readily understood what he wanted and modified her gift giving to match his desires. His birthdays have gone much better since then.

There is one more level of complexity we want to point out here. The role of initiator is actually a little more complex than we have presented it so far. We want to make it clear that the initiator's role, when played fully and well, isn't just about starting something. The initiator should also pay close attention to her partner's response. This will help her know how effective her initiation was and whether she needs to tweak it in any way. So the initiator actually starts a chain of responses in which she herself becomes involved. This chain may be a short one, or it may go on for quite some time. In the example of the chocolates we have been examining, we've pointed out how James might have responded better. There is also a way Suzie might have responded differently. When she saw James's response to her giving him the chocolates (always saying thank you and then pocketing them), she might have gone through the three steps of response herself, becoming aware of James's behavior, assessing its value for her and for the relationship, and then acting in such a way as to continue the spirit of her original initiation. Seeing him always pocketing the chocolates, she might have asked him kindly why he did so. That would have given James an opening to come clean about his lack of a taste for chocolate.

So when we advocate initiation, we advocate bold and creative action. We also advocate curiosity and sensitivity. This means not treating your offers as something your partner must accept and love simply because they came from you, or because of the thought and effort you put into them, but rather thinking of them as experiments, carefully attending to the results, and recognizing them as opportunities for learning more about your partner and yourself and for strengthening your relationship.

Let's pause here to put these ideas into practice with some exercises.

KINDNESS PRACTICE EXERCISES

1. **Cultivate Kindness**
   Given the importance of kindness in relationships, what might you do to cultivate this strength in your life? One challenge we recommend from Lyubomirsky's research is to carry out five new acts of kindness one day per week for the next six weeks.

2. **Contextualize Kindness**
   Think about the role of kindness in your romantic relationship. How could you use this strength to support your partner and grow your relationship?

3. **Assess Your Kindness Initiations**
   Identify some kind things you do for your partner. Consider how your partner responds to them. Based on his or her responses, what are some things you might do to make your initiations of kindness even more effective?

4. **Assess Your Kindness Responses**
   Are there any kind things your partner does for you that are well intended but ineffective? How might you communicate authentically with your partner to continue the spirit of the kindness but not its ineffectiveness?

STRATEGIES FOR USING THE INTERACTION MODEL WELL

Now that we have gone over the roles and steps of the Interaction Model of Relationships, we would like to end this chapter by describing three helpful aids for using this model well.

MINDFULNESS

Awareness is one of the most important aspects of a successful dance. You have to know what's happening in your own body and in the body of the person you are dancing with, and how your movements interact so you don't step on each other's toes. Similarly, in the dance of romantic relationships, it's crucial to be aware of your own—and your partner's—passions, emotions, and strengths, and of how they interact with each other so you can move gracefully together.

Although it seems simple, awareness is particularly challenging for human beings. One reason for this is because of our very limited bandwidth. As we saw in chapter 6, there are way more things going on inside and around us at any given moment than we could possibly attend to. If you don't believe us, take a moment to notice all the things around you that you have not been paying attention to while reading this book. All the objects and the colors within your field of vision; all the sounds, loud or soft, that you can hear; and all the sensations you can feel in your body, including the pressure of your clothes on your skin and the support of the chair you are sitting on as you read. Our conscious experience of any given moment turns out to be a very small sampling of the richness of the world around us.

Our attention is like a narrow-beam flashlight inside a large, dark room. With it, we can pick up only a small part of what's going on inside that room at any time. Some people, concerned that there might be vermin in the room, keep their narrow beam concentrated in the corners of the room. Others point their beams at the walls to see if there is any artwork hanging on them. Still others flash their beams around to see if there are any other individuals in the room they might connect with. The first group of people are more likely to pick up on disgusting things that might be lurking in the room, the second group is more likely to appreciate the aesthetic qualities of the room, and the third group is more likely to connect with other people. Given the different experiences each of these groups has, interviewing them might lead us to conclude that they were in three different rooms. And chances are none of them would be aware of the extent to which their own choices of where to focus their attention shaped their experience.

When we apply these insights to relationships, we can see that it makes a huge difference where you train your attention. You can focus on the dark corners and unpleasant elements in your relationship or you can home in on the strengths and positive qualities of your partner and the uplifting moments of connection in your relationship. Although there are extreme situations in which individuals need to confront the dangers in their relationships for their own safety, for most of us the path to being happy together no doubt lies in the direction of focusing more on the positive aspects of our relationships.

One powerful tool for learning to gain voluntary control over our attention is mindfulness meditation. We are fortunate to live in Philadelphia, where Michael Baime founded the Penn Program for Mindfulness more than twenty years ago. For decades, he has been delivering Mindfulness-Based Stress Reduction training to a wide scope of individuals, from medical caregivers to cancer patients, from university students to retirees, from artists to stressed-out businesspeople. Based on the work of his friend and colleague Jon Kabat-Zinn and developed through his own expertise in the field, Baime's classes are in great demand and have been very well received. To explore the power of mindfulness meditation in our relationship, we decided to sign up for one of his eight-week courses.

Each week we met for two and a half hours with a class of about twenty people. Baime taught us the theoretical aspects of mindfulness meditation, led us in various mindfulness meditation practices, invited us to share our experiences with the group, and assigned us homework for the coming week. Our homework included reading chapters of Kabat-Zinn's powerful and widely acclaimed book, *Full Catastrophe Living*. In this book, Kabat-Zinn details the Mindfulness-Based Stress Reduction program he developed and tested, which has been scientifically shown to help decrease stress and enhance well-being. This was truly inspirational stuff, and we both eagerly devoured the book. The second part of our homework was not quite as easy: meditating for forty minutes each day. At first, as we can both attest, it was very difficult to sit still, do nothing, and focus on our breath. Suzie would often sneak glances at her smartphone to see how much time had passed and would be dismayed when what felt like eons had been only a few minutes. (What then is time, anyhow?) As we continued practicing, however, the experiential part of the homework got easier. Indeed, as we got into the habit of meditating, we actually began looking forward to it. We were also pleased and motivated by the positive changes we began to see in ourselves, in each other, and in our relationship. Among the most important of these changes was our ability to be less reactive and more responsive to each other. Instead of reacting quickly and automatically, we were better able to pause and reflect, and this allowed our responses to be more thoughtful, kind, and helpful.

Something else we noticed was how much clearer and more powerful our awareness seemed to be. As James described it, he felt like he had been driving down the highway for a long time and hadn't noticed how dirty his windshield had gotten. Mindfulness practice was a way of cleaning his windshield, and he was amazed by how clearly and brightly he could see again. Baime pointed out that mindfulness meditation practice can help us take more voluntary control over where we direct the beam of our attention. He went on to say that our practice can also increase the power of the beam itself, helping us notice things in our awareness much more clearly. This was certainly our experience.

As we continue with our meditation, we notice a difference when our practice wanes. We can get so busy and distracted with other things that we don't prioritize it like we should. And then we notice that our communication is not as focused and patient, and that we are falling back into old patterns of acting and reacting. This is why meditation is called a practice. Like going to the gym, it's not something you do once and then you're done. Rather, it takes daily practice to maintain the considerable benefits of gaining greater voluntary control over our attention. It's one thing to know cognitively the value of intentional awareness, as we did before signing up for Dr. Baime's course. It's quite another thing to engage in the practice, which enables us to increase our awareness of the things that truly matter for Aristotelian lovers.

RELATIONSHIP RULES

When you read the words *Relationship Rules*, your mind may immediately go to the popular book *The Rules*, which details how to land a guy by playing hard to get and then lays out what to do and what not to do to make the relationship successful. Whatever you think about that book, we want to make clear that this is not what we have in mind here. We are not going to provide a list of dos and don'ts for being amazing lovers and partners. Instead, we want to talk about the basic, overarching principles we use to guide our relational lives—principles that inform our everyday actions and behaviors, the habits we cultivate, the decisions we make about how to treat our partners, and the expectations we have for how we ourselves should be treated. Let's begin with the most famous and familiar of these: the Golden Rule.

The Golden Rule

The Golden Rule is perhaps the most well-known ethical rule in existence. It can be found in some form in virtually every religion and ethical tradition. Ancient Egyptian, Chinese, Indian, Greek, Persian, Roman, and Near Eastern cultures emphasized it, as have Judaism, Christianity, Islam, Hinduism, Buddhism, and many other religions. Sometimes it is expressed in a directly positive, green-cape way: Do unto others as you would have them do unto you. Or treat others as you would like to be treated. And sometimes it is expressed in an indirectly positive, red-cape way: Do not do unto others what you would not wish them to do unto you. Or don't treat others as you would not want to be treated. This is a very easy and basic rule to understand. And it has been of great value to many people living in a wide range of societies throughout time. Both of us grew up being taught the Golden Rule, and we suspect you probably did, too.

Valuable as the Golden Rule is, though, it also has some limitations. The most basic limitation is the one Suzie ran into when she gave James the chocolates. While her intentions in gifting chocolates to James were good and honorable, we all know that good intentions in themselves are not enough to establish healthy relationships. Taken at face value, the Golden Rule asks us to treat others as though they were in our shoes. But they aren't in our shoes. They are their own unique persons. And in quite a number of areas, they actually don't want what we want. So giving it to them will not produce the same positive results, and may even cause problems.

Participants in our workshops have told us similar stories, in which the Golden Rule was being applied in a well-meaning way, but was not actually working. One woman told us how disappointed and puzzled she was by her son's responses to the Christmas presents she bought him. Every year, she would excitedly purchase presents for him and eagerly give them to him. But each time, he would react with indifference. She was really surprised by his response, since she couldn't imagine why he wouldn't find the gifts as remarkable and interesting as she did. Finally, after this pattern persisted for several years, she decided to stop giving him what *she* would want, and instead start asking *him* what *he* actually wanted. This changed everything! When she got him the things he wanted, he was eager and pleased to receive them.

This problem is a common one across relationships. We've no doubt all been in situations in which we have given our partners something we thought they would want, only to realize our choice was based on the faulty assumption that they would want the same thing we would. So what should we do in these situations? Fortunately, there is another Relationship Rule we can use: the Platinum Rule.

The Platinum Rule

The Platinum Rule instructs us to treat others as *they* wish to be treated. This seems like a much more direct way of proceeding. It can only work, though, if you actually know what the other person wants. The Golden Rule can give us at least a rough approximation

of how to treat people in virtually all circumstances. Often its guidance is very accurate, but sometimes it's significantly off. The Platinum Rule is more restricted, since it works only when we actually
know what the other person wants. But in these cases, it is likely to
be much more accurate than the Golden Rule, and we ought to use
it when we can. In the case of the chocolates, if Suzie had used the
Platinum Rule instead of the Golden Rule, she would have realized
that James would have preferred something else—perhaps a piece
of gum, for example.

Just like the Golden Rule, however, the Platinum Rule can get
us into trouble. We may easily go astray if we try to use it in cases
where the other person isn't actually sure what he wants. And in
some circumstances the Platinum Rule can actually lead to harmful actions. What if what the other person wants is not good for
him? If we treated our son, Liam, the way he wants to be treated,
he would stay up way too late, eat far more ice cream than is healthy,
and spend much more time playing video games than would be
good for him!

In sum, using the Platinum Rule in our relationships is likely to
be an advance over the Golden Rule in many cases. But on some
occasions, it, too, is likely to lead us astray. On those occasions we
need another Relationship Rule: what we have coined the Aristotelian Rule.

The Aristotelian Rule

The Aristotelian Rule instructs us to treat the other person as her
best self would want us to treat her. This rule encourages us to focus
on the good we see in others and treat them in such a way that it will
help that good to grow and develop. In other words, the Aristotelian
Rule is oriented toward helping each person in a relationship build

his or her own character and become a better person. The Aristotelian Rule for relationships is more difficult, of course, than either the Golden Rule or the Platinum Rule. The Golden Rule asks us to think about what we would want in a particular situation, and the Platinum Rule asks us to think about what our partner would want. It may well be more challenging to think about what our partner's best self would want in a particular situation, since this involves a fair amount of speculation. Knowing your partner's strengths, however, can be of great help here. Although not always easy, a consideration of your partner's best self can yield important insights for guiding your actions as an Aristotelian lover.

There are several ways in which the Aristotelian Rule can not only help each partner grow but can also strengthen their relationship. First, since Aristotelian lovers are attracted to each other by the good they see in their partner, as that good grows, they are likely to be even more attracted to each other. Second, since each Aristotelian lover is committed to his own growth, the more his partner and their relationship help him achieve that growth, the more he will appreciate them. And finally, the more partners grow and the more their characters improve, the more long-lasting and fulfilling their relationship is likely to be.

STRENGTHS CONVERSATIONS

Our final aid for using the Interaction Model well takes us back to something we emphasized in chapter 7: having frequent conversations with our partners about our strengths and the ways we are using them in our relationship. Taking seriously the cultivation, contextualization, and construction involved in the initiation role of the Interaction Model is important. So, too, is focusing on the awareness, assessment, and action in the response role. These roles and their attendant steps are ones each partner in a relationship should work on. It's also something partners can work on together, in whatever way is best for their particular relationship. Some couples may prefer to have lots of quiet time for individual reflection on these steps, others may elect to have structured time to discuss various initiatives and how they went, and still others may just want to have informal and impromptu conversations while making dinner or exercising together. But making at least some time to check in on these topics is important so that neither partner is left guessing or shooting in the dark for too long.

We hope this chapter has been helpful to you as you think about ways in which to include more of your strengths in your relationship. We encourage you to practice each step in the Interaction Model carefully, keeping in mind that receiving well is just as important as giving well. To help you use the Interaction Model effectively, remember to practice mindful awareness, rely on the Aristotelian Rule of relationships to address the limitations of the Golden Rule and the Platinum Rule, and have frequent strengths conversations with your partner. We're not claiming, of course, that this is easy. It takes a lot of effort, patience, and perseverance. But do stick with it so that you and your partner can reap the rewards of your hard work in the happier, healthier, and more deeply satisfying loving relationship you cultivate.

INTERACTION MODEL EXERCISES

1. **Mindfulness**

   If you don't have a regular mindfulness practice, we encourage you to develop one. (If you're in the Philadelphia area, we highly recommend the Penn Program for Mindfulness, directed by Dr. Michael Baime.) In the meantime, we recommend you spend some time each day cultivating awareness by focusing your attention on something in a sustained way. One easy way to begin is by practicing Dr. Baime's Twenty Breaths exercise. To do this exercise, sit upright in a chair and spend a few minutes focusing on your breath. The point is not to meditate for twenty breaths, but rather to meditate fully on one breath twenty times in a row. At the end of each breath, pause, silently note the number of that breath, and then take the next breath. To reach twenty, count up to ten and then back down to zero.

2. **Relationship Rules**

   Earlier in this chapter, we invited you to practice thinking about ways you can incorporate kindness into your romantic relationship. Keeping the Aristotelian Rule in mind, go back to that exercise and reconsider it. How could you use the Aristotelian Rule as a guide to use kindness more effectively to support your partner and grow your relationship? How might the Aristotelian Rule help you put other strengths into play more in your relationship, as well?

3. **Strengths Conversations**

   Of all the ideas we have explored in part 2, which ones do you think are most important for your relationship? Set aside some time to have a strengths conversation with your partner and talk about these ideas, then take concrete steps to incorporate them into your relationship. In whatever way works best in your relationship, set aside regular time for strengths conversations on an ongoing basis.

Love Is an Action Verb

WE HOPE YOU have enjoyed your journey through this book, and we're curious to know what you found most helpful for your own quest to be happy together. We began by examining the ideal of Aristotelian love. This is different from the popular view of romance in which we look to our partners to complete us. It also differs from the all-too-common approach of entering into a relationship for the profit or pleasure we can derive from it. Instead, as Aristotelian lovers, we are attracted to our partners because of the good we see in them, and this motivates us to want to become better people and to support our partners in their quest to become better people themselves. In this book, we have focused on green-cape approaches to help us in these endeavors—not because red-cape approaches are not important, but because most of us tend to underutilize the green side of our reversible cape.

In part 1, we looked at three specific ways in which positive psychology research can help Aristotelian lovers flourish. First, we saw the importance of harmonious passion, in which Aristotelian lovers are able to avoid the negative consequences of obsessive relationships, where each partner is out of control, losing him- or herself in the relationship in an unhealthy way. Cultivating harmonious passion, by contrast, can lead to better mental health, a better sex life, and a more stable and mature relationship. We are still able to enjoy the romance of a relationship, but without the corrosive—or explosive—negative consequences of obsessive passion.

Second, we explored the value of positive emotions in relationships and noted the importance for Aristotelian lovers of prioritizing positivity. Going beyond a simple focus on pleasure, Aristotelian lovers actively seek opportunities that allow them to experience and cultivate positive emotions, such as joy, gratitude, hope, serenity, and love. They understand that positive emotions provide a powerful foundation for healthy relationships. Although the emotions themselves may be fleeting, they can help partners broaden their perspectives and build long-lasting physical, psychological, and social resources that can be enjoyed in the present and also provide much-needed stability down the road when things get tough.

Third, Aristotelian lovers don't just wait around for happiness to be delivered to them by thunderbolts from the sky. They can appreciate at least as much as anyone else unexpected moments of magical connection. But they are able to use those moments much more than most couples to grow and maintain strong bonds into the future. They realize that savoring those moments, as well as the much more plentiful moments of everyday positivity, can help them maintain a healthy focus on the good things in their relationship. Furthermore, being open to the present moment with their partner allows them to take in positive experiences more fully and enjoy them more deeply.

In part 2, we turned our attention to the importance of character for Aristotelian lovers. We looked at Aristotle's position on virtue and William James's discussion of the importance of voluntary attention for developing the habits that constitute our character.

Then we introduced one of the foundational research projects in positive psychology: the VIA Classification of Character Strengths and Virtues. We used the VIA Survey to identify our signature strengths, and we looked at ways of cultivating those strengths and using them in our relationships as Aristotelian lovers. We thought of Aristotelian lovers as dancers who must be carefully attuned to each other to dance well together, and we turned to the Interaction Model of Relationships to break down some of the steps of that dance, emphasizing the importance of both initiation and response in our life together.

We have thought of the exercises throughout this book as a series of workouts in a relationship gym. We use this metaphor intentionally since building relationships is a lot like building muscles. It can be quite fun, but there's no escaping the hard work involved. In contrast to the fairy tales that permeate our culture and hold up effortless connection and perpetual honeymoons as the marital ideal, real relationships take effort. And it's crucial to direct that effort wisely. In this book, we have relied on positive psychology research, philosophy, our own ideas and experiences, and what participants in our Romance and Research™ workshops have shared with us to create this workout plan.

As we did at the beginning, we want to emphasize again here at the end that we did not write this book because we have the perfect relationship and can teach you how to have one, too. We don't believe that a relationship is the kind of thing that ever can be "perfect." The word *perfect* actually comes from two Latin words meaning "thoroughly done." And no relationship, as anyone who has ever been in one can attest, is ever thoroughly done. It can be over, of course, when one or both of the individuals decide to pull out of it or to stop trying, but as long as it's a living relationship, it's continually changing and growing. Although we don't think "perfect" is a good goal for a relationship, we do believe "better" is.

There is always something to learn about ourselves, our partner, and our relationship that can help us deepen and strengthen our connection.

We also want to emphasize here, as we did at the outset, that this is not a complete book on relationships. Relationships are far too complex to support the expectation that a single volume, no matter how long, will tell us all we need to know about them. In this book, we have been able to include only a part of the rich literature in positive psychology that is important for relationships. And that literature itself is changing and growing. Science is never thoroughly done. As new scientific results are obtained, we will learn more about harmonious passion, positive emotions, effective savoring, and character strengths—and about how these important areas of research connect with and inform relationships. With regard to philosophy, this book hardly scratches the surface of what has been written over the millennia on topics of great importance for relationships.

Given the complexities of relationships and relationship science, we have not tried to write a comprehensive book with the final word on relationships. Rather, we have worked to give you a head start toward building, strengthening, and enjoying your relationship with your partner, no matter what stage you're in or how long you've been together. Ultimately, this book is our way of developing and communicating—for ourselves and for like-minded couples— a powerful and underemphasized approach to cultivating successful romantic relationships: thinking of them as ways of connecting with and supporting the good we see in our partners and in ourselves. The process of writing this book together has helped us in our own quest to become Aristotelian lovers, and we hope reading it has been a similar help to you in your relationship. If so, this book has achieved its purpose.

To those of you who see your current relationship along the

lines of Aristotelian lovers, who would like to develop that kind of relationship with your partner, or who would like to find someone with whom to create such a relationship, we wish you every success. As we close this book, we would like to offer a few additional observations and suggestions.

First, we believe becoming Aristotelian lovers is part science, part philosophy, and part art. Science can create much useful knowledge for those of us intent on becoming Aristotelian lovers. But that knowledge needs philosophical perspectives to be understood and ordered in the most helpful ways. And neither scientific knowledge, which typically seeks to learn from the experiences of large groups of people, nor philosophical wisdom, which typically focuses on important conceptual distinctions, is sufficient for providing all we need to improve our relationships. The effective application of scientific knowledge and philosophical insights requires nothing short of art. Informed by empirical studies and intellectual perspectives, each of us must use our hearts and our best understanding of ourselves and our partners to optimize our efforts to become Aristotelian lovers. Mistakes are inevitable. Much more important than trying to avoid all mistakes is a mutual commitment to learn from them in our quest to make our relationships better.

Second, we believe meaning is at the core of being happy together. Meaning is what connects us to something larger than ourselves. And that is precisely what relationships do. Moreover, Aristotelian lovers know the importance of connecting to things that are even larger than their relationship. They are brought together by a mutual love of the Good. This is why they respond so strongly to the good they see in their partner's character, and why they prioritize the cultivation of the good in themselves and their partner. Meaningful relationship rituals can be a powerful way of reminding ourselves of our commitment to the Good and of our recognition and support of it in each other.

Third, we believe in the importance of a community of Aristotelian lovers. Connecting to like-minded couples is a large part of our motivation for writing this book. We encourage you to find other couples you can connect with around these ideas and who are interested in exercising with you in the relationship gym. We recommend you find experienced couples who embody the principles of Aristotelian love and who can mentor you in your own development, as well as couples you can mentor, who can benefit from the experiences and insights you have gained on your own journey. And we invite you to connect with us and the larger community of Aristotelian lovers around the world at buildhappytogether.com.

Finally, we invite you to join us in making a formal and public commitment to becoming Aristotelian lovers. We encourage you to tell your friends and family about your commitment to love the good in your partner, to support your partner in the continued development in that good, and to work to become a better person yourself.

As I sit on the balcony, thinking about all that has happened over the years, and what I have learned about romantic relationships, I hear the door open behind me. James sits down beside me, and we look at each other and smile. I ask him if he would read the poem he wrote me for our wedding and that he first read to me at our reception. It's called "A Prayer for Our Marriage," and it beautifully expresses many of the overarching themes we have explored in these pages. In fact, it was an inspiration for our writing this book together. Though it was composed to express his wishes for our marriage, we invite you to adopt it as a prayer for your own relationship, directing it at whatever form the highest Good in the universe takes for you. Or this poem may inspire you to write your own. Either way, we hope this book has helped you strengthen your relationship, and we wish you and your partner many happy, satisfying, and meaningful years together building love that lasts.

A PRAYER FOR OUR MARRIAGE
James O. Pawelski
January 16, 2010

I hold your diamond in my hands,
Watching the light enter,
Prism its way through angled clarity,
Leap into color,
And flash its iridescent beauty into the world.

If beauty is truth, then the truth of this beauty
Is that the world reveals its goodness to us
In moments like these, in flashes and glimpses.
When the light of consciousness is refracted by experience
And we unexpectedly see into another person's soul,
Or we feel the joy that cannot be quieted springing up in our chest,
Or we behold the sacred splendor of a mountain clothed in fall
    oranges and greens
And know we are standing on holy ground.

All my life I have been puzzled by two mysteries:
First, that these moments of epiphany should exist at all
(a mystery for which I have been profoundly grateful)
Second, that these moments of epiphany should melt away so
    quickly
(a mystery by which I have been profoundly disappointed).

As an adolescent, I wondered why fireworks had to end in smoke,
Why lightning flashed and disappeared,
Why sparks fly upward and are extinguished.
I wished that time would stop when the beauty was there,
So I could stay in the epiphany forever.

Diamonds, however, teach a different lesson:
While no colored flash lasts forever,
The diamond's structure creates new and different-colored flashes
    all the time.
It is not a single, static bit of color that makes a diamond special;
But the dynamic generation of ever new and varied flashes of color
    that we find spellbinding.

Like a diamond, a marriage is a structure for generating new
    epiphanic moments;
As two people get to know each other more deeply,
They become more adept at refracting the light of experience
Into each other's wants and likes and needs.
A marriage also provides a way to integrate these moments of
    beauty;
The color doesn't just flash and disappear;
It becomes part of the relationship,
A past event that has ongoing effects.

I hold the diamond in my hands,
Watching the light enter,
Prism its way through angled clarity,
Leap into color,
And flash its iridescent beauty into the world.

Suzie, you have held me in your hands like that,
Opening your heart to the angled clarity of my mind,
Turning facts into feelings,
Stripping away their cold exterior,
Exposing their rosy, pulsing life,
Healing my heart as it sobs in relief.

I have held you in my hands like that,
Cradling, caressing your head,
Gently calming darting thoughts,
Turning them into soothing colors of peace,
The feeling that all is well.

My prayer for our marriage
Is that it be an ongoing source of epiphanic grace
For you, for me, for us, for others.
May we together refract the events of our united life
Into radiant beams of joy and hope and pride and inspiration,
Into strong colors of resilience and focus and determination and
    perseverance,
Into gentle hues of serenity and gratitude and awe and love.

May we savor these experiences,
Holding the memories of all the fireworks, flashes of lightning,
    and romantic sparks we encounter along the way,
And may our lives enrich and be enriched by others in our
    journey,
As we all walk together, becoming the kingdom of God.

Building Happy Together

We invite you to visit buildhappytogether.com to connect with us and others who aspire to the ideal of Aristotelian love in their relationships. You can find additional resources to help you in your relational journey, including updates on scientific research, information on our Romance and Research™ workshops, opportunities for sharing your experiences and insights with others, and stories of role models who are taking seriously the privilege and responsibility of cultivating Aristotelian love.

Building Happy Together

Acknowledgments

One special feature of weddings is the unique opportunity to bring together so many of the most important people in our lives into one physical space. Members of our immediate and extended family, friends of the family, childhood playmates, adolescent buddies, more recent friends we've made in adulthood, classmates, work colleagues, neighbors, and fellow parishioners—people from all these domains and stages of our lives come together to help us celebrate our special day.

In an oddly similar way, writing a book brings together a large number of very important people—not into the same physical space, but into a space of rich meaning. This book has brought together social scientists, philosophers, teachers, mentors, students, workshop participants, work colleagues, editors, publishers, agents, neighbors, friends, and family. People from all these domains and stages of our lives have come together to help us write this book. Some of these individuals provided patient support on a daily basis, others came through at key moments, and still others made valuable contributions without realizing just how much they were adding to the overall endeavor. As we consider the many people whose efforts have helped make this book possible, we are filled with gratitude, joy, and awe. Given the large number of individuals involved and the wide variety of roles they have played, we are mindful that we will be unable to thank everyone adequately. But it will be lovely to try!

We would like to begin by thanking Marty Seligman, whose vision, courage, and inspirational leadership launched the field of positive psychology. This field brought us together, defines our lives in so many personal and professional ways, and has made this book possible. Thank you, Marty, for your support, encouragement, and friendship. And thanks for your kindness in providing the foreword to this book.

We would also like to thank the many researchers in positive psychology whose insights and careful scientific work have led to the empirical results that are at the core of this book. In addition to Marty, we are especially grateful to Bob Vallerand, Barb Fredrickson, Fred Bryant, Joe Veroff, Chris Peterson, and George Vaillant for the pioneering work on which we have relied most heavily. Thank you for the many conversations and email exchanges that have helped us understand your work more clearly and know how to apply it more effectively, and thanks for allowing us to share your empirical scales and surveys in our book. We would also like to thank Sara Algoe, Arthur Aron, Mihaly Csikszentmihalyi, Ed Deci, Ed Diener, Bob Emmons, Shelly Gable, Julie and John Gottman, Jonathan Haidt, Elaine Hartfield, Sonja Lyubomirsky, Donna and Neal Mayerson, Sandra Murray, Ryan Niemiec, Ken Pargament, and Nansook Park for their many scientific contributions of great importance for romantic relationships. We have been able to include some of those contributions in this book, and we look forward to continuing to learn from them and their ongoing work in the years to come.

Next, we would like to thank the many colleagues and friends who encouraged us to develop this material and write this book, some even kindly going so far as to read the manuscript—or portions of it—and give us detailed feedback. We would like to start by extending deep gratitude to Barry Schwartz for his warm encouragement, insightful mentoring, and practical wisdom over many years. And for all manner of support, we express special thanks to Alejandro Adler, Scott Asalone, Tony Baiada, Michael Baime, Aaron Boczkowski, Leona Brandwene, Jer Clifton, Trecia Davis, Stewart Donaldson, Angela Duckworth, Peter Duda, Karen Edelstein, Johannes Eichstaedt, Randi Felberbaum, Sam Foster, Ray Fowler, Nancy Georgini, Lydia Gizdavcic, Christina Grace, Marnie Hall, Shana Heidorn, Scott Barry Kaufman, Kristján Kristjánsson, Piotr Kwiatek, Jeff Leach, Lena Marujo, Virginia Miller, Caroline Adams Miller, Bouchra el Mouatassim, Jeanne Nakamura, Miguel Neto, Kathryn Nordick, Elaine O'Brien, Kristen Ozelli, Mark Policarpio, David Pollay, Shannon Polly, René Proyer, Amy and Reb Rebele, Andrew Rosenthal, Joshua Rosenthal, Paul Rozin, Sydney Rubin, Willi Ruch, Peter Schulman, Anthony Seldon, Mandy Seligman, Marlaine Selip, Georgia Shreve, Sarah Sidoti, Bit Smith and David Yaden, Judy Spiller, Philip Streit, Rick Summers, Margarita Tarragona, Louis Tay, Sunny Thakrar, Caroline Waxler, Ele Wood, and Stephanie Yee and Ryan Weicker.

James would like to thank his many students over the years. Some of the points in this book were developed from material he initially presented in courses he taught at Albright College (Applied Pragmatism), Vanderbilt University (Foundations of Character Development), and the University of Pennsylvania (Foundations of Positive Interventions). It has been a rare privilege to teach—and also to learn with—such open-minded, intelligent, dedicated, and diverse individuals, including nearly five hundred students from some thirty countries on six continents in Penn's Master of Applied Positive Psychology (MAPP) program over more than a dozen years.

James would also like to thank Steve Fluharty, Larry Gladney, Nora Lewis, Dave Bieber, and Ursula Bechert, deans and administrators of the School of Arts and Sciences at the University of Pennsylvania, for their great support of our efforts to bring theory and research to practice.

Gratitude goes to the wonderful audiences we've met when giving talks on these topics around the world, expecially to the participants in the Romance and Research™ workshops over the years. A special thanks to those who, as a part of those events or in different contexts, have shared their stories with us, including Phoebe Tisdale Andrews, Ursula Augustine, Ginny and Charlie Kirkwood, Don Rosenblit, and Anthony Seldon.

We have so much gratitude for Monsignor Robert O'Connor, Reverend Paul Harte, and all those who have supported us as a couple and who have been inspirational models to us—especially Kay and Ernie Boyer, Carol and Ed Diener, Sandy and Ray Fowler, Marjorie and Vincent Gregory, Shirley and John Lachs, Joanna and Anthony Seldon, and Mandy and Marty Seligman. And we wish Bit and David, Stephanie and Ryan, Jess and Carlton, Isa and Noah, Nikki and Taylor, Jamie and Eric, Isabelle and Devin—and all other couples starting their lives together—many years of happiness as they explore the wonders of Aristotelian love.

Suzie would like to thank a variety of people for helping her in her writing career over the years: Peter Himler, Marc Greene, Gail Heimann, and Andy Polansky for giving her the opportunity to hone her writing skills; Ingrid Wicklegren, former senior editor at *Scientific American Mind*, for seeing the importance of applying positive psychology to romantic relationships and publishing "The Happy Couple" feature that led to this book; and Stuart Johnson, Jeff Olson, Deborah Heisz, Donna Stokes, Paula Felps, Emily Miller, Chris Libby, and the entire *Live Happy* team for providing her with an excellent writing platform to disseminate research on positive psychology to a broad and receptive audience. Suzie would like to extend special gratitude to Lori Carlson-Hijuelos, her talented novelist friend and former New York City neighbor, for recognizing her passion and encouraging her to write a book; to Mary Arsenault, for her boundless confidence in Suzie and for giving her an opportunity to write her first column; and to Judy Saltzberg, her superb graduate school adviser, for helping identify her strength of connecting scientific ideas and making them accessible to the public and for her unflagging encouragement along the way, with comments like "You can easily bang out this book!" Although it wasn't easy, it sure helped knowing she had Judy's support. Special thanks, too, to Richard Bank, the prolific author and past president of the Philadelphia Writers' Conference, who took an interest in Suzie's writing, gave her advice, and introduced her to the brilliant Loretta Barrett, who soon became her agent and mentor. Loretta immediately saw the potential for "The Happy Couple" feature to be turned into a book and trumpeted the idea to her colleague Nick Mullendore, who wholeheartedly agreed and continued to support the project when he took over the agency after Loretta's passing. Loretta's bright eyes, hearty laughter, and encouraging words are very much with us, as the book she helped envision is now complete. Thank you, Loretta!

We are profoundly grateful to Nick, our incredibly kind and astute agent, for championing this book and working strategically and patiently to make sure it landed with the right publisher. We would also like to thank our marvelous editors at TarcherPerigee: Stephanie Bowen, for her sharp editing skills and uncanny eye for detail that helped tighten the book and make it flow much better, and Amanda Shih, for her grace and dedication in smoothly taking over the reins from Stephanie, and deftly guiding us to a successful finish. Thanks also to our enthusiastic publicists, Danielle Caravella and Keely Platte, our creative cover designers, and the entire outstanding TarcherPerigee and Penguin Random House teams.

An energetic thank-you to Ross and the Relentless Fitness team and all of Suzie's exercise buddies (and fellow moms) who worked out with her and cheered her on throughout the marathon writing process: Amy, Christina, Claudia, Donna, Leslie, Liz, Marci, Marie, Michele, and Page.

Huge appreciation goes to Suzie's dear Tabard Society gals (Betsy, Clancy, Erin, Grace, Heather, Jen, Lisa, and Stephanie), whom she's grateful to have had as close friends since freshman year of college and who continue to inspire her.

We would like to thank Erica, David, and Nate Rose for their incredible friendship, unwavering support of us, and outstanding care for Liam when we were busy writing. Thanks, too, to Uncle Johnny for his calm and continued support and to Aunt Adele for her understanding when her brother kept being stolen away for child care.

Finally, Suzie would like to thank her parents. Her father, Tom, for ingraining in her as a young girl that she could do anything she set her mind to, and her mother, Liz, for being her rock and continuing to encourage her when the going got tough. She would also like to thank her incredibly loving siblings, Lisa (and husband, Ernie), Jim (and wife, Debbie), and Ted, along with their families, for their ongoing support. Family means the world to her!

James would like to thank his parents, John and Ruth, for their steadfast loyalty and support. The exemplary care and commitment they have brought to their relationship for more than sixty years have resulted in much comfort and joy for them, their family, and the countless lives they have touched. James would also like to thank his siblings, Hope, Dan (and wife, Kim), and Paul (and wife, Anita), and their families, for the caring connections that hold them close across the miles.

And last, lots of love to our favorite boy in the whole wide world, Liam, and gratitude for his utmost patience while we sat in front of various computer screens for long hours. You are our greatest blessing, Liam. We love you more than infinity!

Resources

RECOMMENDED WEBSITES

Happy Together (http://www.buildhappytogether.com)
Suzie Pileggi Pawelski (http://www.suzannpileggi.com)
James Pawelski (http://www.jamespawelski.com)
Positive Psychology Center (http://ppc.sas.upenn.edu)
Authentic Happiness (https://www.authentichappiness.sas.upenn.edu/)
VIA Institute on Character (http://down www.viacharacter.org)
Humanities and Human Flourishing project (https://jamespawelski.com/grant-for-humanities)
University of Pennsylvania massive open online course specialization in positive psychology (https://www.coursera.org/specializations/positivepsychology)
International Positive Psychology Association (http://www.ippanetwork.org)
Robert Vallerand's Research Laboratory on Social Behavior (http://www.lrcs.uqam.ca)
Barbara Fredrickson's PEP Lab (http://www.unc.edu/peplab/people.html)
Loyola University Chicago: Fred Bryant (http://www.luc.edu/psychology/facultystaff/bryant_f.shtml)
Gottman Institute (https://www.gottman.com) Character Lab (https://characterlab.org)
Character Lab (https://characterlab.org)
Jubilee Centre for Character and Virtues (http://jubileecentre.ac.uk/)
Penn Program for Mindfulness (https://www.pennmedicine.org/for-patients-and-visitors/find-a-program-or-service/mindfulness)
Live Happy (https://www.livehappy.com)

RECOMMENDED READING

Seligman, Martin E. P., and Mihaly Csikszentmihalyi. (2000). Positive Psychol-
ogy: An Introduction. *American Psychologist* 55(1), 5–14. http://dx.doi.org/
10.1037/0003-066X.55.1.5
Pawelski, J. O. (2016a). Defining the "Positive" in Positive Psychology: Part I. A
Descriptive Analysis. *Journal of Positive Psychology* 11(4), 339–356. doi:10.1080/
17439760.2015.1137627
Pawelski, J. O. (2016b). Defining the "Positive" in Positive Psychology: Part II. A
Normative Analysis. *Journal of Positive Psychology* 11(4), 357–365. doi:10.1080/17
439760.2015.1137628.
Pawelski, J. O. (2013). "Happiness and Its Opposites." In S. David, I. Boniwell &
A. Conley Ayers (eds.), *The Oxford Handbook of Happiness*, 326–336. Oxford:
Oxford University Press.
Pileggi, Suzann. (2010, January/February). The happy couple. *Scientific American
Mind*, 34–39.
Symposium (Plato)
Nicomachean Ethics (Aristotle)
*Authentic Happiness: Using the New Positive Psychology to Realize Your Potential for
Lasting Fulfillment* (Martin E. P. Seligman)
Learned Optimism: How to Change Your Mind and Your Life (Martin E. P. Seligman)
Flourish: A Visionary New Understanding of Happiness and Well-Being (Martin E. P.
Seligman)
The Eudaimonic Turn (James Pawelski and D. J. Moores)
The Psychology of Passion: A Dualistic Model (Robert Vallerand)
Positivity: Top-Notch Research Reveals the Upward Spiral That Will Change Your Life
(Barbara Fredrickson)
Love 2.0: Finding Happiness and Health in Moments of Connection (Barbara Fredrick-
son)
Savoring: A New Model of Positive Experience (Joseph Veroff and Fred B. Bryant)
The Dynamic Individualism of William James (James Pawelski)
Character Strengths and Virtues: A Handbook and Classification (Christopher Peterson
and Martin E. P. Seligman)
A Primer in Positive Psychology (Christopher Peterson)
Flow: The Psychology of Optimal Experience (Mihaly Csikszentmihalyi)
Thanks! How the New Science of Gratitude Can Make You Happier (Robert Emmons)
Adaptation to Life (George Vaillant)
Aging Well: Surprising Guideposts to a Happier Life (George Vaillant)
Triumphs of Experience: The Men of the Harvard Grant Study (George Vaillant)
The How of Happiness: A Scientific Approach to Getting the Life You Want (Sonja Ly-
ubomirsky)
The Happiness Hypothesis: Finding Modern Truth in Ancient Wisdom (Jonathan Haidt)
Character Strengths Interventions: A Field Guide for Practitioners (Ryan M. Niemiec)
On Human Flourishing: A Poetry Anthology (D. J. Moores and James Pawelski)

Notes

CHAPTER 1

1 Augustine (1960). *The confessions of Saint Augustine.* J. K. Ryan (trans). New York: Doubleday.

2 Schiller, F. (1785). *Ode to joy (An die Freude).*

3 Pileggi, S. (2010, January/February). The happy couple. *Scientific American Mind,* 34–39.

4 Sheldon, K. M. & King, L. (2001). Why positive psychology is necessary. *American Psychologist* 56(3), 216–217. http://dx.doi.org/10.1037/0003-066X.56.3.216; Seligman, M. E. P., & Csikszentmihalyi, M. (2000). Positive psychology: An introduction. *American Psychologist* 55(1), 5–14.

5 Seligman, M. E. P. (1998, January). Building human strength: Psychology's forgotten mission. *APA Monitor* 29(1).

6 Seligman, M. E. P. (1998). *Learned optimism: How to change your mind and your life.* New York: Free Press.

7 Park, N., Oates, S. & Schwarzer, R. (2013). Christopher Peterson: "Other people matter." *Applied Psychology: Health and Well-Being* 5(1), 1–4. doi: 10.1111/aphw.12007; Park, N., & Seligman, M. E. (2013). Christopher M. Peterson (1950–2012). *American Psychologist* 68(5), 403. doi: 10.1037/a0033380.

8 Seligman, M. E. P. (2012). *Flourish: A visionary new understanding of happiness and well-being.* New York: Atria Books.

CHAPTER 2

1 Johnson, B. (producer) & Brooks, J. L. (director). (1997). *As Good as It Gets* [Motion picture]. United States: TriStar Pictures.

2 Brooks, J. L. (producer) & Crowe, C. (director). (1996). *Jerry Maguire* [Motion picture]. United States: TriStar Pictures.

3 Plato (1989). *Symposium*. A. Nehamas & P. Woodruff (trans.). Indianapolis: Hackett Publishing Company.

4 For more on the nature of experiences of sudden connection and insight, as well as an analysis of how they can be connected in healthy ways to the rest of our life experience, see James Pawelski, *The dynamic individualism of William James*, chapter 6.

5 For more on the sense of the sacredness, see Mahoney, A., Pargament, K. I. & DeMaris, A. (2009). Couples viewing marriage and pregnancy through the lens of the sacred: A descriptive study. *Research in the Social Scientific Study of Religion* 20, 1–46.

6 For more information on the importance of interdependence, see Murray, S. & Holmes, J. (2011). *Interdependent minds: The dynamics of close relationships*. New York: Guilford Press.

7 Pawelski, J. (2008). *The dynamic individualism of William James*. Albany, NY: State University of NY Press.

8 Ryan, R. M. & Deci, E. L. (2000). Self-determination theory and the facilitation of intrinsic motivation, social development, and well-being. *American Psychologist* 55(1), 68–78; Deci, E. L. & Ryan, R. M. (2002). *Handbook of self-determination research*. Rochester, NY: University of Rochester Press.

9 Aristotle. (350 BCE; 1934 revised ed.). *Nicomachean ethics*, Loeb Classical Library Edition. G. P. Goold (ed.); H. Rackham (trans.). Cambridge, MA: Harvard University Press.

10 Ibid.

11 Ibid., VIII, xii, 7 (p. 503).

12 Haidt, J. (2006). *The happiness hypothesis*. New York: Basic Books; Haidt, J. (2003). Elevation and the positive psychology of morality. In C. L. M. Keyes & J. Haidt (eds.), *Flourishing: Positive psychology and the life well-lived* (pp. 275–289). Washington, DC: American Psychological Association.

13 Algoe, S. B. & Haidt, J. (2009). Witnessing excellence in action: The "other-praising" emotions of elevation, gratitude, and admiration. *Journal of Positive Psychology* 4(2), 105–127. doi: 10.1080/17439760802650519.

14 Augustine (1960). *The confessions of Saint Augustine*. J. K. Ryan, trans. New York: Doubleday.

15 Pawelski, J. (2014). *The eudaimonic turn*. Madison, NJ: Fairleigh Dickinson University Press.

16 Aristotle. *Nicomachean ethics*.

17 Ibid.

Chapter 3

1 Amit. Personal communication, September 20, 2016.

2 Vallerand. R. (2015). *The psychology of passion: A dualistic model*. New York: Oxford University Press.

3 Vallerand, R. Personal communication, November 2016–May 2017.

4 Vallerand. R. *The psychology of passion*.

5 Baumeister, R. F. & Wotman, S. R. (1994). *Breaking hearts: The two sides of unrequited love*. New York: Guilford Press; Baumeister, R. F., Wotman, S. R. & Stillwell, A. M. (1993). Unrequited love: On heartbreak, anger, guilt, scriptlessness, and humiliation. *Journal of Personality and Social Psychology* 64(3), 377–394.

6 Hatfield, E. & Rapson, R. L. (2009). The neuropsychology of passionate love. In E. Cuyler and M. Ackhart (eds.), *Psychology of relationships*. Hauppauge, NY: Nova Science.

7 Carter, C. S. (1998). Neuroendocrine perspectives on social attachment and love. *Psychoneuroendocrinology* 23(8), 779–818; Hatfield, E., & Rapson, R. L. (2007). Lovesickness. In Y. K. Greenberg (ed.). *The encyclopedia of love in world religions*. Santa Barbara, CA: ABC-CLIO.

8 Vallerand. *The psychology of passion*; Philippe, F. L., Vallerand, R. J., Bernard-Desrosiers, L., Guilbault, V., & Rajotte, G. (December 12, 2016). Understanding the cognitive and motivational underpinnings of sexual passion from a dualistic model. *Journal of Personality and Social Psychology*; Vallerand, R. Personal communication, November 2016–May 2017.

9 Phoebe. Personal communication, June 16, 2016.

10 Jaffe, S. R., Lansing, S. (producers) & Lyne, A. (director). (1987). *Fatal Attraction* [Motion picture]. United States: Paramount.

11 Carbonneau, N., Vallerand, R. J., LaVigne, G. L. & Paquet, Y. (2016). "I'm not the same person since I met you": The role of romantic passion in how people change when they get involved in a romantic relationship. (2016). *Motivation and Emotion* 40(1), 101–107. doi:10.1007/s11031-015 -9512-z.

12   Carbonneau, N. & Vallerand, R. J. (2013). On the role of harmonious and obsessive passion in conflict behavior. *Motivation and Emotion* 37(4), 743–757.

13   Ainsworth, M. S. and Bowlby, J. (1991). An ethological approach to personality development. *American Psychologist* 46(4), 333–341. http://dx.doi.org/10.1037/0003-066X.46.4.333; Bretherton, I. (1992). The origins of attachment theory: John Bowlby and Mary Ainsworth. *Developmental Psychology* 28(5), 759–775. http://dx.doi.org/10.1037/0012-1649.28.5.759.

14   Amit. Personal communication, September 20, 2016.

15   Brickman, P., Rabinowitz, V. C., Karuza, J., Coates, D., Cohn; E. S. & Kidder, L. H. (1982). Models of helping and coping. *American Psychologist* 37(4), 368–384.

16   Vallerand. *The psychology of passion.*

17   The self-expansion model of motivation was developed by leading relationship scientist Arthur Aron, professor of psychology at Stony Brook University. Aron, E. N. & Aron, A. (1996). Love and the expansion of the self: The state of the model. *Personal Relationships* 3(1), 45–58. doi:10.1111/j.1475-6811.1996.tb00103.x; Aron, A., Aron, E. N., & Smollan, D. (1992). Inclusion of other in the self scale and the structure of interpersonal closeness. *Journal of Personality and Social Psychology* 63(4), 596–612.

18   Vallerand. *The psychology of passion.*

19   Ibid.

20   Ratelle, C. F., Carbonneau, N., Vallerand, R. J. & Mageau, G. A. (2013). Passion in the romantic sphere: A look at relational outcomes. *Motivation and Emotion* 37: 106–120. doi:10.1007/s11031-012-9286-5; Carbonneau, N., & Vallerand, R. J. (2013). On the role of harmonious and obsessive passion in conflict behavior. *Motivation and Emotion* 37(4), 743–757.

21   Carbonneau & Vallerand. On the role of harmonious and obsessive passion.

22   Vallerand. *The psychology of passion.*

23   Gottman, J. (2011). *The science of trust: Emotional attunement for couples.* New York: W. W. Norton & Company.

24   Vallerand. *The psychology of passion.*

25   Murray, S. L., Pinkus, R. T., Holmes, J. G., Harris, B., Gomillion, S., Aloni, M., et al. (2011). Signaling when (and when not) to be cautious and self-protective: Impulsive and reflective trust in close relationships. *Journal of Personality and Social Psychology* 101(3), 485–502. doi:doi:10.1037/a0023233.

26 Vallerand. *The psychology of passion.*

27 Vallerand, R. Personal communication, November 2015–May 2017.

28 Amit. Personal communication, January 31, 2016.

29 Vallerand, R. Personal communication, November 2015–May 2017.

30 Phoebe. Personal communication, June 6, 2016.

CHAPTER 4

1 Fredrickson, B. L. (2009). *Positivity: Top-notch research reveals the upward spiral that will change your life.* New York: Three Rivers Press.

2 Ibid.

3 Lasseter, J. (producer), Docter, P. & Del Carmen, R. (directors). (2015). *Inside Out* [Motion picture]. USA: Pixar Animation Studios, Walt Disney Pictures.

4 Fredrickson. *Positivity.*

5 Ibid.

6 Fredrickson, B. L. (1998). What good are positive emotions? *Review of General Psychology* 2(3), 300–319.

7 Fredrickson, B. L. (2001). The role of positive emotions in positive psychology: The broaden-and-build theory. *American Psychologist* 56(3), 218–226.

8 Fredrickson. *Positivity.*

9 Ibid., 56.

10 Ibid., 60.

11 Ibid., 62.

12 Ibid., 21.

13 Ibid., 93.

14 Ibid., 91.

15 Ibid., 92–93.

16 Ibid., 18; Lyubomirsky, S., King, L. & Diener, E. (2005). The benefits of frequent positive affect: Does happiness lead to success? *Psychological Bulletin* 131(6), 803–855.

17 Fredrickson. What good are positive emotions?

18 Fredrickson. *Positivity.*

19 Fredrickson. Personal communication, November 4–5, 2016.

20 Aron & Aron. Love and the expansion of the self; Aron, Aron, & Smollan. Inclusion of other in the self scale.

21 Fredrickson. *Positivity.*

22 Hatfield, E., Cacioppo, J. T. & Rapson, R. L. (1993). Emotional contagion. *Current Directions in Psychological Science* 2(3), 96–100.

23 Barsade, S. G. (2002). The ripple effect: Emotional contagion and its influence on group behavior. *Administrative Science Quarterly* 47(4), 644–675.

24 Ibid.

25 Fredrickson, B. L. & Joiner, T. (2002). Positive emotions trigger upward spirals toward emotional well-being. *Psychological Science* 13(2), 172–75; Frederickson. Personal communication, November 4–5, 2016.

26 Fredrickson, B. L. (2013). *Love 2.0*. New York: Plume, 17.

27 Ibid., 35.

28 Ibid.

29 Ibid., 36.

30 Ibid.

31 Pawelski, J. O. (2016). Defining the "positive" in positive psychology: Part I. A descriptive analysis. *Journal of Positive Psychology* 11(4), 339–356. doi:10.1080/17439760.2015.1137627; Pawelski, J. O. (2016). Defining the "positive" in positive psychology: Part II. A normative analysis. *Journal of Positive Psychology* 11(4), 357–365. doi:10.1080/17439760.2015.1137628.

32 Ibid.

33 Fredrickson. *Positivity*.

34 Kashdan, T. & Biswas-Diener, R. (2014). *The upside of your dark side: Why being your whole self—not just your "good" self—drives success and fulfillment*. New York: Hudson Street Press.

35 David, S. (2016). *Emotional agility: Get unstuck, embrace change, and thrive in work and life*. New York: Avery.

36 Fredrickson. *Positivity*.

37 Ibid.

38 Ibid.

39 Gottman. *The science of trust*.

40 Fredrickson. *Positivity*.

41 Ibid., 47.

42 Ibid.

43 Mauss, I. B., Tamir, M., Anderson, C. L. & Savino, N. S. (2011). Can seeking happiness make people happy? Paradoxical effects of valuing happiness. *Emotion* 11(4), 807–815. doi: 10.1037/a0022010.

44 Catalino, L. I., Algoe, S. B. & Fredrickson, B. L. (2014). Prioritizing positivity: An effective approach to pursuing happiness? *Emotion* 14(6), 1155–1161.

45 Mauss, Tamir, Anderson & Savino. Can seeking happiness make people happy?

46 William James. (1983). The gospel of relaxation. In *Talks to teachers on psychology and to students on some of life's ideals* (pp. 117–131). Cambridge, MA: Harvard University Press.

47 Baumeister, R. F., Bratslavsky, E., Finkenauer, C. & Vohs, K. D. (2001). Bad is stronger than good. *Review of General Psychology* 5(4), 323–370.

CHAPTER 5

1 Tonya. Personal communication, December 13, 2016.

2 Ibid.

3 Ibid.

4 Ibid.

5 Snyder, C. R. (ed.). (1999). *Coping: The psychology of what works*. New York: Oxford University Press.

6 Bryant, F. B. & Veroff, J. (2007). *Savoring: A new model of positive experience*. Mahwah, NJ: Lawrence Erlbaum Associates.

7 Ibid., 2.

8 Ibid., 19.

9 Ibid., 5.

10 Mauss, Tamir, Anderson, & Savino. Can seeking happiness make people happy?

11 Bryant & Veroff. *Savoring*.

12 Bryant, F. B., Smart, C. M. & King, S. P. (2005). Using the past to enhance the present: Boosting happiness through positive reminiscence. *Journal of Happiness Studies* 6(3), 227–260.

13 Bryant, F. B. (2003). Savoring Beliefs Inventory (SBI): A scale for measuring beliefs about savoring. *Journal of Mental Health* 12(2), 175–196.

14 Bryant & Veroff. *Savoring*.

15 Ibid.

16 Ibid., 177.

17 Ibid.

18 Fredrickson & Joiner. Positive emotions trigger upward spirals.

19 Bryant & Veroff. *Savoring*.

20 Veroff, J., Douvan, E. & Hatchett, S. J. (1995). *Marital instability: A social and behavioral study of the early years*. Westport, CT: Praeger.

21 Ibid.

22 Veroff, J. (1999). Commitment in the early years of marriage. In J. M. Adams & W. H. Jones (eds.), *Handbook of interpersonal commitment and relationship stability* (pp. 149–162). New York: Springer.

23 Buehlman, K. T., Gottman, J. M. & Katz, L. F. (1992). How a couple
    views their past predicts their future: Predicting divorce from an oral
    history interview. *Journal of Family Psychology* 5(3–4), 295–318.
24 Harvey, J. H., Pauwels, B. G. & Zickmund, S. (2002). Relationship
    connection: The role of minding in the enhancement of closeness. In
    C. R. Snyder & S. J. Lopez (eds.), *Handbook of positive psychology* (pp.
    423–433). New York: Oxford University Press.
25 Veroff, Douvan & Hatchett. *Marital instability.*
26 Gottman, J. M. & Silver, N. (1999). *The seven principles for making
    marriage work.* New York: Three Rivers Press.
27 Gable, S. L, Gonzaga, G. C. & Strachman, A. (2006). Will you be there
    for me when things go right? Supportive responses to positive event
    disclosures. *Journal of Personality and Social Psychology* 91(5), 904–917.
28 Gable, S. L. & Haidt, J. (2005). What (and why) is positive psychology?
    Review of General Psychology 9(2), 103–110. doi:10.1037/1089-2680.9.2.103.
29 Pileggi, S. (2008). Fred Bryant, as quoted in the monthly newsletter for
    the International Positive Psychology Association, May 2008, 1(2).

CHAPTER 6

1   Aristotle. (350 BCE; 1934 revised ed.). *Nicomachean ethics*, Loeb
    Classical Library Edition. G. P. Goold (ed.); H. Rackham (trans.).
    Cambridge, MA: Harvard University Press.
2   Ibid., Book II, ix, 2.
3   Taylor, Eugene. (2001). Positive psychology and humanistic psychology:
    A reply to Seligman. *Journal of Humanistic Psychology* 41(1), 13–29.
4   James, William. (1890/1981). *The principles of psychology.* Cambridge,
    MA: Harvard University Press.
5   The figure-ground distinction is one of the great classics of perceptual
    psychology. For additional information, see: Rubin, E. (1958). Figure
    and ground. In D. C. Beardslee & M. Wertheimer (eds.), *Readings in
    perception* (pp. 194–203). Princeton, NJ: D. Van Nostrand.
6   James. *The principles of psychology.*
7   Ibid., 127–131.
8   Brickman, P. & Campbell, D. (1971). Hedonic relativism and planning
    the good society. In M. H. Appley (ed.), *Adaptation-level theory: A
    symposium* (pp. 287–302). New York: Academic Press; Lykken, D. &
    Tellegen, A. (1996). Happiness is a stochastic phenomenon. *Psychological
    Science* 7(3), 186–189. doi:https://doi.org/10.1111/j.1467-9280.1996
    .tb00355.x; Kahneman, D. (2000). Experienced utility and objective

happiness: A moment-based approach. In D. Kahneman & A. Tversky (eds.), *Choices, values, and frames* (pp. 673–692). Cambridge, UK: Cambridge University Press; Diener, E., Lucas, R. E., & Scollon, C. N. (2006). Beyond the hedonic treadmill: Revising the adaptation theory of well-being. *American Psychologist* 61(4), 305–314. doi:10.1037/0003 -066X.61.4.305.

9   For more information on this meeting, see the conference archives on the Glasburn Taxonomy Meeting 2000 at http://ppc.sas.upenn.edu/ opportunities/conference-archives.

10 Peterson, C. & Seligman, M. E. P. (2004). *Character strengths and virtues: A handbook and classification.* New York: Oxford University Press.

11 Ibid., 89.

12 Until 2006, VIA referred to Values in Action, but now it simply stands on its own.

13 For more detail, we suggest you consult Peterson, C. (2006). *A primer in positive psychology.* New York: Oxford University Press. We present here a condensed summary of his discussion of the VIA in chapter 6 of that book (pp. 137–164).

14 Copyright 2004–2018, VIA Institute on Character. Used with permission. All rights reserved. www.viacharacter.org.

CHAPTER 7

1   Niemic, R. Personal communication, June 2017; Kashdan, T. B., Blalock, D. V., Young, K. C., Machell, K. A., Monfort, S. S., McKnight, P. E. & Ferssizidis, P. (2017). Personality strengths in romantic relationships: Measuring perceptions of benefits and costs and their impact on personal and relational well-being. *Psychological Assessment.* Advance online publication. http://dx.doi.org/10.1037/pas0000464.

2   Peterson, C. & Park, N. (2009). Classifying and measuring strengths of character. In S. J. Lopez and C. R. Snyder (eds.), *The Oxford handbook of positive psychology* (2nd ed.) (pp. 25–33). New York: Oxford University Press; Niemiec, R. M. (2013). VIA character strengths: Research and practice (The first 10 years). In H. H. Knoop & A. Delle Fave (eds.), *Well-being and cultures: Perspectives from positive psychology* (pp. 11–30). New York: Springer.

3   For an in-depth exploration of applying the science of strengths in families, see: Waters, L. (2017). *The strength switch: How the new science of strength-based parenting can help your child and your teen to flourish.* New York: Avery.

4 It is worth noting that talk of overuse and underuse of signature strengths differs from Aristotle's usage about virtue. For Aristotle, it's not possible to overuse or underuse a virtue, because virtue simply is the right response. Courage is the right response to fear, temperance is the right response to pleasure, good temper is the right response to anger, etc.

5 Haidt, J. (2002). It's more fun to work on strengths than weaknesses (but it may not be better for you). (Unpublished manuscript). University of Virginia, Charlottesville; Haidt. J. (2004). Noble pleasures last longer than self-indulgent pleasures, especially when they match strengths and are socially shared. (Unpublished manuscript). University of Virginia, Charlottesville.

6 Park, N., Peterson, C. & Seligman, M. E. P. (2004). Strengths of character and well-being. *Journal of Social and Clinical Psychology* 23(5), 603–619.

7 Seligman, M. E. P., Steen, T. A., Park, N. & Peterson, C. (2005). Positive psychology progress: Empirical validation of interventions. *American Psychologist* 60(5), 410–421.

CHAPTER 8

1 Peterson, C. & Seligman, M. E. P. (2004). *Character strengths and virtues: A handbook and classification.* New York: Oxford University Press.

2 Emmons, R. A. (2007). *Thanks! How the new science of gratitude can make you happier.* New York: Houghton Mifflin.

3 Peterson & Seligman. *Character strengths and virtues.* 555.

4 Emmons. *Thanks!*

5 Lomas, T., Froh, J. J., Emmons, R. A., Mishra, A. & Bono, G. (2014). Gratitude interventions: A review and future agenda. In A. C. Parks & S. Schueller (eds.), *The Wiley Blackwell handbook of positive psychological interventions* (pp. 3–19). Chichester, UK: Wiley Blackwell.

6 Ibid.

7 Emmons. *Thanks!*

8 Seligman, Steen & Peterson. Positive psychology progress.

9 Ibid.

10 Emmons. *Thanks!*

11 Ibid., 44.

12 Frederickson. Personal communication, August 6, 2009.

13 Algoe, S. B, Gable, S. L. & Maisel, N. C. (2010). It's the little things: Everyday gratitude as a booster shot for romantic relationships. *Personal Relationships* 17(2), 217–233.

14 Algoe, S. B., Fredrickson, B. L. & Gable, S. L. (2013). The social functions of the emotion of gratitude via expression. *Emotion* 13(4), 605–609.

15 Ibid.

16 Ibid.

17 Pileggi Pawelski, S. (2016). The happy couple. *Scientific American Mind* Special Collector's Edition, 25(1), pp. 86–91.

18 Fredrickson. What good are positive emotions?; see also Fredrickson. The role of positive emotions in positive psychology.

19 Seligman, M. E. P. (2002). *Authentic happiness.* New York: Free Press.

20 Vaillant, G. E. (2000). *Aging well.* Boston: Little, Brown.

21 Vaillant, G. E. (2015). *Triumphs of experience.* Cambridge, MA: Harvard University Press.

CHAPTER 9

1 Gottman, J. M. (2001). *The relationship cure.* New York: Three Rivers Press; Gottman, J. M., Coan, J., Carrere, S. & Swanson, C. (1998). Predicting marital happiness and stability from newlywed interactions. *Journal of Marriage and the Family* 60(1), 5–22.

2 Gottman, Coan, Carrere, & Swanson. Predicting marital happiness and stability.

3 Buehlman, Gottman & Katz. How a couple views their past predicts their future.

4 Peterson & Seligman. *Character strengths and virtues.*

5 Gottman, Coan, Carrere, & Swanson. Predicting marital happiness and stability.

6 Lyubomirsky, S. (2008). *The how of happiness: A new approach to getting the life you want.* New York: Penguin Books.

7 Lyubomirsky, S., Tkach, C. & Sheldon, K. M. (2004). Pursuing sustained happiness through random acts of kindness and counting one's blessings: Tests of two six-week interventions. (Unpublished raw data.) University of California, Riverside.

8 Lyubomirsky. *The how of happiness.*

9 Vaillant. *Triumphs of experience.*

10 Hugo, Victor. (1982). *Les Misérables.* Norman Denny (trans.). New York: Penguin Classics.

Index

About the Authors

Tony Baiada

Suzann ("Suzie") Pileggi Pawelski, MAPP, is a freelance writer and well-being consultant specializing in the science of happiness and its effects on relationships and health. Her 2010 *Scientific American Mind* cover story, "The Happy Couple," was selected for inclusion in two special issues of the magazine and became the catalyst for this book. Suzie writes the "Science of Well-being" column for *Live Happy*, where she is also a contributing editor. As a columnist for the newsletter of the International Positive Psychology Association (IPPA), she profiled many of the field's leading scientists and featured their groundbreaking research. Previously, she directed award-winning media relations campaigns for Fortune 500 companies at the New York City headquarters of top global public relations firms: Weber Shandwick Worldwide, where she was a vice president, and Burston-Marsteller, where she received back-to-back media practice awards for her national placements. Earlier in her career, she worked in publicity at Radio City Music Hall and as an associate producer for HBO Downtown Productions and *The Joan Rivers Show*. She gives Romance and Research™ workshops around the world, along with her husband, James. Suzie has a bachelor of arts in communications and a Master of Applied

Positive Psychology (MAPP) degree from the University of Pennsylvania, and is a graduate of the Institute for Integrative Nutrition. She uses her certification in health coaching to help people make better food and lifestyle choices. She lives in Philadelphia with her husband, James, and their son, Liam. Raising Liam is her proudest accomplishment.

James O. Pawelski, PhD, is Professor of Practice and Director of Education in the Positive Psychology Center at the University of Pennsylvania, where he cofounded the Master of Applied Positive Psychology (MAPP) program with Martin Seligman. He is a recipient of Penn's Liberal and Professional Studies Award for Distinguished Teaching in Professional Graduate Programs. The founding executive director of the International Positive Psychology Association (IPPA), and a member of the Advisory Board of the International Positive Education Network (IPEN), he is currently leading a three-year, multimillion-dollar grant investigating connections between the science of well-being and the arts and humanities. Having earned a PhD in philosophy, he is the author of *The Dynamic Individualism of William James*, and coeditor of *The Eudaimonic Turn: Well-Being in Literary Studies* and *On Human Flourishing: A Poetry Anthology*. An international keynote speaker who regularly makes presentations in Spanish as well as in English, he has presented in more than twenty countries on six continents, including Romance and Research™ workshops with his wife, Suzie. He is a recipient of the Practice Excellence Award from the Ministry of Education of the People's Republic of China, as well as the Humanitarian Innovation Award for the Humanities, Arts, and Culture from the Humanities Innovation Forum at the United Nations. He is frequently featured in national and international media, including the *New York Times*, *U.S. News & World Report*, the *Philadelphia Inquirer*, the *Chronicle of Higher Education*, *People's Daily* (China), *El Norte* (Mexico), and *Perfil* (Argentina), and has appeared on the *Today* show, Univision, Globo, and TV Ontario. He lives in Philadelphia with his wife, Suzie, and their son, Liam.